The Politics of Economic Reform in Germany

This new volume situates current debates about economic reform in German in illuminating historical and structural contexts.
Showing how economic reform has become the central issue on the German political agenda, raising contentious issues of policy management and posing deeper questions about political beliefs and identities. It also examines the politics of the reform process, outlining competing views about the root causes of Germany's economic problems, the appropriate policy responses, and the distribution of costs. It situates the reform process in the wider context of the decline of the German economic model (Modell Deutschland) and Germany's transition from European 'pace-setter' to economic 'laggard'.

Particular attention is paid to the following key questions:

- What continuities and discontinuities can be seen in Germany's political economy?
- Are globalization and Europeanization associated with a progressive neo-liberal ascendancy in economic reform?
- How does economic reform in Germany compare with that in other states, notably Britain and France?
- Are there distinctive patterns in the way domestic policymakers negotiate economic reform?
- How do the characteristics of the German labour market and welfare state condition economic reform?
- How much variation exists at the Laender levels?

This book was previously published as a special issue of *German Politics.*

Kenneth Dyson is Research Professor in the School of European Studies, Cardiff University, Wales. He has written widely on European and comparative political economy and public policy.

Stephen Padgett is Professor of Politics at the University of Strathclyde, Scotland. He has written widely on European politics and policy.

The Politics of Economic Reform in Germany

Global, Rhineland or Hybrid Capitalism?

Edited by

Kenneth Dyson and Stephen Padgett

First published 2006 by Routledge
2 Park Square, Milton Park, Abingdon, Oxon, OX14 4RN

Simultaneously published in the USA and Canada
by Routledge
270 Madison Ave, New York, NY 10016

Routledge is an imprint of the Taylor & Francis Group

Typeset in Times by Techset Composition Limited

British Library Cataloguing in Publication Data
A catalogue record for this book is available from the British Library

Library of Congress Cataloging in Publication Data
A catalog record for this book has been requested

ISBN10: 0-415-36679-8
ISBN13: 978-0-415-36679-3

Contents

Notes on Contributors

Andreas Busch is Reader in European Politics in the Department of Politics and International Relations of the University of Oxford and a Fellow of Hertford College, Oxford. His recent books include *Nationaler Staat und internationale Wirtschaft. Anmerkungen zum Thema Globalisierung* (co-edited with Thomas Plümper; Nomos, 1999); *Public Policy and Political Ideas* (co-edited with Dietmar Braun; Edward Elgar, 1999) and *Staat und Globalisierung. Das Politikfeld Bankenregulierung im internationalen Vergleich* (Westdeutscher Verlag, 2003). His recent articles have appeared in *West European Politics, German Politics* and *Politische Vierteljahresschrift.*

Kenneth Dyson is Research Professor in the School of European Studies, Cardiff University, Wales. He has written widely on European and comparative political economy and public policy. His recent books include (with Kevin Featherstone) *The Road to Maastricht: Negotiating Economic and Monetary Union* (Oxford University Press, 1999); *The Politics of the Euro Zone* (Oxford University Press, 2000); the edited volume *European States and the Euro* (Oxford University Press, 2002); and the co-edited volume (with Klaus Goetz) *Germany, Europe and the Politics of Constraint* (Proceedings of the British Academy, vol.119, published with Oxford University Press, 2004). His next book is the edited volume *Enlarging the Euro Area: The Euro and the Transformation of East Central Europe* (Oxford University Press, 2006). He is a co-editor of *German Politics.*

Susanne Lütz is Professor of Political Regulation and Governance at the Open University of Hagen, having previously been Research Fellow at the Max-Planck Institute for the Study of Societies in Cologne. Her recent books include (with Roland Czada and Stefan Mette) *Regulative Politik. Zähmungen von Markt und Technik* (Leske & Budrich, 2004); and *Der Staat und die Globalisierung von Finazmarkten; Regulative Politik in Deutschland, Grossbritannien und den USA* (Campus, 2002). Recent articles have appeared in the *Journal of Public Policy, Politische Vierteljahresschrift* and *Comparative Political Studies.*

Georg Menz is Lecturer in Political Economy at Goldsmiths College in London. He has published recent articles in *Journal of European Public Policy*, *Journal of European Social Policy*, *Journal of Ethnic and Migration Studies*, and *Politique européenne.* His two books, *Contested Borders: National Response Strategies to Europeanization* and *The Future of European Migration Policy*, will be published by Oxford University Press and Lynne Rienner Publishers respectively in 2005.

Stephen Padgett is Professor of Politics at the University of Strathclyde. He has written widely on European politics and policy including the politics of electricity in Europe. His recent publications include *Organizing Democracy: Interest Groups in Post-Communist Society* (Cambridge University Press, 2000) as well as the co-edited volume *Developments in German Politics 3* (Palgrave, 2003). Recent articles have appeared in *Parliamentary Affairs, German Politics, Journal of European Public Policy* and (forthcoming) *British Journal of Political Science.* He is a co-editor of *German Politics.*

Susanne K. Schmidt is Research Fellow at the Max Planck Institute for the Study of Societies, Cologne. Her recent books include (with Raymund Werle) *Coordinating Technology: Studies in the International Standardization of Telecommunications* (Cambridge, MA: MIT Press, 1998), and *Liberalisierung in Europa. Die Rolle der Kommission* (Frankfurt: Campus, 1998). Her recent articles have appeared in the *Journal of Public Policy, Journal of European Public Policy* and the *Politische Vierteljahresschrift.* She is a member of the Editorial Boards of the *Journal of European Public Policy* and the *Journal of European Union Politics.*

Wolfgang Streeck is Director at the Max Planck Institute for the Study of Societies in Cologne, Germany. He was Professor of Sociology and Industrial Relations at the University of Wisconsin-Madison. He is author of *Social Institutions and Economic Performance* (1992) and editor of *Beyond Continuity: Explorations in the Dynamics of Advanced Political Economies* (with Kathleen Thelen; forthcoming 2005); *Germany: Beyond the Stable State* (with Herbert Kitschelt, 2003); *The End of Diversity: Prospects for German and Japanese Capitalism* (with Kozo Yamamura, 2003); *The Origins of Nonliberal Capitalism: Germany and Japan* (with Kozo Yamamura, 2001); and *Political Economy of Modern Capitalism: Mapping Convergence and Diversity* (with Colin Crouch, 1997). He was President of the Society for the Advancement of Socio-Economics in 1998–99.

Roland Sturm is Professor and Head of the Department of Political Science at the Friedrich-Alexander University Erlangen-Nürnberg. He has published widely in the fields of German politics, comparative politics and public policy, political economy and European integration.

Christine Trampusch is Researcher at the Max Planck Institute for the Study of Societies in Cologne, Germany. From 1997 to 2000 she was a Ph.D. student on the graduate programme 'Die Zukunft des Europäischen Sozialmodells' at the Centre for Studies of Europe and North America, University of Göttingen. Her doctoral thesis on *Labour Market Policy, Trade Unions and Employers' Associations: A Comparison of the Formation and Transformation of the Public Employment Services in Germany, Great Britain and the Netherlands between 1909 and 1999* (written in German) was published in 2000. She has also published articles and papers on German and Dutch labour market and social policy.

Introduction: Global, Rhineland or Hybrid Capitalism?

KENNETH DYSON and STEPHEN PADGETT

Starting from the premise that economic reform is a political process, this collection analyses the political factors that have shaped German economic reform as it has wrestled with relative economic decline, persisting stagnation and a bottom place in European and international league positions on growth and employment. It situates current German debates about economic reform, and processes and policies of reform, in their historical and structural contexts and analyses how German policy makers negotiate these contexts. The central question that animates the contributions is whether economic reforms indicate the erosion of national policy autonomy and distinctiveness in the face of changing European and global constraints. Alternatively, do policy processes and outcomes suggest a continuing scope for German economic policy makers to define problems and to fashion responses on specifically German terms within characteristically German institutions? More specifically, the contributors address the following questions:

- How much autonomy of action do German economic policy makers possess, how is it used in economic reform, and what conditions its use?
- Is the German model of managed capitalism viable in the face of globalisation and Europeanisation?
- To what extent, and in what ways, do the institutional characteristics of German political economy condition the way domestic policy makers negotiate economic reform?
- How much sector-level and territorial variation is there in processes of economic reform?
- What are the party political constraints that shape economic reform?

CONTEXT

One of the major European stories of the last 15 years has been the transformation in perceptions of the German political economy. Until the early 1990s the German model commanded admiration and respect, evoked a new national pride within Germany, and stimulated emulation across, and indeed outside, Europe. It was understood as the foundation of the post-war 'economic miracle'. Domestically, the German model served as a new, much-needed and thus valued source of security and self-confidence, thereby helping to stabilise the post-war liberal democracy of the Federal Republic and buttressing its new-found 'politics of centrality'. Externally, German economic ideas, institutional models and practices were emulated abroad and made a distinctive contribution to the design of a new European order of integration in competition rules, the single market and Economic and Monetary Union (EMU). Thus German policies enjoyed a striking 'goodness of fit' with the European Union (EU).[1] Economic policy was the one area in which German power was expressed confidently, even assertively.

For these reasons there was considerable scholarly and practical interest in analysing the German model of political economy, variously labelled 'Rhineland', 'coordinated', 'managed', and 'stakeholder' capitalism, but commonly understood to include a number of distinguishing characteristics. First, an 'enabling' or 'facilitating' state created and/or sustained infrastructures of non-market cooperation in areas like finance, labour markets and welfare, which supported the efficient, long-term functioning of the market economy. Second, a powerful independent central bank – the Bundesbank – served to discipline the collective bargaining of strong employer and trade union organisations, thereby securing both price stability (and avoiding disruptive patterns of 'boom and bust') and low unit labour costs (thus ensuring a competitive export sector). Third, the incorporation of employees into corporate governance through co-determination and works councils ensured social peace in the workplace. Finally, a technologically sophisticated, export-oriented manufacturing sector, backed by a tough backbone of small and medium-sized firms (*Mittelstand*), exercised comparative institutional advantage in producing high-quality, technologically advanced products for world markets. The model was understood to rest on a set of mutually supportive elements, in which non-market mechanisms of coordination played a major role.

For at least the last two decades, however, the German model has faced global, European and domestic challenges that have precipitated an increasingly steep decline in economic performance. The challenges stem from the fast-changing configuration of the international economy and, in particular, from increasing competition from low-cost producers. They have been compounded by German unification, EU enlargement and EMU, and by the burden on labour costs of welfare state provision for an ageing population. Economic performance exhibits a Janus-like profile, with a striking disparity between external success – evident in buoyant trade surpluses, a resilient export performance and competitive unit labour costs – and domestic impoverishment. Germany's position at the bottom of the EU 25 league table of economic growth reflects the culmination of a secular trend. Comparison with the US growth benchmark is particularly revealing, a long period of post-war catch-up going into reverse in the early 1980s. Whilst this reversal is common to all the major continental European economies, Germany's recent growth and employment performance has lagged significantly behind that of its neighbours. At the same time, because of this Janus-like quality, the politics of economic reform has not been shaped by an external shock and crisis, of the kind seen in Britain in 1975–76 and in France in 1983 and that led to a radical reappraisal of the trajectory as well as instruments of economic policy. It has been characterised by incremental policy adjustments on a consensual basis, punctuated by occasional 'tipping points' when small-scale changes produced important changes of policy direction.

Domestic impoverishment has altered the parameters of debate, either by shifting the focus away from the German model as obsolete, or by asking new questions about its decline and viability. Cumulative exogenous challenges highlighted the long-term tensions in the model, casting doubt on whether there had ever been a single, unified model. Dyson, for instance, emphasised long-standing conflict between ordo-liberal and managed elements, warning against the risks of reifying the model and of underestimating its complexities, tensions and potential for conflict.[2] His analysis begged the question of whether it had ever been appropriate to speak of 'the' German model. In any case, as Busch emphasises, contest has replaced consensus. Some analysts asserted the continued ascendancy of coordinated or managed capitalism.[3] From this perspective, continued external success attests to the persistence of Germany's comparative institutional advantage in world markets, whilst the decline of the domestic economy is attributed to the burden of unification and/or the fiscal constraints of the EU Stability and Growth Pact.

This 'continuity' position is assailed from two vantage points – those who see globalisation and Europeanisation as factors precipitating a systemic crisis in the German model, and those who identify a new hybrid capitalism emerging out of the complex interaction of globalisation, Europeanisation and the German variety of 'managed' capitalism. Underpinning this contest of beliefs were differences of perspective over how external variables impact upon the German model. For those who stress continuity, and the persistence of national varieties of capitalism, the effects of globalisation and Europeanisation are assimilated into the domestic institutional logic of the model. In the 'declinist' literature, global macro-level variables are driving systemic change, uncoupling the links that held the German model together, and forcing it to converge with more liberal variants of capitalism. 'Hybrid capitalism' identifies a complex interaction between external and domestic forces, pointing towards a synthesis between liberal and 'managed capitalism, and focusing on multi-level processes of economic reform.

TOWARDS HYBRID CAPITALISM?

The 'varieties-of-capitalism' approach draws on the 'actor-centred' paradigm of micro-economics and the institutional perspective of political economy to show that different forms of capitalism have different comparative advantages. The economy is composed of multiple actors, each seeking to advance their interests in a rational way in strategic interaction with others.[4] Crucially, their interaction is mediated by institutions that shape behaviour in a number of ways: by defining power relations between actors, establishing a matrix of sanctions and incentives, and by acting as 'socialising agencies'. The 'varieties-of-capitalism' approach thus focuses on the kinds of institutions that alter the outcomes of strategic interaction and thus distinguish one political economy from another. One of the main contentions of this approach is that because the capabilities of economic actors are ultimately relational, their success depends on their 'coordination capacity'. This is the main strength of the 'coordinated market economy' of which Germany is the archetypical example. Its principal institutional components are close relations between financial institutions and manufacturing industry, an inclusive system of corporate governance, cooperative and consensual industrial relations, collective provision for skill training and technological transfer, and a high level of social protection under the welfare state. The politics of economic reform exhibits an incremental bias, following the logic of appropriateness defined by the institutional framework in which it is encased.

The notion of global convergence has its intellectual foundations in international political economy and identifies a fundamental trend towards market liberalisation. This trend has its origins in three sets of inter-related developments in the world economy.[5] First, an increase in the volume of trade has been accompanied by an intensification of the international division of labour, and a concomitant sharpening of global competition. Second, banking and company finance has been transformed by an explosion of international trading across an increasingly diverse range of capital markets. Third, corporate structures and strategies have been reshaped by the proliferation of multi-national companies. Consequently, national capitalisms are being assimilated into a global process of convergence, to which Europeanisation contributes an added dynamic. In short, the politics of economic reform is driven by systemic change, resulting in 'the end of diversity'. The politics of economic reform reflect a difficult, tortuous and possibly interrupted process of learning that the German model is no longer viable as its component elements erode, even if at different times and speeds, for instance in finance and in labour markets.

This collection illustrates a newly emerging interest in using the concept of 'hybrid' capitalism to understand the changing German political economy. The concept does not claim to offer a unified explanatory account. Instead it offers a way of combining the focus of the global convergence literature on systemic 'drivers' of change with the emphasis on domestic institutional logic found in the 'varieties-of-capitalism' approach. It thus seeks to capture the impact of the global and European economy on the strategic interactions occurring in domestic institutions. The impact can be seen in each of the institutional frameworks identified by the 'varieties-of-capitalism' approach. It is evident first, in shifting power relations amongst economic actors, in the empowerment of mobile actors (who have the credible option of exit from the domestic economy) over the less mobile. A second effect is seen in changing incentive structures as external economic challenges – exposure to European and international competition, or dependence on foreign capital – reshape the strategic interactions of domestic actors. Finally, the socialisation effects of global interaction may weaken the attachment of domestic actors to the norms and values of national political economy.

A particular strength of the concept of hybrid capitalism is its ability to explain sectoral and territorial variations in the scope, the timing and the pace of change. At a general level, the approach draws attention to the reconfiguration of market and non-market elements in German capitalism, and a looser coupling of the constituent elements. Incentives for actors to reshape economic relations, however, vary between sectors according to the intensity of economic and technological challenges, exposure to international competition, the extent of foreign ownership and dependence on foreign capital. Variation is also related to the increasing importance of the service sector and of entrepreneur-based small businesses and a diminished role for export-oriented, high-quality manufacturing as sources of employment and growth. The result is increasing sector-level and regional complexity, for instance in mechanisms for corporate finance and governance, modes of sector-level regulation, social policy, and patterns of wage bargaining.[6] On the territorial dimension, as Sturm shows, variation is evident in the contrasting institutional capabilities of the Länder for industrial policy. Rather than seeking a single pattern of change, then, the hybrid capitalism approach suggests a variable geometry. A central purpose of this volume is to map variations in the patterns of institutional and behavioural change in German political economy, and to relate those changes to power shifts and changing incentive structures arising from global and European change.

A second strength of 'hybridity' is that it helps us to understand ways in which the processes and outcomes of economic reform are shaped by a system of multi-level governance. This concept emphasises the complex interaction between the different European, national and sub-national dimensions of political economy. Opportunities for actors to reshape economic relations change, and constraints will differ between different levels of governance, depending on the availability of veto points and the institutional resources of veto players. Multi-level governance contributes to the variable geometry of change in German political economy. The politics of economic reform is bound up with the different ways in which multi-level governance exhibits itself, for instance in financial policies.

Third, by focusing more sharply on the ways that actors respond to external change, the concept of hybrid capitalism may be able to reveal more about the changing dynamics of German political economy than the 'varieties-of-capitalism' approach. The emphasis of the latter on institutional continuity and the shaping effects of institutions on behaviour may obscure behavioural change. Formal institutional continuity is not incompatible with goal displacement and changing patterns of strategic interaction *within* institutions. Moreover, over time, behavioural change my serve incrementally to redefine institutions without crystallising in a sharply defined critical juncture. As Katzenstein and others have pointed out, continuity in Germany's post-war economic institutions did not preclude adaptive changes in the processes occurring within them; whilst Dyson has identified the role of 'tipping points' in German economic reform.[7]

STRATEGIES FOR ECONOMIC REFORM: BINDING HANDS

The politics of economic reform involves political leadership in playing a multi-level game, one that involves responding to the policy imperatives of global and European competition, including the behaviour of other states, business companies and financial market players, whilst at the same time managing domestic veto players and engaging in domestic electoral competition. Depending on the specific characteristics of a sector, strategies for economic reform operate within a narrow or broad 'zone of acquiescence' on the part of domestic public opinion. Hence governments must finely calibrate their strategies to suit varying and changing contexts. Padgett examines key contextual attributes that shape the scope for economic policy reform, whilst Dyson analyses strategies for reform.

In particular, governments are faced with problems of managing the tensions and conflicts between *economic* and *electoral* incentives. Economic reform involves difficult and complex strategic choices for governments about both the *objectives* and the *mechanisms* of reform. Strategic choices about objectives of reform are embedded within dominant economic policy narratives. In the German case sound money and sound finance policy ideas are institutionalised as canons of economic policy and enjoy such broad public support that economic reformers hesitate to take electoral risks by challenging them or being seen to subvert them. They are embedded in the

Bundesbank (and its successor as independent monetary policy authority, the European Central Bank) and in the EU Stability and Growth Pact that aims at budgets 'close to balance' over the economic cycle. The logic of sound money and finance ideas is a stress on, and political momentum behind, supply-side adjustment through competitive product, services, capital and labour markets. However, employment protection and the Bismarckian welfare state are also deeply embedded in the normative fabric and policy narratives of the Federal Republic, especially in the institutional structures of social partnership through which labour-market and social policies have operated. The strains and tensions between these three normative principles – sound money and finance, employment protection and Bismarckian welfare state – define and constrain the scope and the agenda of economic policy reform. On the one hand, the domination of academic economics by sound money and finance ideas has meant that ideas about Keynesian-style active demand management have figured only marginally in debate about economic reform (with the exception of Oskar Lafontaine's very brief period as Federal Finance Minister in 1998–99). On the other, supply-side reforms to labour markets and the welfare state have been constrained by the perceptions that they entail high political risks. These strains and tensions about normative principles reflect discordant historical memories about the failure of liberal democracy in Germany and its transition into fascist dictatorship.

A striking feature of the politics of economic reform in Germany is the weak linkage between supply-side reforms and macro-economic strategies of demand management, consequent on the power of sound money and finance ideas. In consequence, German policy makers have hesitated to prioritise and use expanding demand, and the attitudes of well-being and confidence that it generates, to reduce the perceived costs of supply-side reforms through higher consumer and investment spending and consequent job creation. Expanding demand would allow the short-term costs of these reforms to be absorbed with lower political risk. As the Schröder governments illustrated, supply-side reforms in a context of stagnation or recession may actually worsen the problems of growth and employment that they seek to address through their negative effects on consumer confidence (not to mention through increasing the numbers counted as seeking work by taking them out of social assistance). The Schröder governments have been caught up in the dilemma of how to make urgently needed supply-side reforms acceptable at a time when deficient demand precluded a demonstration of their short- to medium-term benefits. Busch highlights some negative macro-economic effects from Economic and Monetary Union.

Strategic choices about mechanisms for reform are shaped by the structure of the polity and the inducements and constraints that it offers. In a strongly majoritarian political system, like Britain, single-party governments have the capacity to reform either by direct legislative action or by sustained indirect pressure on interests to act in order to avoid direct government action. Governments can credibly threaten direct action to induce cooperation in reform. This threat is less convincing in the politics of economic reform in Germany. In non-majoritarian systems – with coalition governments, dual legislative majorities, territorial distribution of powers – the temptation is for government to act as an 'honest broker' in economic reform, seeking to broker agreement between different interests, especially employers and trade unions. Hence 'social pacts' have proved an important mechanism for economic reform in states like

Ireland, Italy and the Netherlands. Their success encouraged Schröder and the Social Democrats to believe that an Alliance for Jobs, on the Dutch model, was the most promising strategy for reform in Germany. As Dyson argues here, the distinctive character of the German state, with its non-majoritarian features, makes 'binding hands' a particularly attractive – albeit difficult and problematic – strategy for reform. The result is a bias towards using 'government by commission', exemplified by the Alliance for Jobs, the Hartz Commission and the Rürup Commission. This strategy seeks to open up a policy space beyond internal party, coalition, legislative and federal politics in which enlightened self-interest can evolve and the authority of expertise define the broad parameters of reform. At the same time these examples highlight the limitations of binding hands as a strategy and the specific conditions in which it is likely to succeed.

REFORM PROCESSES AND OUTCOMES: INCENTIVES AND CONSTRAINTS

One of the most striking conclusions of this volume is the extent to which the reform agenda is shaped by changes in the structure of external incentives and constraints. These changes alter the costs and benefits of the domestic status quo, inducing domestic actors to re-orientate their policy preferences, and shifting the balance between reform advocates and their opponents. The preference-shaping effects of external incentives can be seen in three arenas. First, the expansion of global capital markets has created fears amongst domestic actors for the viability of *Finanzplatz Deutschland* and has induced banks and large companies to disengage from domestic practices of corporate finance and governance. Second, Europeanisation has penetrated deeply into domestic political economy in the form of the Single Market, European competition rules, and emerging EU regulatory regimes. A third set of incentives arises from EU enlargement. Low labour costs and low flat-rate tax regimes to the east intensify the competitive pressures on the domestic economy, creating powerful incentives for firms to reshape collective bargaining and to use exit threats to 'discipline' their employees. Thus the policies of governments in Tallinn and in Bratislava assume significance for the politics of economic reform in Germany.

The strongest incentives for actors to adopt new patterns of strategic interaction and to pursue institutional reconfiguration are in sectors like banking, finance and telecommunications, where actors are very exposed internationally. Lutz shows how extensively external forces have eroded the nexus between domestic financial institutions, company finance, and corporate governance. The internationalisation of capital markets and the 'marketisation' of financial services have provided strong incentives for German banks to switch from lending activities to securities trading and to disengage from their role in corporate finance and governance. Simultaneously large German companies and some sections of the *Mittelstand* have embraced international markets as a source of new capital. A 'marketised' environment, she argues, places increased emphasis on short-term profitability and shareholder values, weakening key elements of coordinated capitalism, notably the role of the public savings banks. Even so, German policy makers, especially in the Länder (as Sturm shows) remain focused on retaining financial mechanisms that will underpin a continuing leading role for the *Mittelstand* in the economic structure (see also Busch).

The effects of Europeanisation on the preferences of domestic actors are very apparent in Schmidt's account of liberalisation in the heavily regulated sectors of telecommunications, energy, insurance, road haulage and services. In these sectors, domestic reformers have used European competition rules to push the reform agenda forward, sometimes anticipating European law or judicial decisions that subsequently failed to materialise. In the face of these pressures, and despite their close relationship with domestic regulators, entrenched sectoral interests in road haulage and the craft occupations have been powerless to prevent far-reaching liberalisation. For many actors (especially large firms) the incentives of European markets have reduced attachments to traditional regulatory institutions and specifically German norms. Thus the dynamics of economic reform have been at least as much 'bottom-up' as 'top-down'.

In industrial relations, Menz focuses on changing power relations between business and trade unions. The persistence of a neo-corporatist institutional framework, he argues, obscures far-reaching changes in actor behaviour, with employers exploiting the threat of relocating abroad to coerce trade unions into making concessions on pay and hours. Institutional continuity also masks a tendency to shift key elements of wage bargaining to company level, where concession bargaining is endemic. The result, he concludes, is 'functional adaptation', with existing institutions being recalibrated to serve the purpose of containing wage costs and reducing unit labour costs in the interests of competitiveness. Whilst the formal institutional apparatus remains intact, its foundations are being eroded by an exodus from the employer associations as firms seek to escape from the constraints of collective bargaining. The result is a rebalancing of power within existing institutional structures.

Whilst private actors have responded to the incentive structures of the international economy, state actors are confronted by a more complex set of incentives and sanctions. Government has not been inactive in economic reform. Lutz refers to 'an unprecedented thrust in legislative activity' that has made a significant contribution to the transformation of Germany's financial institutions and to opening up domestic capital markets; whilst Schmidt underlines the scope of change in heavily regulated sectors. In the labour market, as Menz shows, the Hartz IV reforms represent a decisive break from traditional neo-corporatist practice. In key areas of economic reform, however, successive governments have been unable to resolve the conflict of *economic* and *electoral* incentives referred to above. Electoral incentives are stacked against the reform of the welfare state. As Padgett argues here, differences on welfare state reform cut through rather than between the main 'catch-all' parties of Christian and Social Democracy, reducing the incentive to exploit partisan cleavage to shape and mobilise public opinion behind reform. Comparison with Sweden, Denmark and the Netherlands shows the consequences of the parties' failure to find a legitimating discourse that will make painful reforms acceptable to public opinion.

The incentive structure of electoral competition also figures in Streeck and Trampusch's account of the long-term failure of welfare state reform. A public that regards welfare entitlements as a form of private property is a powerful disincentive against the sort of structural reform in pensions and social insurance that is required to alleviate the non-wage labour costs that burden the domestic economy. A second, structural explanation for reform failure relates to Olson's syndrome of self-interested veto coalitions that emerge during periods of economic success and subsequently serve to block reform.[8] In the face of electoral disincentives and a determined rearguard action on the part of interest coalitions, successive governments have resorted to budgetary sleight-of-hand, modest entitlement cuts, and relatively trivial structural adjustments that have left the central institutional principle of the welfare state – the broad equivalence of benefits with earnings – largely intact. The Bismarckian welfare state has functioned as a key systemic constraint on economic reform, entrenching high non-wage labour costs and making the fiscal disciplines of the EU Stability and Growth Pact difficult. Of the central institutional elements in the German model of coordinated capitalism, it has proved the most resistant to reform.

INSTITUTIONAL CONTINUITY, BEHAVIOURAL CHANGE AND THE EXIT THREAT

Another striking theme in this volume is the way in which behavioural change often coexists with formal institutional continuity. This seeming paradox of institutional continuity and behavioural change can be explained by the way in which domestic actors – responding to changing external incentive structures – have sought to exploit the room for manoeuvre available within existing domestic institutions, or to annex new structures as in the regulated sectors and labour markets. 'Functional conversion' and 'institutional layering' suggest that institutions are *malleable*. This conclusion should not come as a surprise to observers of a German model of political economy that is constituted in large part by informal operating procedures and norms that are particularly susceptible to reform from below.

The paradox of institutional continuity and behavioural change can also be explained by the absence of a critical juncture or crisis of economic reform. In this respect Germany differs from countries where it is possible to identify crisis events that redefined the institutional order and transformed the parameters of debate about economic reform. In Britain, the financial crises and industrial relations conflicts of the 1970s served to discredit the institutional framework of public policy, generating a new sense of urgency and a quest for policy leadership. The exchange-rate crisis of 1983 had a similar effect for France, calling its European leadership role into question. To the extent that Germany has a dominant crisis narrative, it is one of sound money and finance that looks back to the hyper-inflations of the 1920s and 1940s. The absence of Keynesianism from post-war economic policy means that it serves neither as a negative lesson for neo-liberals nor as a set of policy prescriptions. The ideational context of economic reform is therefore limited to a new post-war ordo-liberalism that addressed these earlier crises and to a more traditional managed capitalism that could be traced back before 1914.

The absence of a critical juncture or crisis in economic policy has long disguised the fact that post-war German political economy was itself a hybrid of ordo-liberal and managed capitalism, a case of domestic cross-breeding. Globalisation and Europeanisation have propagated new strands of market capitalism onto the domestic hybrid. But hybridisation is essentially a process of experimentation; whilst some new hybrids survive others fail. There are two main questions. The first is whether this pattern of reform will succeed in reversing the impoverishment of the domestic economy by restoring its competitive advantage and expanding the services sector. Failure would lead economic actors to exploit their room for manoeuvre – especially the threat of exit – to exert pressure for more far-reaching institutional reforms and for constitutional change to strengthen the reform capacity of the state. The second question is – even if the hybrid is successful in economic renewal – whether new forms of market-oriented behaviour in financial services, corporate finance and governance, and industrial relations are compatible in the long term with the institutional pillars of non-market coordination. One of the canons of the varieties of capitalism approach is 'institutional complementarity' between the component parts of the coordinated market economy. Change in one component may thus have important 'knock-on' effects in other parts of the model. Thus, at the time of writing, Germany's reform process balances uneasily between success and failure, its political economy poised between distinctiveness and convergence.

NOTES

1. K. Dyson and K. Goetz (eds.), *Germany, Europe and the Politics of Constraint* (London: Proceedings of the British Academy, Vol.119, 2003).
2. K. Dyson, 'The German Model Revisited: From Schmidt to Schröder', in S. Padgett and T. Poguntke (eds.), *Continuity and Change in German Politics: Beyond the Politics of Centrality?* (London: Frank Cass, 2002).
3. Most notably P. Hall and D. Soskice (eds.), *Varieties of Capitalism: The Institutional Foundations of Comparative Advantage* (Oxford: Oxford University Press, 2001).
4. Ibid., p.6.
5. J. Perraton, D. Glodblatt, D. Held and A. McGrew, 'The Globalisation of Economic Acivity', in R. Higgott and A. Payne (eds.), *The New Political Economy of Globalisation*, Vol.1 (Cheltenham: Edward Elgar, 2000), pp.138–58: G. Garrett, 'Shrinking States? Globalisation and National Autonomy', *Oxford Development Studies*, 26/1 (1998), pp.71–98.
6. See respectively S. Lütz, 'Convergence Within National Diversity: The Regulatory State in Finance', *Journal of Public Policy*, 24/2 (2004), pp.169–97; S. Bulmer, D. Dolowitz, P. Humphreys and S. Padgett, 'Electricity and Telecommunications: Fit for the European Union?', in Dyson and Goetz (eds.), *Germany, Europe and the Politics of Constraint*, pp.251-70; and the contributions by Sturm and by Menz to this volume.
7. P. Katzenstein, *Policy and Politics in West Germany: The Growth of a Semi-Sovereign State* (Philadelphia: Temple University Press, 1987); W. Streeck and K. Thelen (eds.), *Beyond Continuity; Institutional Change in Advanced Political Economies* (Oxford/New York: Oxford University Press, 2005). K. Dyson, 'Economic Policy Management: Catastrophic Equilibrium, Tipping Points and Crisis Interventions', in S. Green and W. Paterson (eds.), *Governance in Contemporary Germany: The Semi-Sovereign State Revisited* (Cambridge: Cambridge University Press, 2005), pp.115–37.
8. M. Olson, *The Rise and Decline of Nations: Economic Growth, Stagflation, and Social Rigidities* (New Haven/London: Yale University Press, 1982).

Globalisation and National Varieties of Capitalism: The Contested Viability of the 'German Model'

ANDREAS BUSCH

The debate about globalisation and its effects on the capacity of nation states has been very much at the forefront of political science research over the last decade or so.* At the heart of this debate[1] is the question of whether the process of growing economic integration forces nation states to adopt similar policies – in other words, whether the future is one of convergence, or of continuing diversity.

So far, detailed studies of a variety of policy areas have urged caution with respect to the hypothesis of encompassing convergence and have emphasised more the 'persistence of national variation'[2] and the 'diverse responses to common challenges'.[3] However, these studies have looked at state policies. In recent years, a literature has sprung up that looks at national economic systems (or 'varieties of capitalism') and addresses the question of convergence or diversity at this level. Will globalisation lead to assimilation in the characteristics of (so far diverse) national economic systems, or will they be able to maintain their independence?

This article addresses this question with respect to the 'German model' of capitalism in four steps. First, it gives an overview of the model's characteristics and development, before briefly outlining the main features of globalisation and the debate about it. The third part discusses the future viability of the 'German model', looking both at literatures that proclaim fundamental change as its inescapable fate, and at those that analyse the situation of national economic systems as one of sustainable diversity. The last part draws on examples from recent developments to argue that evidence from the 'decline hypothesis' is so far not conclusive: the case needs further consideration.

THE 'GERMAN MODEL'

The term 'German model' started its life as the 1976 election slogan of the governing Social Democratic Party, and was quickly adopted into social science literature as a convenient shorthand expression for the above all (but not exclusively) economic characteristics of the Federal Republic's system.[4]

The main reason for the model's initial popularity was the same reason for which the SPD adopted the slogan in the first place, namely the comparatively good performance of the Federal Republic's economy in weathering the stormy 1970s (with its multiple shocks of a disintegrating currency system, oil price hikes, ensuing inflationary pressures and rising unemployment) better than most other advanced industrialised economies of a similar size.[5] Even if labour market performance was not stellar (and certainly not as good as the Social Democrats would have wished), it was acceptable; economic growth was average; and inflation performance very good. Compared to countries like the United Kingdom, the United States, Italy and France, Germany performed better. The term 'German model' suggested that other states might be able to learn from the now grown-up country of the 'economic miracle' of the 1950s and early 1960s.

The characteristics of this model were a comparatively prudent fiscal policy, which (partly due to federal structures) did not experiment with Keynesian demand management; a stringent policy of price stability, carried out by a famously independent central bank, the Bundesbank (which did not shrink even from major conflicts with the government of the day); and a very low degree of labour market unrest, leading to low strike rates and thus supporting the low inflation environment.

The challenges of structural change, especially away from historically grown heavy industries, shifted the focus of the model in the 1980s. Here again certain distinctive characteristics were discernible when contrasted with the strategies employed for instance in Thatcherite Britain: namely the emphasis put on coordination and consensus, which were seen as the hallmarks of a system that Rudolf Hilferding had called 'organised capitalism' as early as 1910.[6]

As the Hilferding reference shows, this system has deep historical roots that reach back far beyond the time of the Federal Republic into the second half of the nineteenth century. Alexander Gerschenkron classically described the conditions under which German industry emerged comparatively late: industrialisation took place through heavy industries such as coal and steel, which required high capital investments. These in turn created close connections between large-scale enterprises and banks, resulting in the 'Hausbank' model: 'A German bank, as the saying went, accompanied an industrial enterprise from the cradle to the grave, from establishment to liquidation throughout all the vicissitudes of its existence.'[7] Hans-Ulrich Wehler describes in detail how the cooperation between big corporations and associations created the 'corporativism' of late nineteenth century Germany, how the 'cartel movement' aimed to impose order onto the dynamism (and volatility) of Germany's late industrialisation, and how this encouraged the rise of the 'intervention state' (*Interventionsstaat*).[8]

State support for cartels had disappeared in the Federal Republic with its emphasis on competition (and a powerful Cartel Office to enforce it). However, its 'Social Market Economy' was widely seen as a system in which the role of the market was circumscribed by state and societal forces. This had substantial benefits, as British economist and political scientist Andrew Shonfield pointed out in his famous book *Modern Capitalism.*[9] He asked why the West European economies had been performing noticeably better since the late 1950s than both the United States and Great Britain, and he focused particularly on the institutional characteristics of the German system. Shonfield concluded that Germany's better economic performance was caused by centralised economic decision making, which, contrary to the French system of indicative planning, was not carried out by the state, but by the private sector. He pointed out that the associations had great influence and were thus able to look after long-term interests, thereby fulfilling 'semi-public' tasks[10] (with banks taking on the role of 'prefects'). This had been the case since German industrialisation, and Shonfield pointed to the re-emergence of the three German 'big banks' in the late 1950s despite the American occupying force's attempts at breaking them up.[11]

In the late 1980s and early 1990s the United States was in the throes of a 'decline' debate, fuelled by Japanese economic success, and then slid into a recession; a similar fate befell the United Kingdom. At the same time, Germany seemed to shoulder the economic burdens of unification with relative ease, displaying remarkable growth figures while maintaining low inflation and even reducing unemployment. As a result the 'German model' was seen as something to be emulated abroad: the British journalist Will Hutton recommended the German system for curing the ills of British 'short-termism' and landed an unexpected bestseller.[12]

A more sophisticated (if compared with Hutton, less popular) appraisal of the German system's advantages was produced by Harvard Business School economist Michael Porter. He described the US economic system as marked by deficiencies in the allocation of investment capital – both between and within firms.[13] This constituted a comparative disadvantage, putting at risk the long-term US growth rate. Porter argued that – compared with the German and Japanese economic systems – the US system put too much weight on short-term considerations, which worked as a disincentive for investment in 'intangible assets' – like worker training and re-training, research and development, organisational development, and stable supplier relations that were becoming ever more important for competitiveness.

The main reason, according to Porter, was the fluidity of US capital. Capital was provided primarily by institutional investors with broadly diversified portfolios, and these investors were above all interested in short-term performance. They lacked incentives to obtain inside information about firms, e.g. through seats on a company's board. Accordingly, they lacked influence over firm decisions. Quick portfolio changes were attractive if a company's performance suffered temporarily. German and Japanese systems, however, were setting incentives for 'dedicated' capital, which helped create stable investor relations and a long-term investment and planning horizon for firms.

Admiration for the German case was based upon its performance – not on an intellectual appreciation of a theoretical kind, for there was no coherent theoretical argument behind it. However, just as Hutton and Porter were writing their praises, the German model's performance declined: the Bundesbank applied the brakes to monetary policy in a drastic way, which to a substantial degree was an expression of the conflict over the strategy for the economic handling of German unification. Germany slipped into a deep recession, unemployment shot up, growth dwindled, and the once-coveted 'German model' seemed to have lost its shine in an age dominated by globalisation.

GLOBALISATION, CONVERGENCE AND DIVERSITY

The debate about globalisation has had a very prominent place in both academic and popular discussions over the last decade or so. At its core lies uncertainty over the future fate of the nation state. In the face of growing economic interdependence, would national democracies still be able to determine their own fate, or would they be steered by the power of anonymous markets?

This should not have come as much of a surprise as market economies were becoming ever more closely intertwined. Indeed, this process had been going on for quite some time, but it was the end of state communism and the Cold War that made it particularly evident. Trade had been growing more quickly than GDP for quite some time, and as a result of this greater openness countries became more vulnerable to external economic shocks and influences. Foreign direct investment grew substantially, again increasing the influence that events abroad and multinational firms had over domestic affairs. Liberalised financial markets underwent revolutionary developments, with volumes in certain instruments – particularly so-called derivatives – skyrocketing in only a few years. A good example is the 50-fold increase in currency markets turnover between 1980 and 1995, which reduced central bank reserves to a *quantité négligeable*, symbolising the reduction of state capacities for intervention.[14]

The academic debate about globalisation – a growth industry for many years – focused on the question of whether increased interdependence would enforce increased convergence of policies or whether it would have no such effect. From a theoretical point of view, the answer was unclear.

Scholars favouring the former position argued that governments competed for mobile capital that was seeking the highest net return. This would lead to an international equalisation of net yields and consequently to tax competition between countries seeking to offer the best conditions for business.[15] Competition, however, would not be limited to taxation alone, but extend to labour market, social and environmental regulations – which all have an effect on the expected return on capital – and lead to an equalisation here as well. Since capital was the most mobile factor, it could most easily threaten with exit and thus force government policy to adapt to its wishes.[16] As this process would happen everywhere, convergence of policy would be the result.

Another group of scholars drew the opposite conclusion, based on theoretical arguments that had been developed about path dependence by the institutional and transaction cost schools of economic theory.[17] They argued that specific national characteristics, such as differences in national policy styles or in institutional arrangements, would display a high degree of stability and persistence. These positions found support from scholars of institutional practice who argued that '[i]nstitutions are not simply reflections of current exogenous forces or micro-behaviour and motives. They embed historical experience into rules, routines, and forms that persist beyond the historical moment and condition'.[18]

The academic debate about state capacity under conditions of globalisation has so far arrived at rather cautionary results about the amount of convergence and has emphasised the high degree of diversity in the reactions to common challenges.[19] But public political discourse does not follow the often meandering paths of detailed scholarly argument. In many countries the debate about globalisation was instrumentalised politically and used to push through economic policy reforms. The public 'discursive construction' of globalisation emphasised the need for change and delimited conceptions of what is economically 'possible' towards an agenda dominated by neo-liberal recipes.[20] The focus on restrictions was meant to galvanise support for reforms. Within the German system the gloomy perspective outlined in the previous section led to the conviction expressed by the then chairman of the Bundesverband der deutschen Industrie, Olaf Henkel: 'Nobody wants our model anymore.'[21]

THE DEBATE ABOUT THE VIABILITY OF THE 'GERMAN MODEL'

The Decline Hypothesis

Prognostications of decline were echoed in the scholarly literature. One book title saw the German model moving from being a 'role-model to being a phase-out model'.[22] All in all, an extensive academic literature has sprung up over the last couple of years on the decline of the German model. Notable contributions have especially been made by present or former members of the Cologne Max-Planck-Institute for the Study of Societies, which is why one could perhaps label this position the 'Cologne decline hypothesis'. In brief, it states that changes in constitutive areas of the German system are undermining the latter's functionality and complementarity. Because these changes are 'uncoordinated',[23] they have to have negative consequences, resulting in the 'winding up of Deutschland AG', to quote the subtitle of another book.[24]

Even more radical statements have been made by American corporate law experts: in an influential and much discussed article, two lawyers from Yale and Harvard Law Schools declare nothing less than 'The End of History for Corporate Law'.[25] The US system, they assert, has established itself as the normative role model, and alternative models like the German one had failed.

The main arguments for decline and failure can be summarised as follows:

- In corporate governance the so-called market for corporate control has undergone wide-ranging change since the mid-1990s, above all in corporate strategy, especially in the financial sector. The focus is now on shareholder value, barriers for takeovers have been scrapped and cross-shareholdings largely abolished. Systematic disposal of 'super-ordinated' linkages has led to a 'decline of organised capitalism' or at least its 'disorganisation'.[26]
- In industrial relations, a substantial weakening of associational strength has occurred, both on the trade union and on the employer side. Streeck and Hassel talk of the 'crumbling pillars of social partnership', which has developed from an asset of the German system into a liability.[27] The reason is that both associations and the state are now too weak to push through their own preferred strategies, but still strong enough to block other strategies. As a result, collective bargaining has turned into a policy oriented towards the interests of labour market insiders, but incapable of contributing to the solution of labour market problems, especially high unemployment – as the failure of the 'Alliance for Jobs' negotiations made abundantly clear.

- In the financial system banks have undertaken a change of strategy away from the 'Hausbank' model towards one focusing on investment banking. They have divested their shareholdings in non-financial firms, because of emerging conflicts of interest.[28] Investment banking promises bigger profit, which is why banks sold their investments in corporations and gave up seats on supervisory boards. In the case of Deutsche Bank, in 1996 it held the chair of the supervisory board on no less than 29 of Germany's top 100 corporations. Only two years later, this number had shrunk to 17, and in 2001 the bank declared in its corporate guidelines that it would no longer seek any chairmanships on supervisory boards.[29] The banks, in other words, have also shifted to an exclusive focus on shareholder value.
- Political reforms supported this development. In 1998, the *KonTraG* bill (*Gesetz zur Kontrolle und Transparenz im Unternehmensbereich*) was supported by all parties on the floor of the Bundestag. Strikingly it was originally an initiative of the Social Democrats when still in opposition. Joint criticism from the political left and the political right of the 'power of the banks'[30] meant that 'Deutschland AG' no longer enjoyed any support in parliament. In 2001, budgetary changes resulted in the abolition of capital gains taxation for sales of corporate investments. This measure provided a clear incentive to divest the cross-shareholdings and block-holdings that had been characteristic of Deutschland AG.
- The 'end of history for corporate law' is predicted by two leading American authors, who argue that an international convergence towards a model exclusively oriented towards shareholder interests is not only inescapable and has already widely taken place but is also preferable. They suggest calling this model the 'standard model' forthwith and ascribe this worldwide convergence to the failure of alternatives, such as the 'labour-oriented model' (as they call Germany with its co-determination), and the 'state-oriented model', which includes France and Japan. In their view, bad economic performance and the end of socialism had eliminated the latter model; the conflict of interest between capital and labour (and the unrest springing from it) had rendered the German model uncompetitive.

  Both authors exclusively use corporate law literature for their sweeping assessment. They might profit from a more interdisciplinary approach and a visit to a social science library – where they would likely not only discover foreign trade statistics instructive with a view to German competitiveness, but also a literature on 'varieties of capitalism' and the persistent differences between national economic models – which implicitly puts question marks behind the hypothesis of the decline of the 'Rhenish model' – and even more the hypothesis about 'the end of history'.

National Models of Capitalism and their Persistence

At the same time as domestic popularity of the 'German model' was waning and the discussion about globalisation – and the convergence that it would bring – took off in academic journals and in political commentary, a new literature argued in favour of the persistence of 'varieties of capitalism'. In this literature the 'German model' played a prominent role.

The literature on national models of capitalism is complex and multi-faceted. However, two things are of particular interest: this literature is truly interdisciplinary with contributions from sociologists, economists and political scientists; and it illustrates a growing differentiation of concepts and an active debate. As a consequence, this area of academic investigation has over the last decade grown from more journalistic beginnings into a branch of systematic empirical and theoretically well-founded social science research.

The French economist and then President of Assurances Générales de France (AGF), Michel Albert, began the debate about classifying market economies with his book *Capitalism against Capitalism.* It is probably no coincidence that the debate started briefly after the demise of Communism, when market economies had won a resounding victory over planned economies.[31] Albert distinguished between a 'Rhenish' and a 'neo-American' model of market economy, and left no doubt which of the two he preferred. On grounds of superior economic and social performance, he considered the 'Rhenish' model (of which the German model is the most prominent expression) preferable and advocated its adoption for France. His book undoubtedly hit a nerve and became popular very quickly as well as translated into many languages. It often still serves as a reference point for the debate, as the term 'Rhenish capitalism' demonstrates.

In the following years the analysis was broadened and substantiated with a focus on questions of firm organisation, alternative disciplinary mechanisms and problems of agency in the economic literature.[32] The publication of the edited volume *Varieties of Capitalism*[33] by Hall and Soskice was a milestone, not only because it provided it with a name (at least in political science), but primarily because it provided a sophisticated theoretical grounding. Building on theories from the economics of information and institutional approaches, Hall and Soskice placed the firm in the centre of their analysis. They distinguished two types of market economies: 'coordinated' (comprising such countries as Germany, Sweden, Switzerland, the Netherlands and Japan), and 'liberal' (the Anglo-Saxon countries: USA, United Kingdom, Canada, Australia and New Zealand). Their model was the first to emphasise the complementarity of the constituent partial systems (finance, industrial relations, training, inter-firm relations) for the performance of the system as a whole, distilling from that their hypothesis of 'comparative institutional advantage'. From this hypothesis it follows that convergence should be unlikely, as it would require forgoing existing comparative advantages. Their volume applies the approach to a wide variety of policy areas, ranging from labour market and corporate governance to employers' preferences in social policy, in a way that combines theoretical and empirical inquiry.

More recent contributions add the dimension of discourse[34] and extend the number of countries analysed as well as the number of varieties.[35] But the most important point in this literature is that it finds strong evidence in favour of the existence and persistence of different national economic models – or 'varieties of capitalism' – even if a precise typology of these different systems is still not agreed.

This literature would analyse the German economic system as the interaction of four sub-systems (see Figure 1):

- A system of financing enterprises that can be labelled 'bank-oriented' and provides long-term capital (also described as 'patient capital'). In exchange, banks which provide this capital obtain influence on the business – often via seats on the supervisory board. The stock market – in contrast to the American model – plays only a minor role in corporate finance.

FIGURE 1
THE COMPONENTS OF THE 'RHENISH CAPITALISM' MODEL

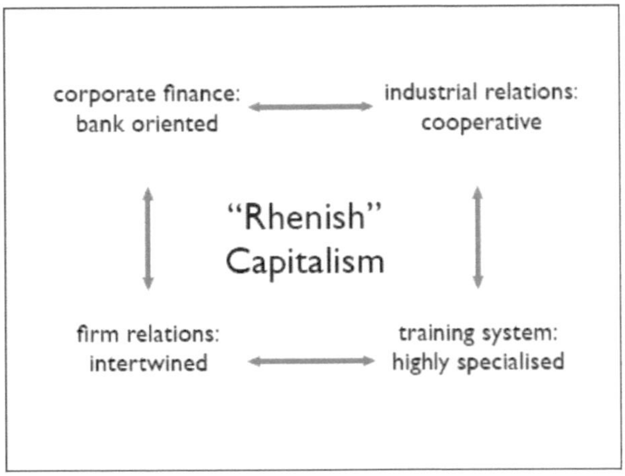

- The system of labour relations is characterised by a strong element of cooperation, which to a large part rests on the comparatively strong role of associations. One result is a high degree of employment protection, which in turn leads to comparatively long periods of employment tenure.
- The system of training combines general and firm-specific skills, which are often highly specialised.
- Relationships between firms are often characterised by an element of cooperation as well as competition, for example when agreeing on standards, where associations play an important role. Cross-shareholdings help to stabilise long-term supplier relations, and interlocking directorships enable firms to gain detailed inside information about each other even without wide-ranging publicity rules.

In short, the German economic system relies to a considerable extent on non-market forms of coordination and strong 'networks'. The constituent parts do not exist independent of each other – in fact, it is only through their functional interaction and their complementarity that they form a system or a 'model':

- 'Patient capital' (which does not have to vie to maximise profit on a quarterly basis) enables businesses to credibly commit to a high degree of employment security, which in turn makes acquiring and investing in firm-specific skills rational for both employees and employers – since they do not have to be afraid of 'sunk investments'.
- Training standards that are the result of cooperation between firms add to this model, because they increase the likelihood of finding suitable employment in the industry (for the employees) and of finding suitably qualified labour (for the firms). In addition, such cooperation makes it possible to obtain inside information about the performance of firms, which means that the correction mechanism of 'hostile takeovers' in the case of failure (which is so typical of the American system)

becomes as unnecessary as it is unlikely because of the prevalence of cross-shareholdings (which are the root cause for the nickname Deutschland AG – Germany, Inc. – that has been given to the system). Safety from takeover bids, in turn, enables firms to take a long-term view of business development, which again is required for the 'patient capital' and its long time horizons (see Figure 1 for a graphic depiction of the system and its interaction).

An economic system characterised by these features will not exclusively focus on the interests of the owners, but take into account the interests of all stakeholders, such as employees, suppliers, customers and society as a whole. It is particularly well equipped for competition in the area of 'diversified quality production', which means incremental improvements in high-quality products with little price competition.[36]

CONTINUITY AND CHANGE IN THE GERMAN ECONOMIC SYSTEM

Does the flourishing literature on 'varieties of capitalism' and their persistent difference imply that the 'Cologne decline hypothesis' is wrong? Perhaps not, though I would argue that at least two criticisms can be made concerning the stability and robustness of their results.

- Many of the conclusions are based on the behaviour (and changing behaviour) of a select group of big enterprises (such as Deutsche Bank, Allianz and – in the case of hostile takeovers – Mannesmann). However, these firms are not typical of the German economy, where the 'Hausbank' relationship is still central to many small and medium-sized enterprises. Indeed, this *Mittelstand* (firms below 500 employees and with a turnover of less than €50 million) comprises a relatively bigger share of the German economy than in Britain or the United States. It accounts for around 70% of employment and about half of gross value production of the enterprise sector.
- More importantly, the results are based on a period of observation that is in many respects an exception rather than the rule – namely the years of the last stock market bubble of the late 1990s and early 2000s. This period has now given way to normalisation. A crucial test will be whether the results will be confirmed during more normal times.

There is evidence of a rollback of some of the developments of the bubble period and of substantial stability in other areas. Hence it remains unclear whether the changes that undoubtedly take place in Germany really hit the core of the systemic functionality of the German economic model and will ultimately cause it to fail. So far, it seems, that case has not (yet?) been made.

Restrictions of space do not allow me here to embark upon a fully fledged empirical test of the various symptoms of the 'decline hypothesis'. They will be covered in more detail in the contributions by Lütz (for the financial sector) and Menz (for labour market reform) in this volume. But in this section I will put forward a couple of observations that would seem to question the hypothesis of systemic change and support the notion of considerable stability at the core of the German system. I will make four points in this respect: one about macroeconomic problems; one about a continuing culture of cooperation; one about evidence for reversal of bubble-period strategies, and one about the importance of political decisions.

While there is no doubt about the weakness of recent macroeconomic performance in Germany, it seems curious that macro-level factors are never used to explain this weakness. As a consequence, the whole malaise of low growth rates and high unemployment is attributed exclusively to microeconomic problems, particularly in the labour market, and the failure to reform those decisively. This is mistaken. There have been substantial macroeconomic disadvantages for the German economy from the introduction of European Monetary Union which contribute to the negative performance.[37] Two disadvantages stand out: Germany lost its privilege of the lowest benchmark rate of interest on government bonds (which sets the floor for the national interest rate); and Germany, traditionally a low inflation economy, now has one of the highest real interest rates in the Euro Zone. The reason for the first problem – the loss of a comparative advantage – is that other Euro Zone countries' long-term interest rates converged on the German rate in the run-up to EMU. The reason for the latter problem is that the ECB only sets the nominal rate of interest for the Euro Zone as a whole. A Euro Zone country with a (comparatively) low rate of inflation, in this case Germany, has consequently a higher real rate of interest than one with a higher rate of inflation. One can only speculate about the reasons for the absence of these facts from public policy discourse in Germany: a fear of further increasing public discontent with the euro would be an obvious candidate; not wanting to distract from the perceived need for domestic reform would be another.

Examining the debate about transformation of the German model, Carola Frege has rightly argued that significant change would be instantiated by change in the traditionally cooperative attitudes in industrial relations.[38] She finds no evidence for that in the surveys that she conducted with trade union officials. In a similar vein, evidence from recent events in collective bargaining also seems to demonstrate a continuing culture of cooperation that produces results without major conflict – in spite of the organisational weakening of both trade union and employers' associations. The cases of Volkswagen, Siemens and DaimlerChrysler in 2004 have all seen painful concessions from trade unions in response to substantial cost-cutting demands from management without major conflict or confrontation. Other examples of continuing cooperative attitudes would be IG Metall joining forces with the metal industry employers in setting up a pension scheme[39] or an agreement between the big German banks to coordinate their ratings for the Mittelstand and thus facilitate lending for that crucial sector of the German economy.[40] If cooperation is at the heart of the 'coordinated market economy' model, then the aforementioned examples would seem to point to significant continuity.

Less continuity is apparent in some of the purportedly seismic shifts in company and particularly bank strategy. Listing German companies on the New York Stock Exchange (NYSE) and shifting bank strategy away from retail banking and towards investment banking seemed to be all the rage in the late 1990s. But not any longer: the 'big' German banks, such as Deutsche Bank (which was accused by *The Economist* of behaving like a 'giant hedge fund'[41]), have pledged to cut down on investment banking and try to win new customers in the retail market. The reason is that income from the retail market is more stable than from investment banking – and that, without such stability, analysts will downgrade the banks, with ultimately negative effects for capitalisation, making them a potential takeover target.[42] Similarly, many German companies discovered that the costs of a listing on the NYSE can easily outweigh the benefits. Therefore, many of them try to de-list – only to find that this is a difficult process.[43]

Finally, it is important not to underestimate the importance of political decisions (as opposed to market decisions) in determining the future viability of national economic systems. Here – in addition to the national level – the European level plays an increasingly important role. Whether and how successfully respective interests influence decisions on that level is of crucial importance. One area of corporate governance regulation demonstrates how influence on political decisions can be used to 'defend' features of the 'German model': The German stock market has a low degree of capitalisation, which means that German corporations are comparatively cheap to buy if foreign shares are used as a currency. A German firm listed on the stock market is rated at only a quarter of a comparable British firm per unit of turnover and at only a sixth per employee.[44] The reason for this divergence is that while a British firm exclusively focuses on profitability, for a German firm profitability is only one goal among several others, such as turnover, market share and employment. What makes a German firm strong in product markets thus weakens it in the market for corporate control.

The European Commission's attempt, driven by the desire for capital market integration, to harmonise the rules for corporate takeover, was accordingly a threat to the German system. It had been on the Commission's agenda since the early 1990s and was the subject of intense negotiations. In 2001, the Commission launched a draft directive – based on British rules – which included the abolition of all defence mechanisms against takeovers (such as restricted voting rights for shares, 'golden shares' or multiple voting rights for certain classes of shares).[45] The German government fought against this proposal, but was voted down three times in the European Council of Ministers by a margin of 14:1. However, a massive political mobilisation ultimately led to a close defeat of the proposal in the European Parliament. Further consultations followed, and in December 2003 the Italian Presidency proposed a compromise in which all regulations concerning defence mechanisms for takeovers were made optional for member countries – an almost complete reversal of the original proposal. The Commission consequently vehemently opposed this compromise, but – in view of the Council's unanimous position – was no longer able to withdraw its original proposal.

CONCLUSION

This essay cannot deliver a definitive verdict on the viability of the 'German model'. By examining the controversy about the viability of 'Rhenish capitalism' and challenging the 'decline hypothesis' with the recent literature on the persistence of differences between national economic models, it demonstrates that, while changes are taking place in the German economic model, evidence for fundamental and long-term change is so far not strong. At the same time it would be unwise to presume an unchangeable stability of the German model.

However, though there are challenges and change, it remains unclear whether such change will affect the core of the German model and disable the positive complementarity of its sub-systems – its 'comparative institutional advantage'. As noted above, in July 2004 the management at DaimerChrysler demanded cost cuts in the order of €500 million per year and an agreement was reached within a week, combining cuts for employees with long-term employment guarantees. This example seems to support the conclusion that patterns of interaction and exchange may be very deeply entrenched and not be affected by a decline in organisational strength on both sides of industry – even though theoretical considerations would lead one to expect less cooperation and growing radicalisation as a result of less 'encompassing' organisations.[46] As Thelen has pointed out, it is not only the trade unions that keep the system alive, but also employers, and for good reasons.[47]

The conclusion that the German system is changing, but not undergoing systemic change, is also supported by recent management studies and economics literature.[48] In addition, the Anglo-Saxon system may lose some of its shine – not only because of obvious system failures like Enron or WorldCom, but also because recent academic studies have raised serious question marks about whether the Anglo-Saxon system really works as it is supposed to work – particularly the nexus between corporate governance and economic performance.[49]

If the Anglo-Saxon model should lose the hegemony that it undoubtedly possessed in public and academic discourse at least since the mid-1990s,[50] German businessmen, as well as politicians and the general public, would have to awaken from the comfortable gloominess into which they have settled recently and assess their economic system more objectively. They will then most likely find that economic systems are far less at the complete mercy of anonymous markets than is often assumed in public discourse about globalisation, for many important decisions concerning economic systems are political decisions. Both the *KonTraG* and European takeover decisions have demonstrated this importance of the political dimension. Whether features that can be defended will be defended depends ultimately on political will and skill. The German political system is a very complex environment in this respect.

NOTES

*For helpful comments to earlier versions of this paper I am grateful to the participants of the workshop on 'The Politics of Economic Reform in Germany' at the University of Cardiff, 16–17 September 2004, and the participants of the conference on 'Die Politische Ökonomie der Europäischen Wirtschafts- und Währungsunion', hosted by the Political Economy section of the German Political Science Association at the Max Planck Institute for the Study of Societies in Cologne, 3–4 December 2004. I have also benefited from detailed comments by the editors of this volume and from Martin Höpner and André Nilsen. I am grateful for all advice, even if occasionally I chose not to follow it. This article was finished during my time as a visiting fellow at the Social Science Research Centre in Berlin (WZB) to which I extend my gratitude.

1. For an introductory overview of the debate see Andreas Busch, 'Unpacking the Globalization Debate: Approaches, Evidence and Data', in Colin Hay and David Marsh (eds.), *Demystifying Globalization* (Basingstoke: Macmillan, 2000), pp.21–48.
2. Colin Hay, 'Contemporary Capitalism, Globalization, Regionalization and the Persistence of National Variation', *Review of International Studies* 26/4 (2000), pp.509–31.
3. Fritz W. Scharpf and Vivien A. Schmidt (eds.), *Welfare and Work in the Open Economy. Volume II: Diverse Responses to Common Challenges* (Oxford: Oxford University Press, 2000).

4. To give a few examples out of many: the 'German model' (or 'model Germany') features in Fritz Scharpf's comparative analysis of Social Democratic economic policy in the 1970s, Fritz W. Scharpf, *Sozialdemokratische Krisenpolitik in Europa. Das 'Modell Deutschland' im Vergleich* (Frankfurt am Main, New York: Campus, 1987); in Karl-Heinz Paqué's description of the long-term challenges to Germany's labour market, Karl-Heinz Paqué, 'Unemployment and the Crisis of the German Model: A Long-Term Interpretation', in Herbert Giersch (ed.), *Fighting Europe's Unemployment in the 1990s* (New York: Springer, 1995); in Kathleen Thelen's insights about the persistence of employers' interests in cooperative relations with trade unions, Kathleen Thelen, 'Why German Employers Cannot Bring Themselves to Dismantle the German Model', in Torben Iversen; Jonas Pontusson and David Soskice (eds.), *Unions, Employers, and Central Banks: Macroeconomic Coordination and Institutional Change in Social Market Economies* (Cambridge: Cambridge University Press, 2000), pp.138–69; and in Helmut Wiesenthal's description of the political system's institutional conservatism, Helmut Wiesenthal, 'German Unification and "Model Germany": An Adventure in Institutional Conservatism', *West European Politics* 26/4 (2000), pp.37–58.
5. See Scharpf, 'Sozialdemokratische Krisenpolitik in Europa' for a detailed description.
6. Rudolf Hilferding, *Das Finanzkapital. Eine Studie über die jüngste Entwicklung des Kapitalismus* (Wien: Verlag der Wiener Volksbuchhandlung, 1910).
7. Alexander Gerschenkron, *Economic Backwardness in Historical Perspective. A Book of Essays* (Cambridge, MA: Harvard University Press, 1966), p.14.
8. Hans-Ulrich Wehler, *Deutsche Gesellschaftsgeschichte. Band 3: Von der 'Deutschen Doppelrevolution' bis zum Beginn des Ersten Weltkrieges: 1849–1914* (München: Beck, 1995), pp.662–80.
9. Andrew Shonfield, *Modern Capitalism. The Changing Balance of Public and Private Power* (London: Oxford University Press, 1965).
10. For the concept of 'parapublic institutions', in which associations play an important role, and which are considered a characteristic of the German political system, see Peter Katzenstein, *Policy and Politics in West Germany. The Growth of a Semisovereign State* (Philadelphia: Temple University Press, 1987) and Andreas Busch, 'Shock-Absorbers Under Stress: Parapublic Institutions and the Double Challenges of German Unification and European Integration', in Simon Green and William E. Paterson (eds.), *Governance in Contemporary Germany: The Semisovereign State Revisited* (Cambridge: Cambridge University Press, 2005), pp. 94–114.
11. On the latter episode see for example Andreas Busch, *Staat und Globalisierung. Das Politikfeld Bankenregulierung im internationalen Vergleich* (Wiesbaden: Westdeutscher Verlag, 2003), chapter 5.1; and Manfred Pohl, 'Die Entstehung und Entwicklung des Universalbankensystems seit der Mitte des 19. Jahrhunderts', in Norbert Kloten and Johann Heinrich von Stein (eds.), *Geld-, Bank- und Börsenwesen. Ein Handbuch* (Stuttgart: Schäffer-Poeschel, 39th edn. 1993), pp.187–93.
12. Will Hutton, *The State We're In* (London: Vintage, 1996).
13. Michael E. Porter, *Capital Choices: Changing the Ways America Invests in Industry* (Washington, DC: Council on Competitiveness, 1992) and Michael E. Porter, 'Capital Disadvantage: America's Failing Capital Investment System', *Harvard Business Review* (Sept.–Oct. 1992), pp.65–82.
14. For more detailed empirical information about globalisation see e.g. Paul Hirst and Grahame Thompson, *Globalization in Question. The International Economy and the Possibilities of Governance* (Cambridge: Polity, 1996); Dani Rodrik, *Has Globalization Gone Too Far?* (Washington, DC: Institute for International Economics, 1997); David Held, Anothony McGrew, David Goldblatt and Jonathan Perraton, *Global Transformations. Politics, Economics and Culture* (Cambridge: Polity, 1999); Busch, 'Unpacking the Globalization Debate'; OECD, *Measuring Globalisation. The Role of Multinationals in OECD Economies, Vol. 1: Manufacturing Sector; Vol. 2: Services* (Paris: OECD, 2001).
15. A survey of the respective economic literature can be found in e.g. Günther G. Schulze and Heinrich W. Ursprung, 'Globalisierung contra Nationalstaat? Ein Überblick über die empirische Evidenz', in Andreas Busch and Thomas Plümper (eds.), *Nationaler Staat und internationale Wirtschaft. Anmerkungen zum Thema Globalisierung* (Baden-Baden: Nomos, 1999), pp.41–89.
16. Jeffry A. Frieden and Ronald Rogowski, 'The Impact of the International Economy on National Policies: An Analytical Overview', in Robert O. Keohane and Helen V. Milner (eds.), *Internationalization and Domestic Politics* (New York/Cambridge: Cambridge University Press, 1996), pp.25–47.
17. Douglass C. North, *Institutions, Institutional Change and Economic Performance* (Cambridge/ New York: Cambridge University Press, 1990); Oliver E. Williamson, 'Transaction Cost Economics and Organization Theory', in Neil J. Smelser and Richard Swedberg (eds.), *The Handbook of Economic Sociology* (Princeton: Princeton University Press, 1994), pp.76–107.
18. James G. March and Johan P. Olsen, *Rediscovering Institutions. The Organizational Basis of Politics* (New York: Free Press, 1989), p.167.
19. See the quotes at the beginning of the article as well as Busch, *Staat und Globalisierung* for a more extensive review of recent results.

20. Colin Hay and Ben Rosamond, 'Globalisation, European Integration and the Discursive Construction of Economic Imperatives', in *Journal of European Public Policy* 9/2 (2002), pp.147–67. See also Tom Conley, 'Globalisation and the Politics of Persuasion and Coercion', *Australian Journal of Social Issues* 39/2 (2004), pp.183–200.
21. Interview in *Die Zeit*, 9 May 1997, p.19, quoted after Roland Czada, 'Reformloser Wandel. Stabilität und Anpassung in politischen Akteursystem der Bundesrepublik', in Thomas Ellwein and Everhard Holtmann (eds.), *50 Jahre Bundesrepublik Deutschland [PVS Sonderheft 30/1999]* (Opladen/ Wiesbaden: Westdeutscher Verlag, 1999), pp.397–412.
22. Jürgen Beyer (ed.), *Vom Zukunfts- zum Auslaufmodell? Die deutsche Wirtschaftsordnung im Wandel* (Wiesbaden: Westdeutscher Verlag, 2003).
23. Jürgen Beyer, 'Einleitung: Unkoordinierte Modellpflege am koordinierten deutschen Modell, in Beyer (ed.), *Vom Zukunfts- zum Auslaufmodell?*, p.11.
24. Wolfgang Streeck and Martin Höpner (eds.), *Alle Macht dem Markt? Fallstudien zur Abwicklung der Deutschland AG* (Frankfurt/Main/New York: Campus, 2003).
25. Henry Hansmann and Reinier Kraakman, 'The End of History for Corporate Law', in Jeffrey N. Gordon and Mark J. Roe (eds.), *Convergence and Persistence in Corporate Governance* (Cambridge: Cambridge University Press, 2004), pp.33–68. (First published in *Georgetown Law Journal*, 89 (Jan. 2001), pp.439–67).
26. Martin Höpner, *Der Organisierte Kapitalismus in Deutschland und sein Niedergang. Unternehmenskontrolle und Arbeitsbeziehungen im Wandel* (Wiesbaden: Verlag für Sozialwissenschaften, 2004), pp.300–321.
27. Wolfgang Streeck and Anke Hassel, 'The Crumbling Pillars of Social Partnership', *West European Politics* 26/4 (2003), pp.101–24.
28. This had become very clear on the occasion of the attempted hostile takeover of Thyssen by Krupp in 1997, when Deutsche Bank advised the 'attacker' Krupp while simultaneously holding a seat on the supervisory board of 'victim' Thyssen.
29. Jürgen Beyer and Martin Höpner, 'Corporate Governance and the Disintegration of Organised Capitalism in the 1990s', *West European Politics* 26/4 (2003). [Special issue on 'Germany: Beyond the Stable State', ed. by Herbert Kitschelt and Wolfgang Streeck].
30. For the historical roots of this criticism and precedents for such cross-party coalitions regarding the 'power of the banks' see Busch, *Staat und Globalisierung*, pp.108–9 and 134–5.
31. Michel Albert, *Capitalism against Capitalism* (London: Whurr, 1993).
32. Pieter W. Moerland, 'Alternative Disciplinary Mechanisms in Different Corporate Systems', *Journal of Economic Behavior and Organization* 26 (1995), pp.17–34; H.W. De Jong, 'European Capitalism: Between Freedom and Social Justice', *Review of Industrial Organization* 10 (1995), pp.399–419.
33. Peter A. Hall and David Soskice (eds.), *Varieties of Capitalism. The Institutional Foundations of Comparative Advantage* (Oxford/New York: Oxford University Press, 2001).
34. Viven A. Schmidt, *The Futures of European Capitalism* (Oxford: Oxford University Press, 2002).
35. Bruno Amable, *The Diversity of Modern Capitalism* (Oxford: Oxford University Press, 2003).
36. Wolfgang Streeck, 'On Institutional Conditions of Diversified Quality Production', in Egon Matzner and Wolfgang Streeck (eds.), *Beyond Keynesianism: The Socio-Economics of Production and Full Employment* (Aldershot: Elgar, 1991), pp.21–61.
37. Focusing on problems here does not mean to deny that there have been substantial benefits as well. The fact that the D-Mark does not alone have to shoulder the recent violent exchange rate fluctuations of the US dollar is only the most readily evident.
38. Carola M. Frege, 'Transforming German Workplace Relations: Quo Vadis Cooperation?', *Economic and Industrial Democracy* 24/3 (2003), pp.317–47.
39. Christine Trampusch, 'Vom Klassenkampf zur Riesterrente. Die Mitbestimmung und der Wandel der Interessen von Gewerkschaften und Arbeitgeberverbänden an der betrieblichen und tariflichen Sozialpolitik', *Zeitschrift für Sozialreform* 50/3 (2004), pp.223–54.
40. *Süddeutsche Zeitung*, 9 Dec. 2004, p.34.
41. *The Economist*, 28 Aug. 2004, pp.65f.
42. *Süddeutsche Zeitung*, 18 Sept. 2004, p.19.
43. *Süddeutsche Zeitung*, 21 Sept. 2004, p.27 and 16 Nov. 2004, p.34.
44. Martin Höpner and Gregory Jackson, 'An Emerging Market for Corporate Control? The Mannesmann Takeover and German Corporate Governance', *MPIfG Discussion Papers*, Vol. 01/4 (Köln: Max-Planck-Institut für Gesellschaftsforschung, 2001).
45. On the case of the EU takeover directive, see e.g. Erik Berglöf and Mike Burkart, 'European Takeover Regulation', *Economic Policy* 18/1 (2003), pp.171–213; Lucian Cernat, 'The Emerging European Corporate Governance Model: Anglo-Saxon, Continental, or still the Century of Diversity?', *Journal of European Public Policy* 11/1 (2004), pp.147–66.

46. Mancur Olson, *The Logic of Collective Action Public Goods and the Theory of Groups* (Cambridge, MA: Harvard University Press, 1965).
47. Thelen, 'Why German Employers Cannot Bring Themselves to Dismantle the German Model'.
48. See for example Marc Goergen, Miguel C. Manjon and Luc Renneboog, 'Recent Developments in German Corporate Governance', *Finance Working Paper*, Vol.41 (Brussels: European Corporate Governance Institute, 2004); Andreas Hackethal, Reinhard H. Schmidt and Marcel Tyrell, 'Corporate Governance in Germany: Transition to a Modern Capital-Market-Based System?', *Journal of Institutional and Theoretical Economics* 159 (2003), pp.664–74; Eva Terberger, 'The German Financial System: Great Institutional Change and Little Effect?', *Journal of Institutional and Theoretical Economics* 159 (2003), pp.707–16. Considering the small, but detectable normative bias the latter two authors have in favour of an Anglo-Saxon style system (a 'modern' system, as the first authors put it, while the second writes about 'limited success of German reforms'), these assessments are particularly interesting.
49. See Mary A. O'Sullivan, *Contests for Corporate Control. Corporate Governance and Economic Performance in the United States and Germany* (Oxford/New York: Oxford University Press, 2000); Marco Becht, Patrick Bolton and Ailsa Röell, 'Corporate Governance and Control', in George Constantinidis, Milton Harris and René Stulz (eds.), *Handbook of the Economics of Finance* (Amsterdam/London: Elsevier/North-Holland, 2003), section 7.1.
50. It should be noted that already Albert spoke of the 'star quality', 'excitement' and 'charm' of the neo-American model, which he contrasted with its inferior performance. Albert, *Capitalism against Capitalism*, p.10.

The Finance Sector in Transition: A Motor for Economic Reform?

SUSANNE LÜTZ

Finance used to be the cornerstone of the German model of managed capitalism. Restricted competition within the banking sector allowed for risk-sharing and a high degree of collective action. A stable network of relations between banks, industry and the Länder was seen as a precondition for long-term investment strategies and regional industrial policy. In general, finance served as an infrastructure for German industry and the state.

From the mid-1980s, however, European and international liberalisation has triggered a massive structural change in global finance. The expansion of cross-border financial markets has intensified competition between domestic financial systems. At the same time, domestic finance has been transformed by a strategic reorientation of banks and companies towards the global capital market as an investment location and as a source of corporate finance. A multilevel system of regulation has redefined the standards of risk management and investor protection, ultimately widening the regulatory role of the state. The adaptation pressures arising from this combination of developments bear particularly heavily on bank-based financial systems like that in Germany.

German finance has experienced a profound transformation. As financial relations have become increasingly short-term, risk-averse and *commodified*, they have lost their former character as infrastructure. The marketisation of finance is accompanied by an increasing amount of public regulation, with the state playing a more active role as *promotor* and *regulator* of the domestic financial marketplace. On the other hand, regional governments have defended the public banking sector against privatisation, and have experimented with public–private structures designed to preserve regional industrial policy networks. The trade unions, moreover, have lobbied very effectively for sustaining co-determination in corporate governance. Thus while the German model of managed capitalism in general is becoming more market-oriented, we observe at the same time that the 'requisite variety' of organisational models within the national model is increasing rather than decreasing.

This study explores the patterns and driving forces of this transformation. It is argued that domestic change was mostly a response to exogenous forces, such as European competition policy, financial globalisation and the re-regulation of financial markets at both European and global level. Changes in global finance led private banks and global firms to change their preferences and business strategies, thereby causing spill-over effects and further adaptation pressures on the small and medium-sized company sector. The system of multilevel governance (particularly EU competition policy) served as an 'opportunity structure' within which advocates of reform were able to constrain the choices of those preferring the status quo.

THE OLD MODEL: FINANCE AS INFRASTRUCTURE

German finance used to be the prototype of a bank-based financial system.[1] As in other continental European countries and in Japan, credits rather than capital markets were the dominating source of corporate finance. The German model differed from the French or Japanese systems, however, in that the framework of corporate financing was defined by coordination among firms, associations and banks rather than the state.

Until now, the German banking sector has been dominated by *group* competition between three main types of institutions; private commercial banks, public or non-commercial savings banks (including the Land banks), and credit cooperatives. All three types of institution are universal banks, permitted to trade in securities and to deal in deposit banking and lending. They vary, however, in corporate structure and business strategy. Unlike private banks, public savings banks and credit cooperatives are also charged, alongside their commercial activities, with the task of promoting the general welfare. One particular task is to ensure that all regions are sufficiently provided with financial services (the principle of *territoriality*). Länder banks are also required to contribute to industrial policy. As public law institutions, the savings and Länder banks are supported in these functions by their respective municipal and state governments. The latter shoulder unlimited liability for their banks, guaranteeing funds to cover any unrecoverable capital losses. For credit cooperatives, the collective purpose of the institutions lies in the support of their members – traditionally private customers and small artisan or retail businesses. As in the savings bank sector, the existence of each institution is guaranteed, since the members of the cooperative are personally liable for the organisation in proportion to shareholding. The umbrella associations of the different banking groups provide collective insurance funds to protect customer deposits against insolvency. Thus the sector exhibits an impressive degree of internal governance, designed to guarantee the continued existence of member firms and thereby the stability of the sector.

Similar structures and functions can also be found in the *Hausbank relationship* between *banks and industry*, based on the multiple ties of ownership and lending.

Banks represent shareholders as a delegated monitor or through proxy votes; they hold seats on supervisory boards and often coordinate rescue operations in the event of corporate crisis. Close relationships between 'big banks' and 'big business' figured prominently in coal, steel, heavy machinery and the electrical industry. (The financial needs of regions and of small and medium-sized *Mittelstand* sector were mostly served by the smaller savings and cooperative banks rather than big universal banks.[2]) *Hausbank* relationships were seen to provide 'patient capital', enabling firms to make long-term employment commitments and invest in projects that generate long-term returns. Providers of such capital are willing to do so because they have access to inside information about the firms, either gained through a significant ownership stake in the company or through extensive long-term lending. The absence of hostile takeovers is widely regarded as facilitating patient capital since the threat of takeover forces firms to maximise short-term profitability. The internal structure of company control (corporate governance) reinforces the capacity for coordination. Due to mandatory labour co-determination, labour spokespersons sit side-by-side with the representatives of shareholders and banks, thus management must be responsive to multiple stakeholders in its strategies.

In a structural model that is based on a pronounced degree of self-regulation by banks, industry and labour, the state does not play a major role, except on the Länder level. The autonomy of the German Federal Bank has been seen as one of the main factors preventing the state from dictating monetary policy.[3] The state is, however, involved in making managed capitalism work, sometimes indirectly and sometimes decisively. For example, the state codifies into law collectively negotiated settlements, such as the capital adequacy standards set by the main banking associations, and makes these compulsory for all sectors of the market.[4] As a partner in crisis cartels, the state provides loan guarantees and thereby compensates its partners for concessions. The closest relationships probably occur at Länder level and in the municipalities. Regional and municipal governments absorb financial risks by shouldering unlimited liabilities for their banks and in turn use the public banking sector for industrial policy purposes.

Overall, in the German model of bank-based finance, firms are embedded in stable networks that limit the influence of shareholders and distribute power among managers, employees, investors, regional authorities, suppliers, customers, creditors and cooperating companies. Risks are internalised through collective self-help, corporate decisions are controlled by an insider network and losers in the structural processes of modernisation are compensated.

EXTERNAL CHALLENGES TO THE GERMAN FINANCIAL MODEL

Since the 1980s, the German model of credit-based finance and the domestic relationship between banks, industry and the state have been challenged by three structural changes in the international environment. First, European competition policy attacks the barriers to market integration and questions the German model of group competition. Second, an increasing share of financial intermediation is taking place through capital markets as opposed to bank lending. Third, re-regulation of capital market relations at both European and global level has redefined the standards of risk management and investor protection, ultimately widening the regulatory role of the state.

The Challenge from European Competition Policy

Since the 1990s, German private banks have used the 'opportunity structure' of European competition policy to question the status of their competitors in the public banking system. In 1994, the German association of private banks, in cooperation with its counterparts in the UK and France, filed a formal objection with the European Commission accusing the government of North Rhine-Westphalia of illegally subsidising the Westdeutsche Landesbank (WestLB, West German State Bank). In 1992, the government had offered the bank a capital infusion in the form of publicly owned housing assets at the rock-bottom interest rate of 0.6 per cent. In November 2002, the EU Commission opened anti-subsidy cases against five other *Landesbanken* that were involved in transactions comparable to the WestLB.[5] In September 2004, after 12 years of struggle on the issue of illegal subsidies, the Commission reached a compromise with the German federal government, state governments, public banks and the association of German private banks that six *Landesbanken* have to repay their state governments subsidies amounting to €4.3 billion. However, the states will have to back up their public banks with fresh capital once the money is paid back, which in turn raises the question of possible commercial disadvantage for the private banking sector and causes a new clash with the Commission.[6]

At the Amsterdam European Council of 1997, Germany won some support for its practice of considering public credit institutions as providers of 'services of general economic interest' exempt from EU competition rules. The following year, however, the Commission argued in a draft Communication that 'it is for the Commission to apply' EU competition rules 'to credit institutions entrusted with the provision of public services'. Given the advent of the single currency, the Commission claimed, the provision of public services may not affect competition in a way harmful to Community interests. Thus, the Commission expressed its opinion that it did not consider the Amsterdam agreement as *carte blanche* for subsidies for all services. Moreover, the Commission announced its willingness to look at existing state aid cases to ensure that a level playing field can be achieved for all competing credit institutions. This announcement was practically a signal to the private banks to take the next move.[7]

In December 1999, the European Banking Federation, the association of private banks in Europe, submitted a formal complaint to the Commission about the unlimited state liability guarantees (*Anstaltslast, Gewährträgerhaftung*) for the *Landesbanken*, which, it said, allowed public competitors higher ratings and therefore discriminated against private banks. In July 2001, the EU Commission, the German federal government and representatives of the German states and banking associations reached the historic compromise to remove public guarantees from state banks by July 2005. The *Anstaltslast* was modified so that infusions of public capital are still possible, but they have to be accepted in Brussels. In return, the public status of the savings banks as well as the principle of territoriality were maintained.

Meanwhile, the debate has shifted to question the public status of savings banks in general. In November 2003, an IMF study criticised the low profitability of the German credit sector and recommended the privatisation of the savings banks and the abolition of regional cartels.[8] The American banking group BGB Capital Partners, which showed interest in buying the Berliner Bankgesellschaft and the Berliner Sparkasse, complained to the EU Commission that the public status of the savings bank sector prevents foreign banks from acquiring majority stakes in public banks and therefore infringes the freedom of capital and services in the European market.[9] In January 2004, the CDU mayor of the city of Stralsund launched an effort to sell the local savings bank to the Commerzbank and the Swedish SEB Bank. The effort was blocked by the PDS government of Mecklenburg-West Pomerania which amended the regional savings banks law to give the Land the final say over the maintenance of public banks.[10] The city of Stralsund, for its part, has submitted a formal complaint to the EU Commission and argues (in line with BGB Capital Partners) that the option of forced mergers within the public savings bank sector, codified in the German savings banks law, inhibits foreign banks from acquiring stakes and therefore challenges the integration of the European financial market.[11]

The Impact of Globalisation: From Bank Lending to Capital Markets

The rise of the capital market since the mid-1980s is one of the core features of financial globalisation, beginning in the 1960s, but intensified in the mid-1970s after the collapse of the Bretton Woods System. Domestic governments retracted exchange controls, dissolved former price and interest rate cartels, lowered access barriers for foreigners to banking activities and stock exchange membership and allowed trading in new financial instruments. The push towards a single European market began in the mid-1980s with a 'European passport' with which banks, stock exchanges, stockbrokers and security brokerages were able to offer their services throughout Europe, subject to minimum standards of capital adequacy and investor protection. The introduction of the euro in January 1999 catalysed further efforts to deepen the European financial market by abolishing remaining regulatory barriers between banking, securities and insurance.

Partly due to this politically induced deregulation, the business of issuing and trading securities has become much more attractive than lending money. For large creditworthy firms in particular, it is often cheaper to acquire capital on international markets by issuing shares or bonds than to seek loans from their *Hausbank* ('securitisation'). Banks are being side-stepped as the classic financial intermediary ('disintermediation'), leaving them to get more involved in the lucrative business of securities trading. Institutional investors have proliferated in the last 20 years, especially in the US and UK, making them major contenders in security markets internationally. Because they act as shareholders in large companies and as security buyers, these insurance companies, pension funds and investment funds have been courted by banks and big business. Institutional investors tend to diversify their portfolios internationally and to adopt short-term investment perspectives.

The Completion of the European Financial Market: Towards a System of Multi-level Governance

The globalisation of financial markets has been accompanied by efforts to harmonise the legal framework of rules governing protection against risk, and transparency in markets and firm behaviour. Hitherto, a multi-level regulatory system has shaped the way that financial markets and the state interact in the domestic political economy.

Multi-level governance first developed in the *banking sector*, aimed at harmonising the rules of risk regulation. In this area the dominant coordinating body is the 'Basel Committee for Banking Supervision', comprising central bankers and regulatory agencies from the Group of Ten (G-10) countries, Spain and Luxembourg. The Basel Committee issues recommendations with the character of 'soft law', but these tend to turn into statutory rules since Basel's recommendations serve as blueprints for the core EU directives in prudential banking supervision. At the end of the 1990s, the Basel Committee developed a flexible and market-based model of risk management designed to align capital charges with underlying risks. A new regulatory framework – 'Basel II' – is due in place in 2006, allowing banks to differentiate risk weights according to assessments of rating agencies or their own ratings. In general, credits to borrowers considered as 'risky' require banks to hold back higher proportions of their own capital as a risk cushion.[12] Moreover, the new approach requires domestic regulatory bodies to test the banks' own risk assessments.[13]

In the 1980s, the multi-level system of regulatory governance was extended to *capital markets*. Regulation was meant to enhance investor protection by creating transparency in markets and firm behaviour and by creating sanctions again malpractices such as insider trading. Re-regulation was much more market-driven than in banking, spurred on by bilateral agreements ('Memoranda of Understanding', MOUs) signed by the US and foreign national watchdogs to ensure reciprocal assistance in cases of cross-border fraud. Institutional investors, sometimes in alliance with the US Securities and Exchange Commission (SEC) put pressure on European countries to prohibit insider trading. At European level, American standards were incorporated in EU directives on 'insider trading' (89/582/EEC) and on 'investment services' (93/227/EEC), prohibiting insider trading and creating a cooperative network of domestic supervisory bodies to regulate capital markets.[14]

Economic and Monetary Union gave new impetus to financial market integration, strengthening the regulatory role of the EU. The Commission's Financial Services Action Plan (FASP) of 1999 listed some 42 measures to be implemented by 2005. The measures focus on relationships between *the company* and its shareholders, investors, auditors and competitors, which are to be structured along the lines of the international capital market. A regulation of 2002 requires companies listed on regulated markets to apply International Accounting Standards (IAS) by 2005. EU adoption makes IAS standards rivals to the US GAAP, prompting US adjustments. Meanwhile, the IAS Committee tasked by the EU with setting accounting standards is currently engaged with the US standard setter FASB in a project designed to converge US GAAP and IAS.[15]

The Commission also intends to reinforce auditor independence and to integrate the auditor more closely into the internal control of a company's financial reporting. Furthermore, its proposed new auditing directive (COM/2004/177) aims at strengthening public oversight of the audit profession by laying down common criteria for national supervisory bodies to ensure that they are sufficiently independent from the profession.[16] The directive is meant to enhance the EU's protection against scandals that have occurred in companies such as Parmalat, Ahold, Enron and Worldcom, but has also to be seen as a response to the US Sarbanes Oxley Act and to US efforts to regulate European auditors of companies listed in the US.[17]

In terms of corporate governance reform in a more narrow sense, the Commission has described its long-term goal as working towards establishing a real shareholder democracy within the EU.[18] Its 2003 Action Plan on 'Modernising Company Law and Enhancing Corporate Governance in the EU' contains a range of proposals to strengthen shareholders' rights and to enhance efficient and independent oversight by the board of directors. As announced in the Action Plan, the Commission issued a recommendation on the role of non-executive or supervisory directors in internal corporate governance in October 2004 (IP/04/1182). However, the content of this recommendation has been substantially watered down due to resistance from member states. The same can be said for the 2003 takeover directive that represented the result of a 20-year struggle by the Commission for a liberal model of takeover regulation based on the British example.[19] Thus the Commission's attempts to harmonise company law has been less successful than in other areas of market integration.[20]

GERMAN FINANCE BETWEEN COMMODIFICATION AND RE-REGULATION

Rising competitive pressures among the different banking groups and the weakening of formerly close relations between banks and industry point to a growing marketisation of finance. The state promotes the market while emphasising transparency and risk-consciousness as new paradigm of financial market regulation.

Structural Change in German Banking

The relationship between the three German banking groups, hitherto a commercial form of peaceful coexistence, is becoming increasingly tense. European market integration has caused margins to fall well below the level banks require to earn both their capital costs and a risk premium. The big banks are seen as potential objects of takeovers because of their low degree of stock market capitalisation. Their consolidation strategy aims at seeking higher returns on capital, including the dissolution of relationships based on shareholdings and problem loans.[21]

As the profit margins in the classic lending and savings deposit business dwindle, savings banks and credit cooperatives are beginning to consolidate their operations, a move that places the markedly decentralised nature of both banking groups in question. The sector of credit cooperatives underwent a wave of banking failures; about 50 firms have to be supported by the association's insurance fund, a further 200 banks are rated as 'extraordinary risk'. The consolidation effort requires more funds than are currently available. This is why the collective insurance system of the credit cooperatives is to be restructured into a pure 'emergency fund' to which the member banks contribute on a risk basis. The umbrella association intends to reduce the number of credit cooperatives from 1,408 to 800 institutions until 2007, in the time-tested manner of fusing banks under its own supervision.[22]

Regarding public sector banks, the loss of the state guarantees by 2005 and the Basel II Accord, due to come into force in 2006, put pressure on banks to adjust their attitudes to risk and the levels of reserves they are obliged to hold. Public banks are required to balance two goals at the same time – achieving a return on the market while adhering to strict risk control mechanisms on the other. The loss of state guarantees requires public banks to become much more risk conscious with regard to the borrowers they get involved with. It is still possible for regional governments to pump capital into public banks in crisis situations, but the practice would be punished by downgraded ratings and higher costs for risk protection. Both the *Landesbanken* and the savings banks have joined forces in issues of risk management. While the *Landesbanken* have set up a collective 'rating provider' to develop internal rating procedures for the wholesale business, the savings banks association (DSGV) runs a 'transparency committee' to define standards of risk measurement and to classify its member firms in different risk categories.[23]

The privatisation of public sector banks or even takeovers of savings banks by private competitors would require a revision of regional savings bank laws, a move that would have to be done state by state. So far, this is very unlikely. In general, the Länder are eager to preserve the *Landesbanken* for matters of industrial policy whilst municipal governments continue for the most part to support their local savings banks which, particularly in structurally weak regions, are often the largest employer, investor and tax payer. In fact, the Länder are currently seeking new models of regional public banking to allow a broader distribution of risk, and to achieve better ratings.[24] This might include the reorganisation of savings banks into joint stock companies (as is being discussed in the state of Saarland) in which private investors are allowed to hold minority stakes.[25] A variety of structures has emerged, reflecting different models of cross-shareholding and therefore power relations between stakeholders such as regional governments, regional banking associations and the *Landesbanken* themselves. In Bavaria, the holding company is jointly owned by the Association of Bavarian Savings Banks and the state of Bavaria, thereby guaranteeing the bank's public-sector character while Rhineland-Palatinate is the only German state so far in which the regional government has withdrawn from the public banking sector.[26] Generally, the savings bank sector seems to pursue a strategy of restructuring through regionalisation. West LB, the public bank of North Rhine-Westphalia, has reduced its exposure to risky international activities, instead offering new types of equity-based finance to the regional *Mittelstand*, a strategy also being followed by the *Landesbanken* of Bavaria (Bayerische Landesbank) and Saxony (Sachsen LB).[27]

The Banks and Industry

The formerly close relations between *banks and industry* are steadily eroding. This holds true in particular for relations between export-oriented firms and big banks. In 1986 the ten largest German banks held stakes of more than 10 per cent in 46 companies; by 1994 this had fallen to just 30.[28] Whereas capital gains tax liabilities previously discouraged the divestment of large stakes, tax reforms initiated by the SPD in 2002 exempted such gains from tax. Banks have reduced stakes through innovative devices such as the Deutsche Bank's 1997 issue of a long-term convertible bond linked to its holdings in Daimler-Benz. Both Deutsche Bank and Dresdner Bank have begun to disengage from the network of interlocking directorates between banks and industry. Deutsche Bank's retreat from the monitoring of non-financial firms was especially noteworthy. In 1996, 29 of the supervisory board chairmen of the 100 biggest firms were representatives of the Deutsche Bank. Only two years later, this number had declined to 17. Indeed, in 2001, Deutsche Bank announced that it would resign from supervisory board chairs altogether.[29] German private banks are shifting away from deposits and industrial loans and have pulled out of lending relationships that do not offer them acceptable risk-adjusted returns on equity.[30]

What are the reasons for the banks' deliberate disengagement from industry? First, banks react to an increasingly competitive European and global environment by pursuing consolidation strategies to eliminate bad loans and under-performing shares from their portfolios, and thus to increase their returns on capital. Second, the flexible and rating-based approach to banking regulation (Basel II) penalises risky engagements with requirements to hold additional capital reserves. Third and probably most important, big banks have oriented themselves towards investment banking and securities trading or the organisation of mergers and acquisitions. Deutsche Bank and Dresdner Bank have both acquired British and US investment banks and shifted their equity holdings to subsidiary companies. Deutsche Bank has even become a trader on its own account after profits from investment banking sagged, thus it acts like a 'giant hedge fund'.[31]

Banks face growing dilemmas regarding their governance role as they shift from traditional *Hausbank* relations to investment banking services. This is well illustrated by the takeover of Hoesch by Krupp in 1991–92. Krupp's 'house bank' (West LB) informally supported Krupp's takeover attempt through its 12 per cent stake in Hoesch. Likewise, Deutsche Bank failed to defend Hoesch despite its role as Hoesch's house bank and its seat chairing Hoesch's supervisory board. Deutsche Bank was again active in advising Krupp–Hoesch in its unfriendly takeover bid for Thyssen in 1997, although its management held a seat on the target's supervisory board.[32] In general, investment banking conflicts with main bank activities because close relationships with domestic industrial companies interfere with reputation-building on international financial markets and impair the ability of a bank to acquire orders from foreign customers.[33]

Large German corporations are increasing their financial autonomy from banks. While corporate borrowing remained high during the early 1990s unification boom, a sharp decline to under 9 per cent of liabilities followed thereafter.[34] Large firms tended to finance their investments internally through retained earnings and pension reserves – pensions representing 15 per cent of their balance sheet and bank credits only 7 per cent in the 1990s.[35] Big firms make use of the capital market as source of financing, seek listings on foreign stock exchanges and follow international (either IAS or US GAAP) standards of accounting.

These globally oriented companies claim to be the vanguard of a corporate policy that includes shareholder value philosophies, such as higher dividend payments and balance sheet disclosure. Shareholder orientation was pronounced in companies where ownership by institutional investors (investment and pension funds) was large. Most important in terms of its influence on firm strategies however, is the composition of foreign ownership in German firms. Foreign investors focus on a narrow segment of export-oriented blue-chip companies with higher market capitalisation and liquidity. In 1998, 24 of the DAX 30 companies showed an average of 31 per cent foreign ownership, compared to 18 per cent at 19 smaller DAX 100 companies.[36]

This suggests that companies in export-oriented sectors like automobiles or electronics that used to be the industrial cornerstones of the German economy are increasingly exposed to the rules of international capital markets.

The close relationships between the public banks, credit cooperatives and small and mid-sized companies appeared to be unruffled by the pressures.[37] While lending business at commercial banks began to deteriorate from the end of 1992, it did not weaken perceptibly at savings banks and *Landesbanken* until the second half of the 1990s.[38] In fact, the savings bank representatives claim to have prevented the German *Mittelstand* from suffering a 'credit crunch'.[39] However, the public banking sector operates in a restrictive environment similar to that of the big banks. Pressures to increase the return on equity are to some extent even higher in the light of the impending loss of state guarantees and the 'market-based' judgements of rating agencies. We might expect that Basel II will push public sector banks to increase the differentiation of credit terms in line with borrowers' creditworthiness. As both commercial and public sector banks try to cut risk-weighted assets and use capital more efficiently, they are likely to concentrate on particularly lucrative business sectors and to give lower priority to less profitable lending in longer-term credit relationships. We can expect variation of lending conditions depending on industrial sector, range of business and, most importantly, on the borrowers' own capital base.[40] Firms in sectors like construction that are sensitive to cyclical downturns can expect lower ratings and increasing loan prices. The core challenge for small and middle-sized firms is to increase their own funds in order to be able to receive loans at acceptable interest rates.[41] Against this background, a new debate centres on alternative sources of company financing, e.g. by 'private equity companies' or 'mezzanine capital'.[42] Taken together, even small and middle-sized German firms are facing an increasingly marketised environment of corporate financing; it has to be seen whether or not the regionalisation strategy of the public sector banks will help to compensate for that.

State Promotion of the Financial Marketplace

Had the *state* not paved the way, none of the changes described above would have been possible. In the older model, the state was more like a partner in a corporatist alliance who approved and codified negotiated solutions. Now it acts as a *promotor* and *regulator* of domestic (financial) markets. However, it is predominantly the federal state, that is, the Federal Ministries of Finance, Economy and Justice which push the adjustment of the domestic financial marketplace to a new restrictive and competitive environment. They collaborate closely with a coalition of globally oriented market actors while the regional governments, more or less irrespective of their party affiliation, are allying with the associations of savings banks and credit cooperatives to retain the public banking sector.[43]

Both Caio Koch-Weser, state secretary in the Federal Finance Ministry and Federal Economic Minister Wolfgang Clement have urged public banks to seek a change in their legal statutes to attract fresh capital and to allow mergers across the three-pillar banking system. German banks should be strengthened in order to be able to compete on the global level.[44] The role of the Finance Ministry in setting up coalitions to promote the German financial market[45] became obvious in April 2003 when Caio

Koch-Weser asked the heads of the German big banks to launch a 'German financial marketplace initiative' (*Initiative Finanzstandort Deutschland, IFD*) to develop specific market-related measures and products.[46]

An unprecedented thrust in legislative activity in the finance sector since the mid-1980s runs completely counter to Germany's image of reform blockage (*Reformstau*). In all, seven laws have been passed, in part to meet European guidelines but more notably to remove the barriers blocking the use of the domestic capital market and the trade of new financial products. Between 1990 and 2002, four laws promoting financial markets were passed, of which the third alone contained 100 different measures. Among the most important measures was the admission of money market funds after the Bundesbank dropped its long-standing opposition and broadened the available legal forms for venture capital funds. In February 2003, the Ministry of Finance announced a new Financial Market Promotion Plan 2006 (*Finanzmarktförderplan 2006*), part of which is the introduction of hedge funds and of a new market for asset backed securities (ABS).[47] These moves reflect the growing securitisation of financial relations since these capital market-based products are meant to allow banks to distribute their credit risks more broadly and to use their own capital more efficiently. In 2004, several German banks established the 'True Sales Initiative' as a market for securitised loans.[48]

Steps to liberalise the financial market were accompanied by attempts to re-regulate its framework. A round of capital market law reforms during the 1990s brought stronger state regulation of the financial markets geared to increasing transparency. Reforms have to be understood as a response to external pressures by foreign, in particular US, regulators and institutional investors, which have ultimately changed the attitudes of the big German banks towards a tighter capital market regulation. A realisation that the old self-regulatory model of 'light supervisory touch' in the capital market was a liability in global competition for investors led the big banks towards 'bringing the state back in' to regulation since 1990.[49]

In 1994, following a bitter battle with the Länder, the federal government assumed responsibility for monitoring the stock exchange for the first time, and a supervisory agency for security trading (Bundesaufsichtsamt für den Wertpapierhandel, BaWe) was established under the jurisdiction of the Federal Ministry of Finance. Two of the tasks given this agency were to crack down on insider trading, which had finally been outlawed, and to ensure that banks and investment businesses complied with the new rules of conduct. In May 2002, the BaFin (Bundesanstalt für Finanzdienstleistungsaufsicht) was founded as a formal umbrella regulator for banking, capital markets and insurance after a turf battle with the Bundesbank. Restructuring should allow for a more flexible payment of the agency's staff since the supervisor's funding is provided by the banks and no longer by the state. The reorganisation was in good part motivated by the need to build up in-house expertise in risk management by hiring practitioners from industry in light of the upcoming implementation of Basel II.[50]

Over recent years, the state's role as regulator has been steadily extended to target financial analysts and hedge funds in addition to banks, insurance and securities firms. Auditors and listed firms are likely to be added to these groups. The Company Account Control Act of 2004 (*Bilanzkontrollgesetz*) establishes a system of 'self-regulation in the shadow of hierarchy' for listed firms. A private body is supposed to control audits and auditing practices. If this form of control fails, the financial regulator may intervene and investigate the books of a company. These legislative measures have to be seen against the background of the scandals which have occurred in firms like Parmalat or Enron and the announcement of the EU Commission to modernise the Company Law Directive on Statutory Audit.[51]

The first legislative measures specifically aimed at overhauling the corporate governance regime were issued in the late 1990s. From 1998 onwards, a series of laws were passed which explicitly supported and promoted the processes of greater market orientation and disentanglement visible at the firm level. An important step towards a more transparent balance sheet was made 1998 with a law (*Kapitalaufnahmeerleichterungsgesetz, KapAeG*) which gave listed companies the option to apply capital market-oriented international accounting standards, i.e. IAS or US-GAAP. Although policy makers refrained from radical measures against the dominance of the banks and other corporations in internal corporate governance, several provisions of the 1998 Control and Transparency Act (KonTraG) weakened the capacities of the traditional 'insiders' to exert influence within the company. For example, the law introduced the 'one share, one vote' rule and imposed restrictions on the voting rights of the banks in the general meeting. At the same time, the KonTraG and another law from 2002 strengthened the *Aufsichtsrat* in its supervisory function, e.g. by mandating more frequent meetings, requiring more extensive reporting of the *Vorstand* to the *Aufsichtsrat* and extending the obligations and powers of the latter in overseeing financial reporting and auditing.[52]

KonTraG marked a watershed in the tradition of company law since it lacked any reference to the stakeholder view of the firm.[53] The law was primarily an initiative of the governing coalition who had consulted with German investment funds, shareholder associations, but also with foreign institutional investors before the legislative proposal was issued.[54] The coalition felt obligated to respond to a number of spectacular failures of control through supervisory boards (e.g., the failures of Metallgesellschaft, Bremer Vulkan, Balsam, plus the Deutsche Bank's large loan exposure to the bankrupt Schneider property development group).[55] However, when the KonTraG was debated in the Bundestag, it turned out that the competition-limiting institutions of German managed capitalism were politically attacked from different directions: the Left criticised interlocking directorates and ownership networks because of the power they gave to banks. The SPD called the KonTraG a law to protect managers against shareholders and demanded stronger shareholder orientation. The liberals interpreted these institutions as welfare-reducing rent-seeking arrangements and complained that they could not push the CDU towards more radical reforms. The course of the debate provides some support for Cioffi and Höpner's argument that corporate governance reforms in Western Europe were pushed by centre-left parties whereas the centre-right's close political alliances with employers (i.e. corporations and their managers) led them to protect traditional features of managerialism favoured by their manager constituents.[56] In the discussion about a more market-driven corporate governance system, the CDU pointed out that the German system was not worse than the American system. In the debate on a new takeover law in 2001, it was the CDU that wanted managements to have more powers in defending companies against hostile takeovers. As far as KonTraG is concerned, no political party would have been willing to veto the reforms, as long as the points of reference were capital ties, the power of banks, transparency and the reduction of capital market restrictions. Nevertheless, KonTraG was held up for approximately one year. Attempts to restrict co-determination of employees by reducing the size of supervisory boards (and thus the number of union representatives) were blocked by trade unions, social democrats and the trade union wing of the CDU.[57]

CONCLUSION

Germany's bank-based financial system has experienced a profound transformation since the beginning of the 1990s. There has been a clear shift towards greater capital market orientation in the business strategy of banks and firms of all sizes. Banks are no longer upholders of a financial infrastructure, supporting and shielding industry from a competitive economic environment, but behave in an increasingly risk-averse way, as firms themselves do. Due to pressures to use their own capital more efficiently, banks have to calculate their lending more carefully (if they decide to lend at all). Firms, on the other hand, have to abide by the rules of the capital market in order to prove that they are a trustworthy client. That these pressures are affecting the small and mid-sized firm segment as well is a recent development with probably far-reaching implications for the future structure of the German economy. In the process of reshaping corporate governance, the interests of foreign investors and small shareholders are being given more weight, whereas the power over company policy held by insider networks is considered less and less legitimate. None of these changes would have been possible without the state. The Federal Ministries of Finance, Economy and Justice act as *promotor and regulator* of the domestic financial market. The measures to reshape the national system of regulation reflect the overriding objective of making the conduct of financial market actors more transparent and risk-conscious. Significantly, the banking associations have shown a remarkable capacity to adapt to the marketised environment, making use, for example, of market principles to distribute the risks and costs of upholding collective deposit insurance systems.

The changes described above contradict the current image of Germany as economic 'laggard' instead of 'pace-setter' in Europe. Why was that possible? In general, the transformation was driven by both market and political forces. Pressures to both reorganise financial business and the regulatory framework of financial markets rose since the mid-1990s, when the trend towards securitisation gained momentum and new actors like institutional investors entered the German scene. The globalisation of finance in general and the big banks' move towards investment banking in particular marked the first step in this process of commodification of financial relations. Institutional investors have put pressure on banks, firms and on regulators to establish a 'transparent' and shareholder value-oriented legal framework. Moreover, the wave of privatisation which accelerated in the 1990s, extended even to those parts of the infrastructure where state ownership had once been regarded as indispensable and catalysed the alteration of the corporate governance framework including accounting, auditing and shareholder–management relationships. In other words, changes in global finance have changed the preferences of domestic market actors, thus feeding back into other parts of the domestic political economy. The integration of the European financial market has accelerated rather than triggered these market changes. In light of the upcoming monetary integration, however, the EU Commission has intensified its efforts to complete the financial market since the late 1990s. A closer look at the dynamics of regulatory reform reveals a process of 'sectoral spill-over', beginning with banking business in the early 1970s, then moving over to capital markets in the late 1980s and eventually to the single corporation whose internal and external relations are to be structured in line with a more capital market-oriented environment. Today, the regulatory framework for both banks and companies emphasises the importance of adequate risk management, disclosure practices as well as the efficient use of own capital. To that extent, banks and firms have become much more similar to each other.

How does politics fit into this? On the domestic level, private banks were the drivers of the capital market reforms of the early 1990s and allied with the federal state for purposes of modernisation of the German financial marketplace. Moreover, it was private banks which used EU competition policy as an 'opportunity structure' to undermine the public status of their domestic competitors. Given the efforts of public banks to restructure their regional organisation in light of the upcoming loss of state guarantees, their 'venue shopping strategy' has to be considered successful. The case of Stralsund shows that even municipal actors make use of this strategy, turning to the European Commission to overcome resistance of their regional government against opening the savings banks sector to foreign investment. Federal government, irrespective of party composition, has promoted the market-oriented transformation of German finance. The reforms of the early 1990s were brought about by the CDU/CSU while the SPD has continued the process of company reform since 1998. The struggles over KonTraG show reduced political support for the competition-limiting institutions of German managed capitalism. Nevertheless, attempts to restrict co-determination were halted by resistance of the trade unions and the trade union wing of both the SPD and the CDU. Moreover, the regional governments are so far the most important veto-players to the privatisation of the public banking sector and upholders of 'regional mercantilism'.

What does all this show us? German finance has gone several steps down the road to a more market-friendly model. Given the global shift towards capital market-oriented business and a regulatory framework that puts a premium on transparency, risk consciousness and shareholder value orientation, it seems unlikely that these changes will be undone. Nevertheless, the German model of managed capitalism will not develop into the twin of its Anglo-Saxon counterpart. Instead, as market elements are built into the system, we see a recombination of 'old' and 'new' parts, leading to a 'hybridisation' of the domestic model of capitalism.[58] The transformation described above suggests that we are witnessing at least three types of institutional change. First, the institutions of managed capitalism are being replaced by elements of market capitalism, especially in the top tier of large firms and financial institutions. Global players are increasingly decoupling from old practices of relational contracting, long-term lending and insider monitoring and reorienting themselves toward global markets and a common set of international capital market rules. This process of 'disembedding' from the domestic institutional environment has in large part been catalysed by government efforts to reorganise the domestic framework of regulation according to demands of international competitiveness. Second, existing elements of stakeholder capitalism are sustained, but turned to new purposes ('functional conversion').[59] Reforms to corporate governance for example have so far upheld elements of co-determination and works councils. Yet in a new marketised environment key elements of the stakeholder model focus to a greater extent on profits and on owner equity. Third, actors use institutional material already available but in new ways or add new institutions on top of existing ones ('institutional layering'). This seems to be the strategy of regional governments, regional banking associations and *Landesbanken* which experiment with different combinations of public–private ownership in order to preserve regional instruments of industrial policy. All in all, the uneven erosion of German managed capitalism suggests that the 'requisite variety' of organisational models is increasing rather than decreasing, with a growing number of 'models within the national model'. Drawing on the observation that the German model is becoming institutionally incomplete we can conclude that it is much more the issue of 'capitalist coherence' than the 'convergence–divergence conundrum' which requires further theoretical attention.

NOTES

1. J. Zysman, *Governments, Markets and Growth. Financial Systems and the Politics of Industrial Change* (Ithaca/London: Cornell University Press, 1983).
2. R. Deeg, *Finance Capitalism Unveiled. Banks and the German Political Economy* (Ann Arbor: University of Michigan Press, 1999).
3. P.A. Hall, *Governing the Economy. The Politics of State Intervention in Britain and France* (Cambridge: Polity Press, 1986).
4. S. Lütz, *Der Staat und die Globalisierung von Finanzmärkten. Regulative Politik in Deutschland, Großbritannien und den USA* (Frankfurt am Main: Campus, 2002).
5. W. Arnold, 'Zur Wettbewerbsdiskussion in der deutschen Kreditwirtschaft', *Die Bank. Zeitschrift für Bankpolitik und Bankpraxis* 8 (2003), pp.516–18.
6. *Frankfurter Allgemeine Zeitung (FAZ)*, 22 Sept. 2004, p.13; 21 Oct. 2004, p.15; 3 Dec. 2004, p.12.
7. 'Banking: Draft Communication to Tighten Controls on German Bank Subsidies', *European Report* of 27 May 1998.
8. International Monetary Fund (IMF), *Germany: 2003 Article IV Consultation-Staff Report, Staff Supplement and Public Information Notice on the Executive Board Discussion.* IMF Country Report No. 03/341 (Washington DC, 2003), pp.32–4.
9. *Süddeutsche Zeitung (SZ)*, 23 Aug. 2003, p.25.
10. *FAZ*, 3 March 2004, p.13.
11. *FAZ*, 20 Jan. 2004, p.10.
12. Basel Committee on Banking Supervision, 'Overview of the New Basel Capital Accord. A Consultative Paper issued by the Basel Committee on Banking Supervision' (Basel: Basel Committee, Jan. 2001).
13. S. Lütz, 'Convergence within National Diversity: The Regulatory State in Finance', *Journal of Public Policy* 24/2 (2004), pp.169–97.
14. S. Lütz, 'The Revival of the Nation-State? Stock Exchange Regulation in an Era of Globalised Financial Markets', *Journal of European Public Policy* 5/1 (1998), pp.157–61.
15. E. Posner, 'Globalization or European Union Politics? Harmonizing Accounting Standards Across Borders'. Paper presented at the American Political Science Association Annual Meeting in Chicago, 2–5 Sept. 2004, pp.28–9; T. Porter, 'Private Authority, Technical Authority, and the Globalization of Accounting Standards'. Paper presented at the inaugural workshop of ARCCGOR, 17–18 Dec. 2004, Vrije Universiteit Amsterdam, p.10.
16. Kommission der Europäischen Gemeinschaften, *Vorschlag für eine Richtlinie des Europäischen Parlaments und des Rates über die Prüfung des Jahresabschlusses und des konsolidierten Abschlusses und zur Änderung der Richtlinien 78/660/EWG und 83/349/EWG des Rates. KOM/2004/177 endg.* (Brüssel: Kommission der Europäischen Gemeinschaften, 2004).

17. F. Bolkestein, 'Ensuring a Robust International Audit'. Address at business breakfast on 'Accountability in the Age of Global Markets' organised by the European Policy Centre, Brussels, 25 March 2004.
18. Kommission der Europäischen Gemeinschaften, *Modernisierung des Gesellschaftsrechts und Verbesserung der Corporate Governance in der Europäischen Union – Aktionsplan. Mitteilung der Kommission an den Rat und das Europäische Parlament. KOM/2003/284 endg.* (Brüssel: Kommission der Europäischen Gemeinschaften 2003), p.17.
19. H. Callaghan and M. Höpner, 'Parties or Nations? Political Cleavages over EU Efforts to Create a Single European Market for Corporate Control'. Paper presented at the 2004 Meeting of the DVPW-Sektion 'Politik und Ökonomie', 3–4 Dec. 2004, Cologne.
20. J. Wouters, 'European Company Law: Quo Vadis?', *Common Market Law Review* 37 (2000), pp.261 ff.
21. *Financial Times Deutschland (FTD)*, 4 July 2003, p.19.
22. *FAZ*, 5 Nov. 2003, p.14.
23. *FAZ*, 3 Dec. 2003, p.13; 17 Nov. 2003, p.139.
24. *FAZ*, 28 Aug. 2003, p.12.
25. *FAZ*, 7 Oct. 2004, p.13.
26. *FAZ*, 3 Feb. 2004, p.14, *SZ*, 28 May 2004, p.24.
27. *FAZ*, 16 Dec. 2003, p.4; E. Wiesel, 'Sparkassen und Landesbanken auf dem Prüfstand des europäischen Wettbewerbsrechts', *Zeitschrift für Bankrecht und Bankwirtschaft* 14/4 (2002), pp.288–99.
28. H.C. Sherman and F.R. Kaen, 'Die deutschen Banken und ihr Einfluß auf Unternehmensentscheidungen', *IFO-Schnelldienst* 23 (1997), p.10.
29. J. Beyer and M. Höpner, 'The Disintegration of Organised Capitalism: German Corporate Governance in the 1990s', *West European Politics* 26/4 (2003), p.184.
30. R. Deeg, 'Institutional Change and the Uses and Limits of Path Dependency: The Case of German Finance'. MPIfG Discussion Paper 01/6 (Cologne: Max Planck Institute for the Study of Societies, 2001); T. Marshall, 'A Splattering of Public Bank Mergers', *Euromoney* (March 2003), p.60.
31. *The Economist*, 28 Aug. 2004, pp.65–6.
32. G. Jackson, 'Corporate Governance in Germany and Japan: Liberalizing Pressures and Responses during the 1990s', in K. Yamamura and W. Streeck (eds.), *The End of Diversity? Prospects for German and Japanese Capitalism* (Ithaca/London: Cornell University Press, 2003), p.282.
33. Beyer and Höpner, 'The Disintegration of Organised Capitalism', p.185.
34. Deutsche Bundesbank, 'Die Beziehung zwischen Bankkrediten und Anleihemarkt in Deutschland', *Monatsbericht* (Jan. 2000), p.39.
35. Sherman and Kaen, 'Die deutschen Banken und ihr Einfluss auf Unternehmensentscheidungen', p.8.
36. Jackson, 'Corporate Governance in Germany and Japan', p.277.
37. Deeg, *Finance Capitalism Unveiled.*
38. Deutsche Bundesbank, 'The Development of Bank Lending to the Private Sector', *Monthly Report* (Oct. 2002), p.34.
39. *FAZ*, 18 March 2004, p.11.
40. Deutsche Bundesbank, 'The Development of Bank Lending to the Private Sector', pp.44–5.
41. *FAZ*, 13 Oct. 2003, p.22; 28 June 2004, p.18.
42. *FAZ*, 13 Oct. 2003, p.22.
43. *SZ*, 1 Dec. 2003, p.23.
44. *FAZ*, 24 Nov. 2003, p.13.
45. The Federal Ministry of Finance played a similar role in the early 1990s, when Finance Minister Waigel announced further promotion of the 'Finanzplatz Deutschland' (Lütz, 'The Revival of the Nation-State', p.163).
46. *FAZ*, 16 June 2004, p.13.
47. Bundesministerium der Finanzen (BMF), 'Eckpunktepapier: Der Finanzmarktförderplan 2006' (Ms, 5 March 2003, Berlin: BMF).
48. *FAZ*, 30 April 2004, p.21.
49. Lütz, 'The Revival of the Nation-State', pp.159–60.
50. Lütz, 'Convergence within National Diversity', pp.183–4.
51. Bundesministerium der Justiz (BMJ), 'Bilanzrechtsreform und Bilanzkontrolle stärken Unternehmensintegrität und Anlegerschutz', Pressemitteilung (BMJ, 2004).
52. C. Berrar, *Die Entwicklung der Corporate Governance in Deutschland im internationalen Vergleich* (Baden-Baden: Nomos, 2001), pp.57ff.
53. Beyer and Höpner, 'The Disintegration of Organised Capitalism', p.191.
54. J.N. Ziegler, 'Corporate Governance and the Politics of Property Rights in Germany', *Politics and Society* 28/2 (2000), p.204.
55. S. Vitols, 'From Banks to Markets: The Political Economy of Liberalization of the German and Japanese Financial Systems', in K. Yamamura and W. Streeck (eds.), *The End of Diversity? Prospects for German and Japanese Capitalism* (Ithaca/London: Cornell University Press), p.253.

56. J.W. Cioffi and M. Höpner, 'The Political Paradox of Finance Capitalism: Interests, Preferences, and Center-Left Party Politics in Corporate Governance Reform'. Paper presented at the 2004 Conference of Europeanists, Council for European Studies, 11–13 March 2004, Chicago.
57. Beyer and Höpner, 'The Disintegration of Organised Capitalism', p.192.
58. See among others Jackson, 'Corporate Governance in Germany and Japan', and R. Deeg, 'Governance and the Nation-State in a Global Era', in S. Lütz (ed.), *Governance in der politischen Ökonomie*, in S. Lütz (ed.), *Governance in der politischen Ökonomie* (Wiesbaden: VS-Verlag, forthcoming 2006).
59. K. Thelen, 'Timing and Temporality in the Analysis of Institutional Evolution and Change', *Studies in American Political Development* 14 (2000), pp.101–8.

Reform in the Shadow of Community Law: Highly Regulated Economic Sectors

SUSANNE K. SCHMIDT

During the 1990s, *Modell Deutschland* has given way to the picture of *Reformstau*, suggesting that the 'institutional pluralism' of the German political system stands in the way of economic reforms needed to confront the double challenge of Europeanisation and globalisation. Yet *Reformstau* is not ubiquitous. As in other EU states, highly regulated monopoly utilities sectors have been liberalised. Despite the many veto points in the German political system, contentious reforms were concluded relatively swiftly. Reforms were an integral part of the EU single market, and it was therefore possible to circumvent national veto players in the multi-level European polity.

This study reviews the impact of European policies on domestic reforms, showing the domestic effects of the EU's approach to market integration. The EU does not distinguish between trans-border and domestic economic exchanges. Instead, it has created a unified regulatory regime, with far-reaching implications for domestic regulation. Although domestic reforms took place in the shadow of community law, however, they cannot simply be seen as top-down enforced adaptation. Rather, top-down pressure combined with attempts of national actors to use the European context as an opportunity structure to pursue their interests.

Beginning with a review of the traditional German approach to sectoral regulation, arguing that actors' interests and institutional veto points represented formidable obstacles to reform at the domestic level, the reform requirements emanating from the European level are then outlined. The ensuing account of domestic reform shows both the scale of adaptation required by the EU legislation, and the importance of European law as an opportunity structure for the domestic advocates of reform.

THE STABILITY OF ECONOMIC SECTOR REGULATION

Governing is difficult in Germany. Policy making is characterised by joint decision making with the attendant danger of joint-decision traps and immobilism.[1] A strong second chamber means that governments have to negotiate with different veto players. Agreement is frequently prohibited by party competition,[2] accentuated by a crowded schedule of 16 Länder elections which puts Germany in a state of permanent electoral competition. In addition, associations play an important role in a pattern of neo-corporatist decision making that operates at sector-specific rather than macro level.[3] Even if bargains can be struck, the powerful constitutional court with its extensive powers for judicial review means that the losers can always try to reverse the deal. Accordingly, the likely position of the constitutional court plays an important role in the deliberations of the Bundestag.[4] It is therefore not surprising that sectoral regulation has been marked by the utmost stability.

Utilities

A characteristic of *telecommunications* until the end of the 1980s was the comprehensive monopoly that the PTTs enjoyed. Provision for telecommunications and postal services were fused under the direct responsibility of a Ministry. The PTT model combined operative, regulative and public power responsibilities. In Germany, the model was particularly protected as Article 87 of the Basic Law gave the exclusive responsibility for posts and telecommunications to the federal administration.[5]

Monopolisation was justified by technical and political arguments relating to the natural monopoly status of network-bound sectors, and to concerns about universal service across the country, including rural areas. Monopoly led also to a very limited range of policy actors beyond the Deutsche Bundespost and the Postal Ministry. A small number of 'court suppliers' cooperated closely with the Bundespost in the development of technologies geared to national technical specifications.[6] The high membership density of the German Postal Union (Deutsche Postgewerkschaft, DPG) gave it an important role in the defence of the status quo.[7] In the face of this broad political consensus-supporting monopoly, far-reaching reforms would have been difficult to enact on a purely national level.[8]

In electricity the absence of competition was justified by very similar natural monopoly arguments. Unlike in telecommunications, and in contrast to the electricity sector in countries like France, the German state did not play a large role as a direct provider of electricity. The sector was extremely fragmented. The market was dominated by eight trans-regional interconnected utilities responsible for over 80 per cent of production. Eighty regional and 800 communal providers concentrated on distribution.[9] Competition was suppressed by a system of contracts between the municipalities and the utilities, and between the utilities themselves. Electricity was exempted from national competition law, and the mandate of the Federal Cartel Office was restricted to preventing abuse of dominant position. The Federal Ministry of Economics was responsible for regulation.[10] Electricity suppliers were organised in the Vereinigung Deutscher Elektrizitätswerke (VDEW). The municipal companies were organised separately in the Verband Kommunaler Unternehmen (VKU). Also important was the Verband Industrielle Kraftwirtschaft (VIK), organising the large electricity users.[11]

Regulated Sectors

Insurance and road haulage both fall in the area of legislation requiring the consent of the Bundesrat. The sectors originally displayed quite similar patterns of meso-corporatist regulation, with close coordination between the regulatory authority and business associations. Regulation concerned market access, tariffs, supervision over operational matters, and (in the insurance sector) products. Markets were characterised by very little competition. There was a congruence of interests between regulated firms and the regulators, with evidence of regulatory capture.[12]

The regulation of *insurance* was marked by a considerable continuity.[13] The insurance oversight act dates back to 1901. In 1951 the Bundesaufsichtsamt für das Versicherungswesen (BAV) was established as regulatory authority, largely modelled on the previous Reichsaufsichtsamt. Originally, competence was located in the Federal Economics Ministry, but the responsibility was moved to the Finance Ministry in 1972. In exercising its regulatory function, the BAV cooperated closely with the different branches of the insurance association (Gesamtverband der Deutschen Versicherungswirtschaft, GDV). The centrality of the association in regulation was reflected in a high degree of cooperation between companies, facilitated by exemption from competition law and the restriction of the Federal Cartel Office to controlling abuse of dominant position.

This pattern of regulation resulted in a market with largely uniform products. It was successful in that no insurance firms went bankrupt. Tariffs, however, were high in international comparison, at least for private contracts which were widely used to subsidise industrial insurance. There were few product innovations, and it was difficult for consumers to terminate contracts in the short or medium term, even if companies raised their tariffs. Consequently, consumer and business associations were critical of the system, advocating reform to make insurance cover more flexible. Different reforms of the cartel law tried to induce more competition but failed due to the powerful opposition of the insurance industry. In the 1980s, the Monopoly Commission and the Deregulation Commission joined in calls for liberalisation. However, the Finance Ministry was deterred from reform initiatives by adamant opposition from the insurance associations and the regulatory authority. Opposition also included the Länder, particularly those that contained important insurance companies.[14]

The regulation of *road haulage* showed similar features of continuity.[15] Founded in 1952 by the Güterkraftverkehrsgesetz (GüKG), the Bundesanstalt für Güterfernverkehr (BAG) regulated the sector in close cooperation with the different business associations. Market access was licensed, with uniform tariffs set by tariff commissions composed jointly of private actors and the Federal Ministry of Transport which had clientelistic links to the sector.[16] This situation of regulatory capture resembled that in insurance. It came at great cost for freight forwarders which stood little chance of avoiding tariffs calculated to be 20 per cent above market prices.[17] Their interest in reform was backed by the Federal Ministry of Economics, but the latter was powerless against the regulatory authority, the Transport Ministry, and the associations which all had stakes in the status quo.

EUROPEAN PRESSURES FOR REFORM

With the move towards the single market, member states lost their ability to regulate their economic sectors at will. Monopoly rights, or cartel-like structures in regulated sectors limited the economic activity of potential competitors in other member states, thereby infringing against the single market. Under the new legislation, such infractions of market competition could only be justified by one of the few exemptions of European competition law.

Compared to other policy fields, *European competition law* is highly supranational in character with few formal opportunities for member state governments to influence the way the Commission handles its powers.[18] Articles 81 and 82 are directed at private actors, prohibiting cartels and the abuse of dominant positions. Governments are involved in decision making through advisory committees, giving the Commission the final power of decision. Articles 86 to 89 restrict the potential of member states to grant special rights or state aid to enterprises. These articles thus target utilities in particular. Although member states lack formal means of influence, in cases of high political salience governments have multiple means to put significant pressure on 'their' commissioners and the Commission as a whole when controversial measures arise, so that they may successfully prevent negative decisions.[19]

In addition to competition rules safeguarding the competitive order of markets, the Single European Act of 1987 upholds the different market freedoms (the mobility of goods, services, capital, and persons) which may be restricted only in exceptional cases. While constraints necessary to realise important national goals are generally recognised, this is granted under the caveat that the internal market is not adversely affected.[20] Accordingly, the Commission has the potential to seriously interfere with the parts of the national economies that are *not* predominantly *structured by market principles.* Similar to the market freedoms, European competition law knows hardly any restrictions. This is very different from national competition law which normally exempts certain areas, such as the classic utilities, and where it is taken for granted that parliament remains free to regulate certain areas of the economy.[21] On the European level, member states are denied this freedom, which would amount to a breach of the single market. Whereas national competition rules are a kind of secondary law, European ones have the status of primary law.[22]

It is important to note how far Treaty rules reach into the national realm. Though the rules only aim to eliminate hindrances to the single market and do not engage with purely national concerns, the likelihood of such disturbances has been interpreted very broadly. Since national restrictions almost always hamper the potential economic activities of other European nationals, there may in fact be few inherently national affairs.[23] *In sum*, while both sets of rules are complementary, referring either to competition or to inter-community trade, they may partly serve as substitutes. Whenever national markets are not fully competitive, they can be liberalised either by applying competition law, or by allowing foreigners to offer their services in this domestically protected market.

Primary law – Treaty rules – is supplemented by secondary law in the form of directives or regulations targeted at specific sectors or issues. Primary law has undergone a history of interpretation since its inception in 1957, often setting it quite apart from the original will of the 'masters of the Treaty'. By contrast, secondary law is now often passed by qualified-majority vote in the Council and co-decision in the European Parliament. The application of secondary law to the single market is a comprehensive one. Although the objective is to facilitate the single market, all economic matters, whether trans-border or simply domestic, are treated in the same way. The single market thereby follows a different regulatory philosophy than the US with the interstate commerce clause. The idea is that companies should not have to fulfil a different set of regulatory requirements if they want to offer products or services on the single market, as this would amount to an additional burden.[24] This however means that the single market enjoys a considerable privilege – in order not to burden trans-border economic activity, all domestic economic activities are regulated in conformity to the single market.

Former Monopoly Sectors: Telecommunications and Electricity

The realisation of the single market for telecommunications and electricity is heavily influenced by the fact that these are sectors very close to the state. In *telecommunications*, the European Commission used its competition law powers (Art. 86) to a previously unknown extent by issuing Commission directives, thereby taking all liberalisation decisions seemingly single-handedly from the late 1980s to the mid-1990s. From 1998 onwards, telecommunications was fully liberalised. In parallel, the Council enacted harmonisation directives.[25] The harmonised legal framework and European competition law contains a catalogue of different rights which can be enforced in national courts or by addressing complaints to the Commission. Within this common framework, national regulatory authorities and parliaments still have competences for shaping the domestic regulatory regime.

A new package of directives being currently enforced aims, *inter alia*, to realise EU licences, allowing companies to offer community-wide services under a single licence (Directive 97/13/EC, 10 April 1997). Previously, companies needed to be licensed in each member state where they aimed to provide services.

In *electricity*, the Commission originally considered following its successful path from telecommunications, but refrained from Commission directives in view of significant opposition from member state governments. Consequently, electricity was liberalised by a Council and Parliament directive, taking the normal course of European legislation. The experience with electricity politics showed with hindsight the extraordinary situation that had facilitated the Commission's telecoms policy. Only the broad support of member states for liberalisation had allowed the European Commission to use its competition law powers to this extent.[26]

It took the Council the determined attempts of four presidencies (German, French, Spanish and Italian) to finally reach a compromise in June 1996. Directive 96/92/EC opened the market incrementally. Starting in 1999 the market share equivalent of users with more than 40 GWh[27]/year consumption was opened, equalling 22 per cent of market share. This level was lowered later to 20 GWh/year, and in 2003 to 9 GWh/year, thus liberalising 33 per cent of the market.[28]

A new directive was agreed in 2003 (2003/53/EC), in order to accelerate market liberalisation. It requires the liberalisation for all business customers from mid-2004, and for all customers from mid-2007 onwards. By mid-2004, member states were obliged to have established an independent regulatory authority. Electricity companies have to organise the distribution of electricity separately, in order to guarantee non-discriminatory network access to competitors. A separate regulation (1228/2003) deals with the trans-border trade of electricity.

Insurance

The single market for insurance services was established mainly through three generations of directives. The freedom of establishment was realised first, followed by the freedom of services for large risks, and later for mass risks from 1994.[29] As with banking services, there is a single European passport: The supervisory authority of the home country regulates all activities of the company in the EU, thus realising the freedom of services. It is sufficient to simply inform the home supervisory authority of plans to enter other member states.

Based on partly harmonised rules, the home member state is responsible for authorisation, legal oversight and financial control. But insurance companies also have to obey several rules of the host country where they offer their services. Examples are general legal rules, consumer protection and insurance contract laws.[30] As insurance services are legally defined products, but insurance contract law is not harmonised, it is impossible to offer unified insurance services on a community-wide scale.[31]

Road Haulage

Member states were much divided about the single market for road haulage. However, pressure from the Commission and member states like the Netherlands that were interested in liberalisation, as well as rulings of the European Court of Justice made it clear that the single market could not be prevented forever.[32] Since 1992, access to trans-border transports is subject to EU licences that are allocated according to qualitative criteria (namely training, reputation and financial assets).[33] Within this harmonised framework, member states regulate market access. Cross-border transport can be offered at freely negotiated tariffs. In addition, partly harmonised social, technical and tax rules apply.[34]

Cabotage services, i.e. the delivery of domestic transport services through EU foreigners, have to be distinguished from cross-border transports. Their liberalisation was particularly contentious in high-cost countries such as the FRG. However, while cabotage was fully liberalised from 1998 onwards, companies have to obey the legal and administrative rules of the host country, relating for instance to tariffs, transport conditions, weights and sizes, and driving and resting times. This means that cabotage and cross-border services are not regulated in parallel. For cabotage, a member state may require stricter driving and resting times than those harmonised in the cross-border context.[35] Differences in competitiveness result mainly from a lack of tax harmonisation (vehicle and fuel), a different intensity of controls of driving and resting times or stricter national rules as well as differences in wages.

NATIONAL RESPONSES TO EUROPEAN PRESSURES

As described above, the traditional regulation of these sectors in Germany was very stable, characterised by congruence of interests between regulators and regulatees that made it difficult for critics to pursue a successful national reform agenda. In contrast to the welfare state,[36] where the pressure of the European Union is limited, the application of single-market rules to these economic sectors led to far-reaching measures for national reform. However, these national reforms were not only a response to top-down pressures. For once, German political actors took part in formulating European sectoral requirements. In addition, the single market programme was an opportunity structure for those reform advocates who lacked the institutional resources to realise their preferences in the domestic context.

Liberalisation of the Utilities

The stepwise liberalisation of *telecommunications* provides the best testimony to the sharp contention that liberalisation could generate. The threat to employee interests provoked large-scale protests by the union. Possible disparities in service levels between cities and the countryside aroused opposition from some Länder.

The liberalisation of telecommunications proceeded in three steps, and is already well documented. The *Postreform I* in 1989/90 liberalised terminal equipment and services but left telephone service and the telecommunications network under monopoly. Regulatory responsibilities were split from operative functions, and the latter were divided in three branches – telecommunications, postal and banking services. The Basic Law did not need changing, since the organisational form of federal administration was retained.[37]

Whilst leaving the extent of liberalisation unchanged, *Postreform II* (1994) took the preliminary organisational steps towards privatisation. All three companies were - converted into independent joint-stock companies. This entailed a change of the Basic Law, which in turn required a very broad consensus. Meanwhile, the huge investment burden of German unity had changed the preferences of many actors regarding liberalisation. Deutsche Telekom ran into serious capital scarcity, hampering its potential for becoming a global player. Also the court suppliers came to realise that the possibility of competitors to invest in networks would be good for them. Moreover, a shares issue offered a much-needed injection of capital into the company. The reform obliged the federal state not to sell any of its shares until the year 2000.[38]

Postreform III followed shortly after in 1996 and prepared to meet the EU requirement for full liberalisation by 1998. At the same time, the Postal Ministry was abolished and the Regulierungsbehörde für Telekommunikation und Post (RegTP) took over as the independent regulatory authority. The political responsibility for telecommunications shifted to the Federal Economics Ministry, by now the Bundesministerium für Wirtschaft und Arbeit, BMWA.

It would, however, be wrong to assume that during these reforms the German administration simply reacted to European demands. In the Postal Ministry there was an attempt to speed up liberalisation by cooperating with the European Commission to put additional pressure on German politicians.[39] This may appear paradoxical given that the ministry was to be dissolved in the process? Normally we assume that corporate actors seek to defend, or even expand their responsibilities.[40] However, liberalisation also held considerable potential for Postal Ministry administrators – new responsibilities in the independent regulatory authority, or in Deutsche Telekom and its competitors – offering much more independence, freedom of action and most likely better pay.

Telecommuncations liberalisation has rendered the corporatist and clientelistic network of actors much more pluralistic. A range of new associations represent the interests of new actors in the field. The association of the providers of telecommunications and value-added services VATM (Verband der Anbieter von Telekommunikations- und Mehrwertdiensten), represents about 50 of the larger competitors of Deutsche Telekom, whilst Breko (Bundesverband der regionalen und lokalen Telekommunikationsgesellschaften) represents regional and local carriers.

Finally, the new telecommunications directives required further reforms (Germany was a year behind the implementation date of mid-2003). Activities requiring a licence no longer need to have prior permission. Regulation now covers all dominant providers, with no bias against Deutsche Telekom. With the exception of those (parts of) markets where competition is not yet functioning, regulation has given way to general competition law under the jurisdiction of the Federal Cartel Office. With the latter assuming a more prominent role, the two regulatory bodies will therefore have to cooperate closely in the future.

In contrast to the incremental liberalisation in telecommunications, the 1998 reform of the Energiewirtschaftsgesetz (EnWG) implemented the European *electricity* directive in one single radical step, liberalising the whole electricity market, including simple household customers. Electricity reform is therefore a very clear example of using the European reforms to realise more far-reaching domestic liberalisation. Alongside the European policy process, the FDP-run Ministry of Economic fostered its own reform ideas. The Monopoly Commission took up the issue in its X. Main Report in 1994, following discussions in the Deregulation Commission and BMWi.[41] Thus, opinion shifted towards treating electricity as a normal economic sector in a competitive market economy. Immediate, full liberalisation could also be justified by the important role in the German economy of small and medium enterprises, which would otherwise have had to wait for the benefits of liberalisation.[42]

Germany faced a problem, however, relating to network access for alternative electricity suppliers. Given the starting point of a very fragmented ownership structure, it was not possible to make a clean break and to establish an independent network holder that would grant non-discriminatory network access to established companies and newcomers alike. This was the solution the UK had been able to take a decade earlier, when it was breaking up its integrated monopoly. In view of the dispersed ownership structure, Germany opted for network access via negotiation between the parties, under the *ex post* control of the Cartel Offices at federal and Länder level. No sector-specific regulatory authority was established, and *ex ante* regulation was kept at a minimum.

Rather than opting for state regulation, the electricity reform relied on corporatist self-governance. Principles of network access and tariffs were negotiated in an associations' agreement (*Verbändevereinbarung*) between the VDEW, VKU on the supplier side and the VIK and the German Association for Industry (BDI) for the users. Germany was alone in the EU in opting for this model of corporatist self-governance. Responding to criticism that it had not taken sufficient care of the interests of new market actors, the first agreement of May 1998 was replaced by a second in early 2000. The associations' agreement was reached 'in the shadow of hierarchy' as the law foresaw regulation by the Federal Economics Ministry should the associations fail to provide for an effective market opening.

Eberlein argues that the electricity reform – despite its radical approach to liberalisation – stood very much in continuity to the existing traditions of the sector.[43] Rather than being seen as the result of regulatory capture, he contends that the resort to a form of self-governance should be understood to mirror several institutional constraints and path dependencies. Thus, the fragmented federal political organisation made it difficult to establish a new regulatory authority at the federal level, where – in contrast to telecommunications – the tradition of a separate ministry was missing. Voluntary self-regulation on the basis of an associations' agreement conformed to the traditional corporatist model of state–society relations under organised capitalism. In this context, it was also possible to cater for environmental issues, employment security, as well as municipal and East German interests, all backed by the idea of a social market economy. Thus, legislators reverted to established routines to cope with the changes entailed by liberalisation.

Meanwhile, a more significant break from sectoral traditions is underway. Heavily criticised by market newcomers and by larger incumbents eager to expand their market shares,[44] the new associations' agreement also came under fire from the European Commission. The voluntary nature of the agreement meant that it was not justiciable and did not fulfil the requirements of the electricity directive. Moreover, since the decisions of the Federal Cartel Office were not legally binding, its interventions led to protracted court proceedings that disrupted efficient sectoral regulation.[45] Consequently, the Commission pushed increasingly for the establishment of an independent regulatory authority (Germany was the only member state which had not taken this step).

The acceleration directive required the establishment of an independent authority by mid-2004. At the time of writing, the German government had agreed on the basic principles of legislation, but it had not yet passed into law. The draft legislation gives responsibility for regulating electricity and gas to the existing regulatory authority for telecoms and post (Bundesregulierungsbehörde für Elektrizität, Gas, Telekommunikation und Post, ReGTP). Meanwhile, it was agreed with the European Commission that the ReGTP would exercise its new responsibilities on an interim basis. Interestingly, the expedient of using ReGTP as the independent regulator for electricity may entail a more radical rupture with past practice than would otherwise have been the case, since the advanced institutional development of telecommunications regulation will now set the pace for electricity.

Beyond the independent regulator, however, the reform has been difficult to agree. The draft law requires electricity companies to operate their transmission networks separately from their supply operations. The *conditions* for network access and tariffs, however, remain undecided, and will appear subsequently as separate regulations to be passed by the BMWA. The form of network access regulation is particularly contentious. The draft law makes provision for Germany to retain a system of *ex post* control of network access. The opposition CDU, however, favours *ex ante* regulation, and its majority in the Bundesrat gives it a potential veto. The government view is that *ex ante* authorisation of network tariffs for 900 or so different operators is unfeasible.[46] With such a large number of network operators, European Commission requirements that tariff approval should be subject to a review of pricing principles would appear to prohibit *ex ante* authorisation.

The draft law was rejected by the Bundesrat in September 2004. Thereafter, agreement became even more difficult to achieve, as the Greens took up the demand for *ex ante* regulation. Coalition disagreement also arose over the extent of subsidies for alternative energies. The future of the law is thus unclear, and the Commission has already initiated infringement proceedings against Germany for its failure to implement the acceleration directive.[47] Despite European pressures for reform, then, the multiple veto points in the domestic political process can entail persistent disagreement and delay, although ultimately the binding nature of European requirements make reform inevitable.

Liberalisation of the Regulated Sectors[48]

European insurance liberalisation required very far-reaching changes from Germany. Parallel to liberalisation, the directive prohibited the *ex ante* control of insurance conditions and services which had been at the core of the German regulatory model. Regulatory oversight switched from the control of products to the solvency of companies. In addition, the monopoly insurers that existed in some of the Länder had to be abolished.

As mentioned above, the dominant sectoral actors – the associations, companies and the regulatory authority – were all opposed to these changes in the regulatory structure. The Federal Ministry of Finance, however, backed by the cabinet, did not oppose European liberalisation, since it offered opportunities for *Finanzplatz Deutschland.* Furthermore, in the aftermath of unification, Germany wanted to dissipate the concerns of its European partners – particularly France – that the new East German market would be closed to outsiders.

Thus, insurance liberalisation exemplifies Moravcsik's argument that European integration strengthens member state governments by offering a negotiating arena that bypasses national veto players.[49] This is particularly true in the case of monopoly building and fire insurance, where some of the Länder originally considered appealing to the ECJ.[50] The reduced influence of the associations also stands out, since as insurance products ceased to be regulated, their cooperation with the regulatory authority was no longer needed. Their resistance was undermined by an increasing diversity of interests amongst insurance companies, as the larger ones began to see liberalisation as an opportunity to expand market share against smaller competitors.

Unlike insurance, the Federal Ministry of Transport opposed the liberalisation of *road haulage* until the end. Nevertheless, some domestic reforms were enacted in the early 1990s to prepare the domestic sector for a liberalisation which was seen as inevitable given European pressures. The inevitability of liberalisation in cabotage services led Germany to begin lifting some of its road haulage regulations, fearing that otherwise a reverse discrimination of nationals (*Inländerdiskriminierung*) would take place. Restrictions on market access could result in barriers to *Germans* doing business in *German* transport markets in which *EU foreigners* could be active. Consequently, lorries under 3.5t (previously 0.75t) were freed from licensing requirements, and the number of licences was considerably increased. The licence system was retained, however, despite a coalition agreement in 1990 to liberalise all licence requirements and tariffs.

The case was different for tariffs, providing a very interesting example of the way domestic reforms can take place. Parliament abolished the system of regulated tariffs from January 1994, under the impression that the ECJ would rule the existing system to be in violation of European competition law. The question was raised by the *Landgericht Koblenz* in a preliminary proceeding (C-185/91) of a case concerning a company that had transported goods below the official tariffs and at the same time declined the penalty payments that the BAG had foreseen for such cases – if detected. Instead, the freight forwarder started the court case, supported by the relevant association, with the explicit aim of overturning valid national rules with the help of European competition law.[51] In the legal literature, the assumption had been common that the fact that the associations took part in the tariff commissions meant that tariff decisions could be seen as an illegal cartel under European competition law.[52] Legal uncertainty over regulated tariff systems under European law was aptly exploited by liberalisation advocates like the FDP, which argued in parliament in favour of altering the domestic system immediately rather than waiting for a ruling from the ECJ that was expected to be negative. In anticipation of the Court ruling, tariff liberalisation was carried out. Given the imminent liberalisation of cabotage, it was seen to be necessary to prepare the road haulage industry for competition. Paradoxically, the anticipation was incorrect – the Court ultimately ruled that the tariff commissions could be kept, since it was the formal responsibility of the Minister of Transport to set the tariffs.

Reform of the German Crafts Law

In contrast to the other liberalisation processes, the reform of the German crafts law was only indirectly connected to European politics. Some domestic adaptation was necessary, since the single market entailed Community-wide freedom of establishment for EU foreigners who had been active in a craft for six years in a member state. The German crafts law of 1953, however, restricted this privilege of establishment (and of training apprentices) to individuals having a *Meisterbrief* (master craftsman's diploma) involving expensive long-term training additional to the basic craftsmanship training as *Geselle*. Both the red–green coalition and the opposition agreed that EU foreigners would have to be granted this opportunity, and that potential reverse discrimination against nationals (*Inländerdiskriminierung*) must be kept to a minimum.[53]

There were significant cross-party differences, however, over the extent of liberalisation to a crafts law that was – by international standards – extremely regulated. The Greens had already argued for an end to the *Meisterzwang* at the time of the previous reform under a conservative government in early 1998. Despite two years of discussion, this reform made only minor changes to the definition of crafts, the resistance of the craft associations preventing any noticeable liberalisation.[54]

Part of *Agenda 2010*, the 2004 reform of the crafts law was much more far-reaching. A minor amendment, not requiring the consent of the Bundesrat, allowed persons established as *Ich-AG*[55] being able to offer simple craftsmanship services requiring no more than two to three months of training. This was accompanied by a major amendment with a more explicit liberalisation goal. In order to cut red tape and to provide new impetus for growth, Economics Minister Wolfgang Clement proposed to abolish the *Meisterzwang* for all those crafts where more advanced training could not be justified by safety concerns. In addition, *Gesellen* working in a craft still falling under the *Meisterzwang* should be able to establish themselves after a certain period of employment in a responsible position. Along with the requirements of European law, this proposal reflected concerns over relatively slow growth in the crafts sectors, and a belief that over-regulation had fuelled the 'black economy' and curtailed employment.[56]

The debate among the parties centred on two questions – how many of the 97 crafts on the list would be excluded from the *Meisterzwang*, and how many years of employment as a *Geselle* would be accepted as an equivalent? Acting as guardians of craft interests, the CDU/CSU and FDP tried to keep as many crafts as possible within the *Meisterzwang*, and to restrict the possibility of equivalence. The opposition parties argued that alongside safety concerns, environment, consumer protection and the extent of apprenticeship training should be taken into account.[57]

The government conceded to the opposition that both reforms would be negotiated together – despite the fact that only the major one required the consent of the Bundesrat.[58] At the same time, however, the government emphasised its determination to reconfigure the major reform so that many of its parts could be passed without Bundesrat consent, should the opposition not refrain from obstruction.[59] Thus, while Clement originally planned to restrict the *Meisterzwang* to 29 crafts, the CDU wanted to allow 53 and the FDP 47, the final reform adopted in 2003 settled on 41 crafts. Alongside safety criteria, the crafts remaining under the *Meisterzwang* are those with a training rate of 50 per cent or more above the average. Despite the reform, 90 per cent of the craft sector is still covered. Without *Meister*, a *Geselle* must have worked for two years, with an additional four in a management position, to be able to establish their own enterprise.[60]

At the time of writing the reform is still too recent to determine its impact. In the first six months since liberalisation in January 2004, 16,000 new establishments were counted, 11,700 of which were in crafts liberalised from the *Meisterzwang*.[61] It should be emphasised that quite far-reaching changes were achieved relatively quickly – the first reading in the Bundestag was in late June 2003 – despite fierce resistance from craft associations and reservations about the extent of liberalisation on the part of opposition and some SPD-governed Länder. Nevertheless, the apprenticeship criterion means that only a small percentage of crafts have profited from liberalisation. Most widely-practised crafts like baker, hair-dresser, butcher or painter remain highly regulated.

The Services Directive

Reform of the crafts law has thus shown once again just how difficult reforms are in the Federal Republic. Although much was achieved, it was still too little to make a significant impact on the crafts which matter quantitatively. This explains the turmoil that the European Commission's proposal for a services directive has generated in Germany, especially since services make up about 50 per cent of all economic activity across the member states. Launched in early 2004, the directive is meant to realise the single market freedoms of services and of establishment in all those service sectors where specific measures have not yet been taken. Very few exceptions are envisaged. The principle of home-country control means that member states must mutually recognise services regulated in other member states as equivalent to their domestically regulated services. The directive proscribes excessive regulatory requirements for establishment. Given that most service sectors are very highly regulated, the directive has a significant deregulatory potential. As former Commissioner Bolkestein has put it:

> We cannot expect European businesses to set the global competitiveness standard or to give their customers the quality and choice they deserve while they still have their hands tied behind their backs by national red tape, eleven years after the 1993 deadline for creating a real Internal Market. Some of the national restrictions are archaic, overly burdensome and break EU law. Those have simply got to go. A much longer list of differing national rules needs sweeping regulatory reform.[62]

In view of the many problems he experienced in the crafts law reform, Economics Minister Clement originally welcomed the directive as an opportunity to overcome the obstacles. More recently, however, Germany has been very vocal in its opposition to the directive, with Chancellor Schröder demanding exemptions for services that are close to the state, such as health or education, and insisting on special provisions to protect environmental and work-place safety. The *Deutsche Gewerkschaftsbund* opposed the directive from the start. Since the EU's eastern enlargement, the freedom of services has proven problematic for Germany. Thus, in German slaughterhouses, Germans have been laid off in large numbers to be replaced by East European service providers with personnel on low pay working under deplorable conditions. While Germany opted to delay freedom of movement for East Europeans for some time, service providers have immediate entry into the country.[63]

It remains to be seen in what form this directive – part of the Lisbon strategy for EU competitiveness – will emerge from the EU policy process, if indeed it does so at all. It seems clear, however, that it would have noticeable impact on the German government's *Agenda 2010* programme. The bargains the government had to face when reforming the crafts law would probably pale into insignificance compared to the likely deregulatory potential of this directive.

CONCLUSION

In the highly regulated economic sectors, many reforms in Germany have taken place – and are still in process – in the shadow of Community law. Of course, it is always difficult to prove the counterfactual point that reforms would not have happened had it not been for the requirements of the EU. However, the high level of ministerial autonomy in German government,[64] close meso-corporatist cooperation with the relevant associations in sectoral regulation, and the scope for Länder veto through the Bundesrat all made reforms highly unlikely. Moreover, domestic criticism of the extent of regulation has largely been absent, with the most relevant regulatory actors preferring the status quo. Liberalisation advocates – users, the FDP and the Economics Ministry – were generally too marginal in the policy process to force measures through. Thus, it has been argued that the liberalisation of road haulage would not have occurred without the pressure of the EU. In the case of Germany, European transport liberalisation was in fact vital for overcoming the stability of sectoral corporatism and for the switch to a liberal transport policy approach to be achieved.[65]

The requirement to conform to European law has brought about far-reaching changes in highly regulated economic sectors. This is due in large part to a comprehensive approach to the single European market that regulates domestic and trans-border activities alike according to the same set of rules. Thus, in insurance, Germany could not restrict product authorisation to companies active only on the domestic market. This approach privileges the single market, even where cross-border trade of services is relatively insignificant. Thus, cabotage services in road haulage made up only 0.76 per cent of total road transport in 2001. In France and Germany, where most of road haulage takes place, it made up 1.6 per cent and 1.1 per cent of domestic road transport respectively.[66] In the German insurance market in 2000, 3.2 per cent of market share was made up by cross-border service providers or secondary establishments of EU foreigners. In contrast, foreign-controlled companies (at least 50 per cent) had a market share of 13 per cent in 2000.[67] As these are establishments in Germany, they fall under any additional national regulation and would not have needed the complicated European rules to realise the freedom of services in the single market.

It would be wrong, however, to perceive Germany as responding only passively to the demands of European liberalisation. In several regulated economic sectors – telecoms, electricity, insurance, road haulage, and the crafts – domestic reforms have gone beyond European requirements. The fact that once reforms became necessary these went beyond requirements shows how locked in previous sectoral regulation had been. With its multiple veto points, the German polity privileges a blocking minority over the majority, facilitating the defence of regulation against reform even where it is supported only by a minority of actors. Once the veto position of the minority was circumvented through the need to implement European requirements, however, it became apparent how far away from the balance of actor preferences the previous regulatory regime had been.[68] Furthermore, the case studies presented here show the way in which liberalisation can change actor preferences. For actors that had previously been united in support of highly regulated regimes – large insurance and electricity companies – the advent of liberalisation led to a reconsideration of preferences as the market opportunities became apparent. Thus, those actors set to profit from liberalisation came to support it.

Finally, it is interesting to note that the same forces of lock-in and stability typical of the German polity have set in again after the reforms. This becomes apparent when comparing the German to the French case. Details are beyond the scope of this study, but comparison shows that French political actors have been much more able than their German counterparts to grasp the autonomy that remains under European law to realise domestic regulatory objectives.[69]

NOTES

This essay draws on the results of my habilitation project (S.K. Schmidt, 'Rechtsunsicherheit statt Regulierungswettbewerb: Die nationalen Folgen des europäischen Binnenmarkts für Dienstleistungen', Habilitationsschrift, Hagen, 2004). I would like to thank Fritz Scharpf for his comments to this project. Additionally, I am indebted to the editors, Kenneth Dyson and Stephen Padgett, and to Ines Läufer for research assistance.

1. F.W. Scharpf, 'The Joint-Decision Trap: Lessons from German Federalism and European Integration', *Public Administration* 66/3 (1988), pp.239–78.
2. G. Lehmbruch, *Parteienwettbewerb im Bundesstaat. Regelsysteme und Spannungslagen im politischen System der Bundesrepublik Deutschland* (Wiesbaden: Westdeutscher Verlag, 2000).
3. H. Voelzkow, 'Korporatismus in Deutschland: Chancen, Risiken und Perspektiven', in E. Holtmann and H. Voelzkow (eds.), *Zwischen Wettbewerbs- und Verhandlungsdemokratie* (Wiesbaden: Westdeutscher Verlag, 2000), pp.185–212; R. Czada, *Dimensionen der Verhandlungsdemokratie* (Hagen: Polis, 2000).
4. K. v. Beyme, *Der Gesetzgeber* (Opladen: Westdeutscher Verlag, 1997).
5. S.K. Schmidt, 'Taking the long Road to Liberalization. Telecommunications Reform in the Federal Republic of Germany', *Telecommunications Policy* 15/3 (1991), pp.209–22; E. Grande and B. Eberlein, 'Der Aufstieg des Regulierungsstaates im Infrastrukturbereich. Zur Transformation der politischen Ökonomie der BRD', in R. Czada and H. Wollmann (eds.), *Von der Bonner zur Berliner Republik* (Wiesbaden: Westdeutscher Verlag, 2000), pp.631–50.
6. A. Cawson *et al.*, *Hostile Brothers: Competition and Closure in the European Electronics Industry* (Oxford: Clarendon Press, 1990).
7. Schmidt, 'Taking the Long Road to Liberalization', p.213.
8. D. Webber, 'Die ausbleibende Wende bei der Deutschen Bundespost', *Politische Vierteljahresschrift* 27 (1986), pp.397–414.
9. B. Eberlein, 'Institutional Change and Continuity in German Infrastructure Management: The Case of Electricity Reform', *German Politics* 9/3 (2000), pp.81–104 (p.84).
10. E. Grande and B. Eberlein, 'Der Aufstieg des Regulierungsstaates im Infrastrukturbereich', p.639.
11. Eberlein, 'Institutional Change and Continuity in German Infrastructure Management', p.86.
12. G. Stigler, 'The Theory of Economic Regulation', *Bell Journal of Economics and Management Science* 2 (1971), pp.3–21; S. Peltzman, 'The Economic Theory of Regulation after a Decade of Deregulation', *Brookings Papers on Economic Activity* (1989), pp.1–41.
13. M. Krakowski, 'Regulierung der Versicherungsmärkte', in M. Krakowski (ed.), *Regulierung in der Bundesrepublik Deutschland. Die Ausnahmebereiche des Gesetzes gegen Wettbewerbsbeschränkungen* (Hamburg: Verlag Weltarchiv, 1988), pp.423–97.
14. Interview No. 5.
15. Wacker-Theodorakopulos, 'Regulierung des Verkehrssektors', in M. Krakowski (ed.), *Regulierung in der Bundesrepublik Deutschland. Die Ausnahmebereiche des Gesetzes gegen Wettbewerbsbeschränkungen* (Hamburg: Verlag Weltarchiv, 1988), pp.287–345.
16. D. Garlichs and E. Müller, 'Eine neue Organisation für das Bundesverkehrsministerium', *Die Verwaltung* 3 (1977), pp.343–62 (p.344f).
17. G. Aberle, 'Sektorale Deregulierung – Die EG-Integration erzwingt veränderte ordnungspolitische Strukturen auf den Straßengüterverkehrsmärkten', *Hamburger Jahrbuch für Wirtschaft- und Gesellschaftspolitik* 32 (1987), pp.157–74 (p.164); Deregulierungskommission, *Marktöffnung und Wettbewerb* (Stuttgart: Poeschel, 1991), p.46f.
18. D. Allen, 'Competition Policy: Policing the Single Market', in H. Wallace and W. William (eds.), *Policy-Making in the European Union* (Oxford: Oxford University Press, 1996), pp.157–83.
19. G. Ross, *Jacques Delors and European Integration* (Cambridge: Policy Press, 1995), pp.130–35; S.K. Schmidt, 'Commission Activism: Subsuming Telecommunications and Electricity under European Competition Law', *Journal of European Public Policy* 5/1 (1998), pp.169–84.
20. P. Behrens, 'Die Konvergenz der wirtschaftlichen Freiheiten im europäischen Gemeinschaftsrecht', *Europarecht* 2 (1992), pp.145–62 (p.149).
21. S.K. Schmidt, *Liberalisierung in Europa. Die Rolle der Europäischen Kommission* (Frankfurt: Campus, 1998), p.66.
22. F.W. Scharpf, 'Democratic Policy in Europe', *European Law Journal* 2/2 (1996), pp.136–55.
23. F.W. Scharpf, *Governing in Europe: Effective and Democratic?* (Oxford: Oxford University Press, 1999).
24. P. Troberg, 'Niederlassung', in H. v. d. Groeben, J. Thiesing and C.-D. Ehlermann (eds.), *Kommentar zum EU-/EG-Vertrag, 5. Aufl.* (Baden-Baden: Nomos-Verlag, 1997), pp.1303–440 (p.1414).
25. Schmidt, *Liberalisierung in Europa.*

26. Schmidt, 'Commission Activism'.
27. Hours of gigawatt (i.e. 40,000,000,000 watt).
28. Schmidt, *Liberalisierung in Europa*, p.251.
29. J.H.-E. Badenhoop, 'Binnenmarkt der Versicherungen', in W. Weidenfeld (ed.), *Binnenmarkt '92: Perspektiven aus deutscher Sicht* (Gütersloh: Bertelsmann Stiftung, 1988), pp.103–6 (p.103).
30. U. v. Criegern, *Die Bedeutung der Dritten Schadenrichtlinie unter aufsichtsrechtlichen Gesichtspunkten für die Dienstleistungsfreiheit der Versicherungsunternehmen in dem Binnenmarkt* (Frankfurt *et al.*: Lang, 1997), pp.157, 160, 171; G. Wagner, 'The Economics of Harmonization: The Case of Contract Law', *Common Market Law Review* 39 (2002), pp.995–1023.
31. It also has to be kept in mind that insurance services are very context-dependent: thus, accident insurance for cars has to regard national accident statistics, and life insurance national death tables.
32. D. Kerwer and M. Teutsch, 'Transport Policy in the European Union', in A. Héritier *et al.* (eds.), *Differential Europe* (Lanham: Rowman & Littlefield Publishers, 2001), pp.23–56.
33. J. Basedow and M. Dolfen, 'Verkehrs- und Transportrecht', in M.A. Dauses (ed.), *Handbuch des EU-Wirtschaftsrechts* (München: Beck, 1998), pp.1–148, No.158–60.
34. Social harmonisation includes for instance driving and resting times; technical harmonisation relates to size and weight; also there are minimum taxes for fuel and vehicles See J. Basedow and M. Dolfen, 'Verkehrs- und Transportrecht', No.188.
35. J. Basedow and M. Dolfen, 'Verkehrs- und Transportrecht', No.176. Interview No.12.
36. See Streeck and Trampusch, this volume.
37. Schmidt, 'Taking the long Road to Liberalization'; R. Werle, 'Liberalisation of Telecommunications in Germany', in K.A. Eliassen and M. Sjövaag (eds.), *European Telecommunications Liberalisation* (London/New York: Routledge, 1999), pp.110–27 (p.112).
38. R. Werle, 'Liberalisation of Telecommunications in Germany', p.112f; S.K. Schmidt, 'A New German Public Sector?' in A. Benz and H.G. Klaus (eds.), *A New German Public Sector?* (Aldershot: Dartmouth, 1996), pp.45–70.
39. Schmidt, *Liberalisierung in Europa*,.p.151f.
40. U. Schimank, 'Spezifische Interessenkonsense trotz generellem Orientierungsdissens', in H.-J. Giegel (ed.), *Kommunikation und Konsense in modernen Gesellschaften* (Frankfurt: Suhrkamp, 1992), pp.236–75.
41. Deregulierungskommission, *Marktöffnung und Wettbewerb* (Stuttgart: Poeschel, 1991).
42. R. Eising, *Liberalisierung und Europäisierung* (Opladen: Leske & Budrich 2000), pp.268–90.
43. Eberlein, 'Institutional Change and Continuity in German Infrastructure Management', pp.96–8.
44. *FAZ*, 14 Dec. 2000, p.20.
45. Christian Theobald, 'Wettbewerb mit Strom und Gas', *FAZ*, 10 March 2001, S.15.
46. *FAZ*, 29 July 2004, p.9.
47. *FAZ*, 13 Oct. 2004, p.13; 18 Oct. 2004, p.15; 19 Jan. 2005, p.12.
48. See S.K. Schmidt, 'Rechtsunsicherheit statt Regulierungswettbewerb: Die nationalen Folgen des europäischen Binnenmarkts für Dienstleistungen', chapter 4 in *Fachbereich Kultur- und Sozialwissenschaften* (FernUniversität Hagen, 2004).
49. A. Moravcsik, 'Warum die Europäische Union die Exekutive stärkt: Innenpolitik und internationale Kooperation', in K.D. Wolf (ed.), *Projekt Europa im Übergang?* (Baden-Baden: Nomos, 1997), pp.211–69 (p.220).
50. *Handelsblatt*, 7 May 1993.
51. M. Teutsch, 'Regulatory Reforms in the German Transport Sector: How to Overcome Multiple Veto Points Differential Europe', in A. Héritier *et al.* (eds.), *Differential Europe* (Lanham: Rowman & Littlefield Publishers, 2001), pp.133–72 (p.143).
52. J. Basedow, 'EG-Recht und Verkehrspolitische Handlungsspielräume der Mitgliedsstaaten nach 1992', *Das deutsche Transportrecht an der Schwelle zum Europäischen Binnenmarkt: Symposium der Deutschen Gesellschaft für Transportrecht Wiesbaden 1991* (Neuwied/Berlin: Luchterhand, 1993), pp.155–79 (p.166); Monopolkommission, *Wettbewerbspolitik vor neuen Herausforderungen. Hauptgutachten 1988/89* (Baden-Baden: Nomos, 1990), p.307.
53. *FAZ*, 7 May 2003, p.11.
54. *FAZ*, 5 Feb. 1998, p.18; 14 Feb. 1998, p.14.
55. If unemployed persons establish their own business, their social security is financed by the *Bundesanstalt für Arbeit* and they have to pay only 10 per cent taxes until a yearly income of €25,000.
56. *FAZ*, 28 Nov. 2003, p.12.
57. *FAZ*, 11 Dec. 2003, p.13.
58. *FAZ*, 8 Dec. 2003, p.2.
59. *FAZ*, 17 Oct. 2003, p.7.
60. *FAZ*, 16 Dec. 2003, p.12; 18 Dec. 2003, p.11.

61. *FAZ*, 8 Sept. 2004, p.9.
62. Rapid press release IP/04/37, 13 Jan. 2004: Services: Commission proposes Directive to cut red tape that stifles Europe's competitiveness.
63. *FTD*, 9 Feb. 2005, p.27; 'Der Osten kommt', *Der Spiegel* 7/2005, pp.32–5. However, the services freedom only covers temporary cross-border activities. Permanent activities fall under the freedom of establishment and then the relevant rules of the country of establishment have to be applied. It could therefore well be that Germany could enforce its standards if East European service providers are active on a permanent basis. See S.K. Schmidt, 'Die nationale Bedingtheit der Folgen der europäischen Integration', *Zeitschrift für Internationale Beziehungen* 10/1 (2003), pp.43–68.
64. R. Mayntz and F.W. Scharpf, *Policy Making in the German Federal Bureaucracy* (Amsterdam: Elsevier, 1975), pp.42, 69, 74.
65. D. Kerwer and M. Teutsch, 'Transport Policy in the European Union', p.131.
66. See Eurostat, Statistiques en bref, Transport, Theme 7-7/2003, Josefine Oberhausen: Le cabotage routier de 1999 à 2001. http://europa.eu.int/comm/eurostat/Public/datashop/print-product/FR?catalogue = Eurostat&product = KS-NZ-03-007-__-N-FR&mode = download.
67. Bundesanstalt für Finanzdienstleistungsaufsicht, 'Geschäftsbericht 2001 Teil B' (Bonn: Bundesanstalt für Finanzdienstleistungsaufsicht, 2003); OECD Statistics (CD-ROM), 'Financial and Fiscal Affairs, Insurance Statistics', Paris, C3131–C3112.
68. Schmidt, 'Die nationale Bedingtheit der Folgen der europäischen Integration'.
69. Schmidt, 'Rechtsunsicherheit statt Regulierungswettbewerb'.

Economic Reform and the Political Economy of the German Welfare State

WOLFGANG STREECK and CHRISTINE TRAMPUSCH

Contrary to widespread belief, the German economy does not suffer from a lack of international competitiveness.[1] Despite the high value of the euro, the trade surplus continues to rise. Employment in exposed sectors, while declining as elsewhere, continues to exceed that in any comparable country, indicating that German industry has maintained its outstanding competitive performance. Industrial wages are high, but are offset by high and fast-rising productivity.[2]

Nor does the German economy face particular difficulties with respect to internationalisation. Notwithstanding employment protection, co-determination and high wage levels, inward foreign investment remains buoyant, attracted by an excellent infrastructure, a high skill workforce and peaceful labour relations.[3] German firms have substantially expanded their activities abroad in order to compete for market share. During the past decade, firms like Siemens, BASF, BMW, Volkswagen, Daimler-Benz, and Hoechst, have evolved into true multinationals. Well into the 1990s, the domestic employment effects of outward investment have been generally benevolent. A decline in low-skilled jobs has been compensated by growth in high-skilled employment, resulting in an upgrading of the employment structure with only minor losses in the volume of employment.[4]

Nevertheless, there is a severe and worsening employment problem, and it is here that an analysis of malfunction in German economic institutions must begin. For almost two decades now, high unemployment has been combined with low participation in the labour market, resulting in a remarkably low *rate of employment.* Given that employment in industry is above the international average, the explanation is low employment growth in services, especially domestically traded services.[5] While this has long been known, it has been largely neglected for a number of reasons. Above all, many of those outside employment have been supported by comparatively liberal unemployment benefits, or attractive early retirement terms.[6] Others were kept out of the labour market by extended periods of education.[7] Moreover, a low rate of female participation in the labour market turned the family into another holding pen for those unlikely to find employment in a stagnant labour market.[8]

It is now obvious, however, that the country can no longer afford to treat a low employment rate as a matter of political choice, or as the expression of a national preference for industrial rather than service-sector occupations. Taking surplus labour out of the market on comparatively comfortable terms has become less and less possible due to an endemic financial crisis of the state. The resultant benefit cuts make non-employment increasingly unacceptable to a growing number of people. Not only does this cause political discontent, but it also sets in motion a transformation of the employment system from below, in the form of the emergence – unprecedented in the post-war German economy – of a sizeable number of 'working poor'.[9]

These problems are compounded dramatically by the slow growth of the German economy.[10] Slow growth contributes to a crisis of public finance that is exacerbated by downward pressure on public revenues resulting from tax competition with other countries and the perceived desire of citizens for tax cuts. Tax cuts coincide with the obligation incurred under European Monetary Union to consolidate public finances, resulting in an apparently unending series of austerity budgets. At the same time, governments at all levels are faced with business demands for a well-developed infrastructure and high levels of education as a condition for continuing to produce in Germany.

There are also indications that Germany is beginning to lag behind other countries in high-technology sectors and high value-added products.[11] Moreover, low-cost competition from potential high-quality producers in Eastern Europe is making it harder for German production sites to compensate for high costs through superior productivity and product quality. In short, not only are the old ways of living with low employment becoming gradually unviable, but the highly productive employment that in the past paid for the pacification of the unemployed may be about to break away at a much faster pace.

Where does an affluent country facing slow impoverishment begin with economic reform? An often-cited suspect is Germany's vast and expensive welfare state. Indeed, comparative research has produced convincing evidence that it is the particular characteristics of the Bismarckian welfare state – funded through social security contributions and geared to status maintenance rather than protection from poverty – that depresses the level of employment by inflating the costs of labour. High non-wage labour costs interact with unemployment in a vicious circle. By making labour more expensive, they induce firms to downsize their labour force, in the past typically through early retirement. They also prevent employment growth in labour-intensive sectors, especially in services. Alternatively they drive labour into the black economy, reducing the revenues of the social insurance funds, thus pushing up contribution rates. The same effect is caused by unemployment and non-employment, to the extent that individuals are supported by the pension or the unemployment insurance system. As rates rise in response to declining employment or increasing entitlements, labour costs also rise, reducing employment even more. In the end, the very instruments which used to make unemployment socially acceptable become a cause of even more unemployment.[12]

Cutting non-wage labour costs in order to raise employment is, however, not an easy feat to accomplish as it must involve one or more of three things: cuts in the entitlements of future and, especially, current beneficiaries; a shift from public to private provision paid for by individuals with no contribution from their employers; and a change in the funding base of the welfare state from contributions to taxes. Given the demographics of an ageing population, the same applies in principle when the objective is much less ambitious and involves no more than freezing non-wage labour costs at the current level.

Freezing, however, is clearly not enough. Apart from the fact that it leaves the relationship of mutual reinforcement between high labour costs and low employment intact, it would require growing infusions of tax money that would be urgently needed for investment in the physical infrastructure and in research and innovation. This is another, more recent way in which welfare state compensation for unemployment and low employment contributes to exacerbating the problem that it is supposed to remedy. For example, by the early 2000s the budget of the Federal Labour Office (around €50 billion) was almost double the combined budget of all German universities (about €27 billion).[13] Thus a fundamental precondition for a successful defence of German prosperity is moving resources from the satisfaction of mostly consumptive entitlements into investment in productive capacities. It is for this reason that economic reform must focus above all on the welfare state.

THE RISE OF NON-WAGE LABOUR COSTS

The German welfare system consists of four major elements: pension insurance, unemployment insurance, health insurance and long-term care insurance. Whereas pension and unemployment insurance receive federal subsidies, health insurance was until 2003 exclusively funded by contributions, and long-term care insurance still is. Long-term care insurance was introduced in 1995, at a time when the social insurance system was already beginning to crumble under the burden of German unification. The main period of expansion of the German social insurance system was during the heyday of *Modell Deutschland* in the 1970s and early 1980s, the success of which was based on a subtle interaction between the welfare state, the system of collective bargaining and the federal budget.[14] Social security supported the remarkably successful adjustment to declining mass production and later helped the country cope with the socio-economic and political challenges caused by German unification. The latter brought West German welfare standards to East Germans nearly overnight, allaying any political discontent that might have arisen from the dismantling of state socialism.

The West German welfare system responded to the economic crisis after unification by transforming East Germany rapidly into a state-supported secondary labour market and a society of early retirees. Owing to decades of extensive use of the social insurance system to absorb surplus labour created by high wages, low wage dispersion and German unification, combined social insurance contributions steadily increased, and by 1996 they exceeded the magic figure of 40 per cent of gross wages (Table 1). Between 1990 and 1998 alone, the combined social insurance contribution rate grew by six and a half percentage points, from 35.5 per cent to 42.1 per cent, of which German unification accounted for about three percentage points.[15]

One of the typical characteristics of the German social insurance system is its fragmentation into four separate budgets. This allows the government to mask financial difficulties by complex fiscal manoeuvres involving the different parafiscal social insurance funds and the federal budget. Since the early 1980s, the government has with

TABLE 1
CONTRIBUTION RATES BETWEEN 1949 AND 2003, AS OF THE END OF THE YEAR

Year	Unemployment	Pension	Health care	Total*	Year	Unemployment	Pension	Health care	Total*
1949	4.0	10.0	6.0	20.0	1977	3.0	18.0	11.4	32.4
1950	4.0	10.0	6.0	20.0	1978	3.0	18.0	11.4	32.4
1951	4.0	10.0	6.0	20.0	1979	3.0	18.0	11.2	32.2
1952	4.0	10.0	6.0	20.0	1980	3.0	18.0	11.4	32.4
1953	4.0	10.0	6.0	20.0	1981	3.0	18.5	11.8	33.3
1954	4.0	10.0	6.2	20.2	1982	4.0	18.0	12.0	34.0
1955	3.0	11.0	6.2	20.2	1983	4.6	18.5	11.8	34.9
1956	3.0	11.0	6.2	20.2	1984	4.6	18.5	11.4	34.5
1957	2.0	14.0	7.8	23.8	1985	4.1	19.2	11.8	35.1
1958	2.0	14.0	8.4	24.4	1986	4.0	19.2	12.2	35.4
1959	2.0	14.0	8.4	24.4	1987	4.3	18.7	12.6	35.6
1960	2.0	14.0	8.4	24.4	1988	4.3	18.7	12.9	35.9
1961	0.0	14.0	9.4	23.4	1989	4.3	18.7	12.9	35.9
1962	1.4	14.0	9.6	25.0	1990	4.3	18.7	12.5	35.5
1963	1.4	14.0	9.6	25.0	1991	6.8	17.7	12.3	36.8
1964	1.3	14.0	9.7	25.0	1992	6.3	17.7	12.5	36.5
1965	1.3	14.0	9.9	25.2	1993	6.5	17.5	13.2	37.2
1966	1.3	14.0	10.0	25.3	1994	6.5	19.2	13.3	39.0
1967	1.3	14.0	10.1	25.4	1995	6.5	18.6	13.1	39.9
1968	1.3	15.0	10.2	26.5	1996	6.5	19.2	13.7	41.1
1969	1.3	16.0	10.5	27.8	1997	6.5	20.3	13.4	41.9
1970	1.3	17.0	8.2	26.5	1998	6.5	20.3	13.6	42.1
1971	1.3	17.0	8.2	26.5	1999	6.5	19.5	13.6	41.3
1972	1.7	17.0	8.4	27.1	2000	6.5	19.3	13.6	41.1
1973	1.7	18.0	9.2	28.9	2001	6.5	19.1	13.6	40.9
1974	1.7	18.0	9.5	29.2	2002	6.5	19.1	14.0	41.3
1975	2.0	18.0	10.5	30.5	2003	6.5	19.5	14.3	42.0
1976	3.0	18.0	11.3	32.3					

*Total: from 1995 including long-term care. Until June 1996 the contribution rate was 1.0 per cent. In July 1996 it increased to 1.7 per cent.

Source: 1949 to 2002: 'Christine Trampusch, Ein Bündnis für die nachhaltige Finanzierung der Sozialversicherungssysteme: Interessenvermittlung in der deutschen Arbeitsmarkt- und Rentenpolitik', *MPIfG Discussion Paper 03/1* (Köln: Max-Planck-Institut für Gesellschaftsforschung, 2003); for the data on health insurance in 2002 and 2003: BDA, Beitragssätze zur Sozialversicherung, http://www.bdaonline.de/www/bdaonline.nsf/id/GraphikBeitragssaetzezurSozial/$file/Beitragssätze.pdf (6 Dec 2004).

increasing skill hidden rising contribution rates and avoided spending cuts by means of financial transfers between the social insurance funds and by infusing federal tax money into the social insurance system. For example, in 1977 the government made the unemployment insurance fund pay pension contributions for recipients of unemployment benefit. It was thus able to keep the pay-as-you-go pension system liquid without an increase in the contribution rate, at the price of creating additional future entitlements. Similarly, from 1992, the unemployment insurance fund has to pay pension insurance contributions for participants in job creation measures in eastern Germany. While this increased the revenue of the pension insurance fund, it caused a long-term increase in unemployment insurance contributions. Moreover, to stabilise the combined social insurance contribution rate between 1981 and 1991, the government several times balanced a rise in one contribution rate by lowering another, causing long-term fiscal problems for those systems whose contribution rates were lowered.

A second means of avoiding increased contributions was to subsidise social budgets through federal grants to the pension and unemployment insurance funds (Table 2) and by federal transfers of benefits not calculated according to actuarial principles. Between 1981 and 2003, federal support for the pension insurance system increased from 18 to 26 per cent of the latter's total revenue (€14 to €61 billion; Table 2). In 1993, the then Bundesanstalt and now Bundesagentur für Arbeit, which runs the unemployment insurance system, received a federal grant of €13 billion to cover the extra costs of German unification. In the 1990s, short-term consolidation of the social insurance budgets by means of federal subsidies was often financed by tax increases. At the end of 1997, an increase in the pension contribution rate was avoided by raising the value added tax from 15 to 16 per cent. In 1999, federal subsidisation of the pension

TABLE 2

FEDERAL SUBSIDIES FOR PENSION AND UNEMPLOYMENT INSURANCE FUNDS, 1981–2003

	Federal subsidy to pension insurance fund		Federal expenditure on unemployment assistance (*Arbeitslosenhilfe*)		Federal subsidy to unemployment insurance fund	
Year	**In €m**	**In % of total revenue of pension insurance fund**	**In €m**	**As % of total expenditure of unemployment insurance fund***	**In €m**	**In % of total expenditure of unemployment insurance fund**
1981	13,933	17.75	1,457	10.1	4,197	29.1
1982	15,737	19.47	2,564	15.0	3,581	21.0
1983	15,888	19.76	3,642	17.6	806	4.8
1984	16,776	19.66	4,458	29.6	0	0.0
1985	17,155	19.03	4,666	30.7	0	0.0
1986	17,591	18.56	4,683	28.7	0	0.0
1987	18,203	18.79	4,617	25.1	0	0.0
1988	18,866	18.63	4,318	20.7	459	2.2
1989	19,532	18.38	4,195	20.6	987	4.8
1990	20,371	17.71	3,879	17.3	361	1.6
1991	25,808	18.51	3,648	9.9	524	1.4
1992	29,820	19.84	4,656	9.7	4,571	9.6
1993	31,978	20.58	7,145	12.8	12,485	22.3
1994	36,651	21.36	8,912	17.5	5,186	10.2
1995	37,470	20.90	10,486	21.1	3,522	7.1
1996	39,454	20.98	12,386	22.9	7,033	13.0
1997	42,229	21.41	14,315	27.3	4,895	9.3
1998	49,214	24.09	15,563	30.8	3,947	7.8
1999	49,822	23.52	15,581	30.1	3,739	7.2
2000	49,795	23.21	13,161	26.1	867	1.7
2001	53,342	24.21	12,778	24.3	1,900	3.6
2002	56,657	25.34	14,756	26.1	5,600	9.9
2003	61,173	26.38	16,532	31.1	6,200	11.7

*Unemployment assistance is not included in the budget of the unemployment insurance fund.
Source: Pension insurance: VDR (Verband der Deutschen Rentenversicherungsträger), *Einnahmen der Rentenversicherung*, http://www.vdr.de/internet/vdr/statzr.nsf/($URLRef)/5F0E1B53C4AC2A6FC1256A390043F88D (22 Nov 2004); Bundesagentur für Arbeit: Bundesministerium für Gesundheit und Soziale Sicherung (BMGS), *Statistisches Taschenbuch, Arbeits- und Sozialstatistik* (Bonn, 2004), http://www.bmgs.bund.de/download/statistiken/stat2004/Stb8_14.xls (22 Nov 2004); Bundesagentur für Arbeit, *Haushaltsplan Haushaltsjahr 2004* (Nürnberg, 2004); Bundesagentur für Arbeit, Referat IIIc2 (Haushaltsreferat, Finanzauswertungen und Finanzplanung) Diplom-Verwaltungswirt Dieter Spetzke.

fund was continued by the Red–Green government with the introduction of the eco-tax on energy and gasoline, whose fifth and last stage came into effect in 2004.

As a result of the decade-old practice of parafiscal burden-shifting and of balancing the social insurance funds by federal tax subsidies, the different social insurance budgets and the federal budget are now closely intertwined. Changes in contribution rates and benefit reductions in one of the social insurance schemes affect not only the other social insurance schemes but often the federal budget also. Lowering contributions in one branch of the social insurance system may require increases in another and is thus unlikely to have a discernible effect on total contributions. Put another way, structural reforms of only one of the four social insurance systems may merely exacerbate the crisis in the social insurance system as a whole.

The recession of 1992–93 changed the interaction between the budgets of the welfare state and the federal government, underlining that a social insurance system that had hitherto imposed no discernible cost to economic growth had become a burden. High non-wage labour costs had created a strong impediment to economic growth and a disincentive to private sector job creation, especially in labour-intensive service sectors. Additionally, European Stability Pact limits on state deficits had reduced the government's room for fiscal manoeuvre to subsidise the social insurance budgets. Rising non-wage labour costs and high unemployment also strained the loyalties of the constituencies of employer associations and trade unions.[16] By the mid-1990s, pressures for reform had grown enormously.

Reform, however, is not easy in the German political system. German unification increased the number of Länder to 16, with independently scheduled Länder elections turning national politics into an almost permanent election campaign.[17] During Schröder's first term there were 15 state elections, seven in 1999, two in 2000, four in 2001, and two in 2002. In addition there was the European election of 1999. In the first Land election after its accession to power (in Hesse in early 1999), the Red–Green government lost its majority in the Second Chamber, the Bundesrat. Since the February 2003 election in Lower Saxony, the opposition had held a solid Bundesrat majority that gives it veto power over all major legislation.

One way of lowering the costs of labour is moderation in collective wage bargaining. Here Germany has, on the whole, done surprisingly well.[18] In a Bismarckian welfare state, however, lower labour costs also require lower contributions to the three main sectors of the welfare state: pensions, unemployment insurance and labour market policy, reducing the financial burden imposed by the state on the employment relationship. Since coming to power in 1998, the Red–Green government has initiated a series of measures for welfare state reform in an effort to control public spending and increase employment. As we will show in the following sections, all of them have failed and indeed the entire political capital the government had available for welfare state reform had to be spent on keeping contributions at the level of 1998.

PENSIONS

Until recently the basic principle of Germany's contribution-financed statutory pension system was maintaining the living standards of workers during retirement (*Lebenstandardsicherung*). Entitlements were calculated on the basis of the length of their insurance record and the amount of contributions paid (calculated as a percentage of income, up to a cut-off point). In addition, the 1957 pension reform linked pensions to changes in the gross pay of active workers. The main aim of the government's pension policy was to adjust the revenues of the pension insurance funds to the expenditure required to serve the entitlements of those drawing pensions.

Since public pensions maintained living standards, the statutory pension system became the institutional core of the early retirement regime.[19] High public pensions allowed firms to restructure and close down plants without harsh conflicts with trade unions. Redundancies were chosen so as to make early retirement possible for older employees.[20] The manufacturing industry in particular soon learned how to make use of early exit options.[21] Early retirement policy allowed unions to adhere to their high-wage strategy because it absorbed surplus labour. It is not surprising that early retirement soon began to account for a growing part of the expenditure of the pension system. The result was both increasing statutory non-wage labour costs and higher government subsidies for pension funds, which were partially financed through higher taxes. Whereas in 1970 the federal budget accounted for 18.9 per cent of the total revenue of the pension insurance system, by 2000 this had risen to 23.2 per cent.[22]

In 1997, under pressure from rapidly increasing non-wage labour costs (Table 1; Figure 1), the Kohl government broke with the traditional consensus style of pension policy.[23] A reform aimed at stabilising the rate of insurance contribution introduced

FIGURE 1
CONTRIBUTION RATES TO PENSION, HEALTH AND UNEMPLOYMENT INSURANCE, 1949–2003

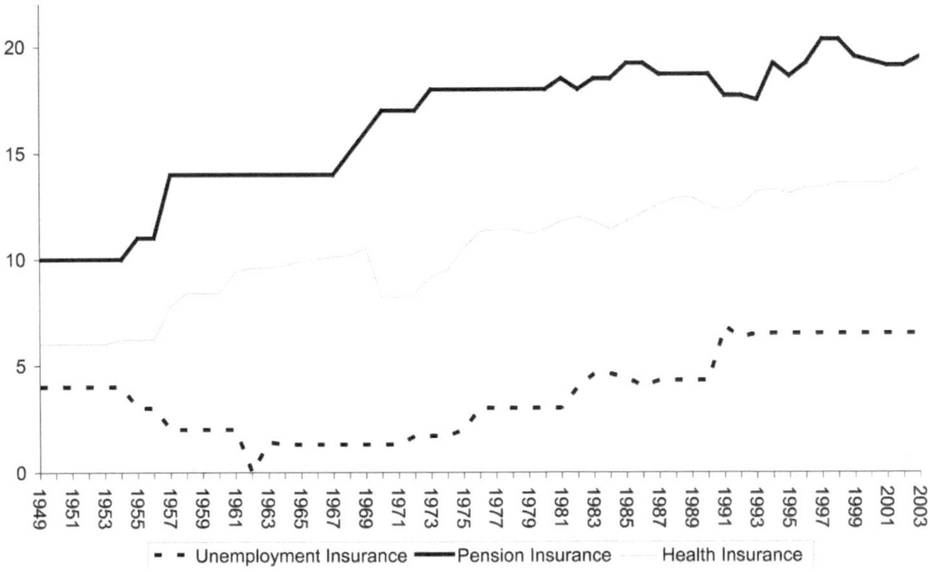

Source: See Table 1.

the principle of *einnahmeorientierte Ausgabenpolitik*, where benefits depend on revenues rather than vice versa, as previously.[24] Against the resistance of the opposition SPD a so-called 'demographic factor' was introduced, aimed at taking into account the increase in life expectancy. The demographic factor was to reduce the replacement rate of the 'standard pensioner' from 70 per cent in 1999 to 64 per cent in 2030. Moreover, disability pensions were cut by actuarial deductions.

The Kohl reforms contributed to the success of the Social Democrats in the 1998 Bundestag election.[25] During the campaign the SPD had promised to undo the cuts in benefits. Immediately after its accession to power, it delivered on its promise with the 1998 'Act to Correct Social Insurance and Guarantee the Rights of Employees' (*Gesetz zu Korrekturen in der Sozialversicherung und zur Sicherung der Arbeitnehmerrechte*). The law suspended the demographic factor and removed the cuts in disability pensions. The government also lowered the rate of contribution to pension insurance from 20.3 to 19.5 per cent, even though the suspension of the Kohl reforms was bound to cause higher expenditure. Schröder believed, however, that revenues could be increased by extending compulsory social insurance to certain categories of self-employed, which were declared to be pseudo-self-employed (*Scheinselbstständige*). In addition, in April 1999 the government introduced social insurance contributions for jobs in the low-wage sector, hoping that this would also generate revenues for the pension insurance scheme (*630-DM-Reform*). However, both reforms had the opposite effect as they added to the rigidity of the labour market and created new incentives to work in the underground economy.[26]

Suspension of the demographic factor was followed by numerous *ad hoc* measures aimed at stabilising the contribution rate without having to cut benefits. Most important among these were the ecological tax reform; a pension freeze in 2000–01, which tied pensions to consumer prices instead of wages; coverage out of the federal budget of a pension supplement for time spent child-rearing; and federal reimbursement of the pension funds for payments to specific groups of pensioners in the former GDR. The measures were accompanied by further reductions in the rate of contribution, from 19.5 to 19.3 per cent in 2000 and from 19.3 to 19.1 per cent in 2001. All in all, the government managed to lower the pension contribution rate between April 1999 and January 2001 by 1.2 percentage points. Taxation required to subsidise the pension system, however, took the estimated overall contribution rate of the average employee to around 28 per cent of gross wages.[27]

Having stretched the federal budget to its limit,[28] the measures of 1999 unintentionally forced the government to consider structural reforms that went beyond short-term fiscal remedies. It faced opposition, however, from trade unions like IG Metall that demanded a reduction in the statutory age of retirement to age 60 (*Rente mit 60*), which would have greatly accelerated the collapse of the social insurance system. Nevertheless, in June 1999 Labour Minister Walter Riester announced a major overhaul of the pension system to limit the contribution rate to a maximum of 22 per cent in 2030. At the core of his proposal was a mandatory private pension, which would have allowed the public pension to decline. This, in turn, would have held employer contributions constant, alleviating pressure on non-wage labour costs. The proposal was at loggerheads with social democratic plans to extend mandatory pension insurance to additional groups of employees and to other forms of income than wage.[29] Unions, the opposition and the public violently objected to an obligatory private 'third pillar', and with the SPD suffering recurrent defeats in Länder elections, the government was forced to make concessions. Rather than making supplementary pensions obligatory, it adopted a more expensive strategy of liberal tax subsidies for workers choosing to buy supplementary pension plans. Nonetheless, polls showed that no more than 18 per cent of the voters regarded the SPD as the most credible party on pension policy.[30]

Against all expectation, the pension reform, enacted in 2001, became one of the more lasting achievements of Schröder's first term. The so-called *Riester-Rente* encouraged workers to take out private or occupational supplementary pension plans, helped by a government subsidy of up to €10 billion a year. Employees can now put a maximum of one per cent of their pay into a private savings account, rising to four per cent in 2008. Subsidies for these *Entgeltumwandlung* accounts, however, are conditional on the existence of a collective agreement signed by unions and employers (the so-called *Tarifvorrang*). The reform signalled a cautious move from a public pay-as-you-go system towards a privately funded system. In addition, a new formula for calculating pension benefits was introduced to reduce the pension level for the so-called 'standard pensioner' to 67 per cent of net income by 2030. Due to the high cost of government subsidies for private and occupational pension plans the reform will not really save money. It does, however, help keep non-wage labour costs in check.[31]

Still, pension reform and the energy tax failed to reduce overall non-wage labour costs during Schröder's first term. The most that was accomplished was a brief respite.[32] Shortly after its surprising re-election in 2002, the government had to recognise that the pension system needed yet more money. Its response was to plug the holes in social insurance budgets with a confusing mix of tax increases, spending cuts, higher contributions and new borrowing. On pensions, the most important measures of the so-called 'Act to Stabilise Contribution Rates' were an increase in the contribution rate by 0.4 percentage points to 19.5 per cent, which the Greens opposed; an increase in the income ceiling for contributions to the statutory pension system; and a reduction of the fluctuation reserve (*Schwankungsreserve*) of the statutory pension insurance system from 80 to 50 per cent of monthly expenditure (*Monatsausgabe*). To keep the contribution rate at 19.5 per cent, further emergency measures were put into effect, including another pension freeze in 2004 (*Nullrunde*), a further lowering of the minimum required fluctuation reserve from 50 to 20 per cent, and full contributions by pensioners to long-term care insurance from 2004 onwards. In addition, the disbursement of pensions was shifted from the beginning of the month to the end. As result, net pensions were effectively cut by 0.85 per cent in 2004.[33]

Whilst failing to bring about a lasting reduction of non-wage labour costs, the haphazard emergency surgeries performed on the pensions system since 1999 entailed major risks for the federal budget. In May 2003, the federal subsidy to the pension insurance system amounted to no less than €54 billion, and the Ministry of Finance forecast that by 2050 it would rise to more than half the federal budget if nothing were done.[34] By 2004 it was obvious that the limits of piecemeal tinkering had been reached and that more fundamental changes were required, although the direction these would take was far from clear. Ironically, the government seems to have returned to its starting point. The 2004 law that adds a 'sustainability factor' to the pension formula to take into account the declining birth rate and the increasing life expectancy bore an uncanny resemblance to the Kohl government's 'demographic factor'. The measure had been suggested by a government-appointed expert commission in mid-2003. In addition, the commission proposed cutting pensions to 40 per cent of average gross earnings, from the present 48 per cent; a gradual increase in the statutory retirement age from 65 to 67 by 2035; and a capping of pension contributions at 22 per cent of gross monthly pay.[35]

THE LABOUR MARKET

Like the pension system, unemployment insurance played a crucial role in the traditional management of the German employment crisis.[36] The very expensive labour market programmes of what is now the Bundesagentur für Arbeit removed surplus labour from the market by providing unemployment benefit over long periods of time and extensive subsidies for short-term work, job creation and further training. In effect this created a huge secondary labour market at public expense. Next to the pension insurance system, the Bundesagentur für Arbeit (governed on a tripartite basis by the state and the social partners) became the focal institution for German social policy in the aftermath of unification. Labour market programmes expanded to unprecedented levels,[37] adding to non-wage labour costs and generating a spiral in which the very policy that was to fight unemployment became a potent contributor to it. In 2002 the Bundesagentur had a staff of 90,000 and a budget of €50 billion, around 40 per cent of which it spent on so-called 'active labour market policies'.[38]

Throughout its first term, the Red–Green government left labour market policy and the unemployment insurance system almost entirely untouched. The Chancellor delegated labour market reform to the tripartite talks of the Bündnis für Arbeit, which began in December 1998. Deadlocked almost from the beginning,[39] the Bündnis achieved nothing of significance apart from the so-called *Job Aqtiv-Gesetz* and two symbolic pilot projects to improve the labour market situation of low-skilled workers, the long-term unemployed and low-income families. *Job-Aqtiv* promised minor improvements in placement services for the unemployed. It also introduced what was sold to the public as the 'Danish job rotation model' and pretended to improve the control and evaluation of active labour market measures. At the same time, it extended publicly funded employment programmes. None of the measures produced any effect before they were overtaken by the so-called 'Hartz reforms' after the 2002 election.

In addition to the deadlocked Bündnis für Arbeit, another reason for inactivity on labour market policy in Schröder's first term was that Minister of Finance and party chairman Oskar Lafontaine insisted on following through election promises to the trade unions that made reform of the labour market practically impossible. For example, the government suspended a rule forcing firms to reimburse the unemployment insurance fund for benefits paid to workers sent into early retirement. Moreover, the government rescinded legislation obliging unemployed persons to show up at the job centre four times a year and to accept job offers that required them to commute for up to three hours a day. Further, employment protection was restored for workers in firms with between five and ten employees, and low-paid part-time jobs were made subject to social insurance contributions. In addition, and in accordance with what he regarded as a 'Keynesian' economic policy, Lafontaine encouraged high wage claims from unions outside the public sector, thereby undercutting Schröder's attempts to use the tripartite talks of the Bündnis for wage moderation.

With the Red–Green government abstaining from labour market policy reform, the unemployment insurance system was just as starved of cash as the pension and health insurance systems. Soon after the 1998 election victory, the government had to implement measures to stabilise the unemployment insurance contribution rate and to limit its own payments to the Bundesagentur.[40] From June 2000 to July 2002, unemployment benefits were frozen in real terms, no longer rising with average wages as in the past. In addition, in 1999 the government abolished *Originäre Arbeitslosenhilfe*, a special form of unemployment assistance paid by the federal budget – a measure that the SPD had opposed under the Kohl government. At the same time, to limit youth unemployment the government passed the Emergency Programme to Reduce Youth Unemployment (*JUMP*) subsidising 100,000 jobs and apprenticeships for workers up to 25 years of age, which again imposed a burden on the federal budget.

A first step towards a reform of the public employment service was provoked by the so-called placement scandal at the Bundesagentur für Arbeit. In February 2002, when the government faced certain defeat in the upcoming federal election, it discovered what had long been widely known among insiders, that the statistics of the public employment service on its rate of success in job placement were largely fictional. To show the public that he was taking action 'to clean up the mess', Schröder created the 'Hartz Commission', named after its chairman, Peter Hartz, the personnel director at Volkswagen. The commission represented a break with the tripartite philosophy of the Bündnis für Arbeit[41] in that its 21 members included no more than two trade union representatives and only one official of a small-firm business association, the Federation of Craft Associations (Zentralverband des Deutschen Handwerks). The commission proposed a list of 13 reform measures, ranging from a weakening of the tripartite structure of the Bundesagentur to a rather vague appeal to the 'elites of the nation' to assist in creating employment opportunities for the unemployed. The commission's most important recommendations were to integrate unemployment assistance (*Arbeitslosenhilfe*) and social assistance (*Sozialhilfe*)[42] and to turn the job centres into temporary-employment agencies (*Personalserviceagenturen*). Anyone still jobless after six months was to be placed by the agencies in a private firm to perform temporary work. Hartz claimed that the commission's proposals could halve Germany's unemployment within three years and slash the costs of unemployment benefit by two-thirds.

After the 2002 election, two 'Acts Promoting Modern Labour Market Services' (commonly referred to as 'Hartz I' and 'Hartz II') were passed, tightening the rules determining which jobs an unemployed worker was allowed to reject (*Zumutbarkeit*), and the conditions for claiming unemployment assistance. In addition, workers facing unemployment were required to report earlier to the local employment service. Moreover, the reform raised the earnings limit for low-paid work exempt from social insurance contributions (*Mini-Jobs*) and introduced a scale of rising contribution rates for monthly incomes between €400 and €800. Also, various measures were passed to promote the employment of older people and the transition of jobless workers to self-employment (the so-called *Ich AG*). Finally, the legislation provided for the creation of temporary employment agencies on the Hartz model.

In March 2003, shortly after the opposition had gained a solid majority in the Bundesrat by winning the Land election in Lower Saxony, Chancellor Schröder announced 'Agenda 2010' – a package of measures intended to make the German economy more 'flexible' and competitive. In addition to tax cuts and vague promises to make it easier for firms to opt out of sector-wide industrial agreements, the 'agenda' focused on pensions, health care and unemployment insurance. It included a reduction in Germany's generous unemployment and sickness benefits and proposed making it easier for small companies to hire and fire new workers. The measures that were ultimately introduced included a tax cut of €15 billion, a change in employment protection rules for companies with up to ten employees, and two more Acts to Promote Modern Labour Market Services (Hartz III and IV). To gain the agreement of the opposition, Schröder had to reduce the tax cuts which were intended above all to appease the public – something that CDU and CSU were not willing to let the government pay for by increased borrowing.

Agenda 2010 reinforced long-existing internal divisions between 'modernisers' and traditionalists among German trade unions. Germany's leading union, IG Metall, refuses as a matter of principle to take changes in non-wage labour costs into account when negotiating industry-wide wage increases. It was and still is bitterly opposed to Agenda 2010, running advertisements in national newspapers attacking the reforms as 'one-sided' and 'unfair'.[43] Its position is reflected in the DGB, whose chairman, Michael Sommer, labelled the reforms as 'dismantling the welfare state'.[44] On the other hand, the head of the chemical workers union IGBCE, Hubertus Schmoldt, urged unions to 'play an active role in a search for compromise',[45] proposing that the most controversial reforms should be tested in a pilot phase. Indeed IGBCE had already in 1999 concluded collective agreements that included private, supplementary pension plans and was eager to protect its approach. While the trade unions were debating, Germany reached the fourth-highest unemployment rate of all OECD countries, at 9.4 per cent, surpassed only by Poland, the Slovak Republic and Spain.[46]

Hartz III and IV relaxed employment protection for small firms and shortened the duration of unemployment benefit (*Arbeitslosengeld*) to 12 months (18 months for persons aged 55 or more), instead of 32 months in the past. The new rule, however, will not come into force until 2006.[47] The most far-reaching measure of the Hartz reforms was the amalgamation of unemployment assistance and social assistance into a single, flat-rate and means-tested benefit calculated according to principles of social assistance (*Arbeitslosengeld II*).[48] It also involved ending the dualism between labour exchanges on the one hand and social assistance offices on the other, for those receiving social assistance other than unemployment benefit. Both the amalgamation of unemployment assistance and social assistance and various measures for a further tightening of work availability requirements (*Zumutbarkeit*) were diluted in the legislative process. Nevertheless, on the day the Bundestag passed the bills, the Federal Minister of Economics and Labour, Wolfgang Clement, predicted that unemployment would drop by 20 per cent once the reforms were reality.[49]

The Hartz reforms were designed to lower the threshold of *Zumutbarkeit* for the unemployed, and in general to make labour market policy more 'activating' by increasing incentives to work. Reform of the Bundesagentur für Arbeit, however, foundered in the face of resistance from SPD backbenchers, trade unions and employer organisations that fear for the funding of their extensive further education empires. It remains to be seen how much the Hartz measures will in fact lower expenditure for unemployment benefit and labour market policy, and with it the unemployment insurance contribution rate.

The same holds for whether the Hartz reforms will result in lower unemployment. According to the Council of Economic Experts (*Sachverständigenrat*), 'any attempt to forecast the volume of unemployment in 2005 is subject to major uncertainty',[50] not only because of low economic growth but also because Hartz IV will change the way unemployment is measured. It is even possible that the number of those registered as unemployed may rise by 300,000, especially in early 2005, due to the fact that Hartz IV includes former social assistance recipients in the statistics of the Bundesagentur. In November 2004, the research institute of the Bundesagentur announced that in 2005 unemployment may reach the politically devastating mark of five million.[51] Uncertainty about the development of unemployment makes the expected reduction in 2005 of the federal grant to the Bundesagentur from €6.2 to €4 billion unlikely. This being the case, a reduction of the unemployment contribution rate seems to be out of reach.

Nevertheless, Agenda 2010 has scared the electorate and made it even more volatile. It caused devastating defeats for the SPD in the state elections in Bavaria in September 2003 and in Hamburg in March 2004. To add to this, in January 2004 the supervisory board of the supposedly reformed Bundesagentur – composed of union, employer and public sector representatives – stated that it had 'lost confidence' in the agency's new chairman, Florian Gerster, an SPD politician appointed by Schröder in the aftermath of the 2002 scandal. While officially Gerster was blamed for minor irregularities over contracts for consultants, in fact he was punished for having tried to weaken the influence of the social partners. During all of 2004, the Bundesagentur remained in turmoil over its reorganisation. Beginning in 2005, it must pay the government a per capita lump sum of nearly €10,000 for each and every former recipient of unemployment benefit now reassigned to the new, tax-financed *Arbeitslosengeld II*[52] – at a total annual cost of €6.7 billion.[53] Apparent flaws in the new software designed for the disbursement of *Arbeitslosengeld I* and *II* caused additional costs in good will as well as in cash. In spite of having added thousands of employees to its staff of over 90,000 to cope with the reform, job placement by the Bundesagentur has come to a virtual standstill.[54]

HEALTH CARE

In the 1990s, the costs of the German health care system spiralled out of control. Between 1991 and 2002 spending on health care increased by 36 per cent.[55] The increase was attributable not only to the extension of the health care system to the new Länder but also to disproportionate growth in expenditure on pharmaceuticals and the introduction of long-term care insurance.[56] The rise in spending resulted in growing contribution rates. Between 1991 and 2002 contribution rates in the old and new Länder increased from 12.2 and 12.8 per cent to 14 per cent.[57] During the 1990s it was health insurance that contributed most to the rise in the overall contribution rate to social insurance.[58] Currently health insurance contributions account on average for 14.3 per cent of gross wages, the second largest deduction after pensions.

A large part of the increase in health care expenditure is attributable to a lack of efficiency incentives and transparency and to over-capacities. The self-governing structure of the health care system allows doctors and pharmaceutical producers a great variety of strategies to circumvent government efforts to contain costs. Doctors enjoy considerable autonomy in writing bills for treatment and setting fees for their services. For example, pharmaceutical producers may respond to legal regulation forcing doctors to prescribe less expensive generic drugs by increasing the size of packages,[59] so as to defend their volume of sales.

Since health insurance funds may set contribution rates autonomously within the context of statutory provisions, the government has even fewer ways of bringing contribution rates in line with the goals of economic reform than is the case with pension and unemployment insurance. As it is the Länder which are primarily responsible for inpatient care, especially in hospitals, the capacities of the federal government are additionally limited by far-reaching legislative powers of the Bundesrat. Health care reform is further complicated by the fact that the Christian Democratic parliamentary party has always been deeply divided on the issue, particularly on health care finance. Whereas CDU leader Angela Merkel prefers funding health care by a flat rate to be paid by everybody (*Prämienmodell*), the labour wing of her party and the CSU favour the extension of the insurance-based system to additional groups of employees and forms of income.

That health care reform is especially difficult in Germany is due also to the self-governing character of the health care system and the effective organisation of the many interests involved in it, including big pharmaceutical companies, the doctors' lobby, the health insurance funds, and the hospitals. The KBV, the main doctors' association, is particularly effective in defending its clients. Its power derives from the fact that it functions as a statutory link between the doctors and the health insurance funds. Thus, the KBV collects the bills on behalf of the doctors and negotiates collective contracts with the funds. Because of the KBV system, the funds have practically no control over the treatment doctors provide. Health care funds are reduced to the role of 'passive financers' rather than 'active purchasers of health services from suppliers on behalf of the patients'.[60]

As in pension and unemployment insurance, shortly after its election in 1998 the Red–Green government suspended some of the health care reforms of the Kohl government.[61] The 1998 'Act to Strengthen Solidarity in Health Insurance' rescinded cuts in the statutory reimbursement for dentistry and dropped co-insurance payments for drugs and other treatment-related costs. It also cancelled the automatic rise in co-payments with increases in contribution rates. At the same time, to stabilise the federal budget the government changed the calculation of the contributions paid by the unemployment insurance fund to the health insurance funds on unemployment insurance benefits, which resulted in lower revenues for the health insurance system.[62] The overall effect of the measures was to increase expenditures whilst simultaneously reducing revenues, making further reforms inevitable.

Measures for cost containment subsequently devised by Health Minister Andrea Fischer, however, were mostly abortive. Proposals for a global ceiling on spending and the abolition of dual financing for hospitals were killed off by the opposition in the Bundesrat. All the government was able to obtain was a reform of hospital finance. Instead of a standard daily fee per patient, hospitals now receive a lump sum reflecting the type of treatment, regardless of the length of stay (*diagnose-orientierte Fallpauschalen*). Opposition in the Bundesrat was accompanied by a large-scale campaign involving all the major players in the health sector: doctors' associations, the pharmaceutical industry, and the health insurance funds,[63] not to mention the voters. Soon after, in early 2001, Fischer resigned, ostensibly over the BSE crisis.

The new minister, Ulla Schmidt (SPD), lifted the budget caps for prescribed drugs. Introduced in 1993, this measure had been under constant attack from doctors' associations. Schmidt replaced them with a system under which doctors' associations and health care funds set spending limits at the regional level. In effect, those responsible for the increase in expenditure were made responsible for controlling it. With no sanctions against non-compliance, however, the new arrangement for containing spending proved ineffective.[64] In 2002, self-regulation at the implementation level was further strengthened by the introduction of so-called Disease Management Programmes (DMPs) for chronic diseases. Under these programmes, an advisory board defines care standards that are then made obligatory by the federal government. With the exemption of some minor rule-changes, further reform measures were put on hold until after the election at the express instruction of the Chancellor.[65]

After the 2002 election had been won, the government could no longer avoid confronting the continuing crisis of health care finance. In the first of a series of emergency measures, the 'Act to Stabilise Contribution Rates' raised the upper income limit for the assessment of contributions to the statutory health insurance system to €5,100 per month and obliged health insurance funds to lower their contribution rates. Moreover, it imposed a zero per cent increase (*Nullrunde*) for the incomes of doctors and hospital workers. However, to relieve the federal budget by cutting the deficit in the unemployment insurance fund the same Act lowered the rate of health care contributions for persons drawing unemployment assistance, which reduced the revenue of health insurance funds. Although the Act made it illegal for funds to raise contribution rates, the Minister for Social Affairs of the Land of Bavaria encouraged the local health care funds to do exactly this.

The year 2003 became the year of health care reform. Scandals involving financial conspiracies between doctors, insurance funds and drug companies alerted the public to the vulnerability of the health insurance system to abuse and fraud. Among other things, doctors had used their professional autonomy to mislead health care funds about the costs of treatment, importing cheap products from abroad but charging full German prices. With the 'Act to Modernise the Statutory Health Insurance System' (*GKV-Modernisierungsgesetz*), the government sought to address inefficient practices in the health care system and prevent an expected increase in the contribution rate to up to 15 per cent in 2004.

The CDU/CSU having by then captured a solid majority in the Bundesrat, the final legislation could only be passed in agreement with the opposition. It introduced various measures to control expenditure (such as cancelling funeral benefit) and to strengthen competition among providers. Overall, however, it imposed most of the burden on patients rather than doctors or drug companies. Trade unions regarded the reform as a historical departure from the principle of parity financing by workers and employers, and from the principle of solidarity. In part this reflected the fact that from 2006 onwards sickness benefit (*Krankengeld*) is to be financed solely by the insured. Equally controversial was the fact that the reform raised health insurance contributions on company pensions, which partially counteracted the government's objective of promoting company pensions as a supplement to declining public pensions. Taken as a whole, the Act sought to reduce the expenditure of the statutory health care funds by €20 billion, for example through higher supplementary co-payments, flat-rate charges for visits to doctors' offices, and the total exclusion of dentures from the list of standard services.

While cutting the health insurance contribution rate to 13.6 per cent in 2004, the Act also started a move towards subsidising health care through transfers from the federal budget. The new transfers, financed mainly through a three-stage increase in the tobacco tax, are supposed to cover various non-actuarial benefits (*versicherungsfremde Leistungen*). However, as demonstrated in pension insurance, such transfers can become self-perpetuating. In addition, once introduced, tax-financed transfers may constrain future fiscal policy.[66] With no explicit link to the extent of *versicherungsfremde Leistungen*, federal subsidies are likely to seep away in an inefficient system with an endless appetite for fresh cash.

Since the beginning of the 1990s, health care reform in Germany has mainly amounted to successive increases in co-payments by patients and in government support, which have hitherto failed to generate lower contribution rates. Government proposals to expand the funding base, on the model of the *Bürgerversicherung*, are being blocked by the CDU, reflecting the traditionally close relations between the party and the pharmaceutical industry and the associations of doctors and pharmacists.[67] In November 2004, after long and painful internal discussions, CDU and CSU presented a reform concept that tries to combine premium, contribution and tax-based forms of funding. It proposes a monthly premium of €109 to be paid by every insured person, supplemented by an additional €60 paid by employers – whose share would be limited to 6.5 per cent of gross wages – and by tax-financed subsidies to individuals with low income.

While there is deadlock on the financing side, cost-cutting on the supply side continues to meet with effective resistance from providers and the drug industry. Short-term emergency measures have reached their limit, and the view is gaining ground that nothing short of major restructuring will help. How such restructuring can be made to happen politically, however, is a mystery. Instead of a decline in contribution rates, the reform of 2003 will at best provide for stability over two or three years, although even this seems uncertain, as major health insurance funds have stated publicly that they see no possibility of cuts in contribution rates in 2005.

CONCLUSION AND PROSPECTS

In 1995 at the latest, with non-wage labour costs approaching the magic threshold of 40 per cent, cutting the economic burden imposed by the Bismarckian welfare state on the employment relationship in a changing economy and society became a central concern of German domestic politics, for the last Kohl cabinet as well as for the two successive governments of the Red–Green coalition under Gerhard Schröder. However, after eight years of sometimes dramatic political conflict over welfare state reform, by 2003 non-wage labour costs, far from having come down, had risen further by two percentage points, with no end in sight (see Table 1).

If reforming the German welfare state continues to be as hopeless as it was for almost a decade, Germany's economic prospects are bound to deteriorate further. For some time, such deterioration may still proceed gradually and will therefore remain barely perceptible in the short-term view that dominates politics, public commentary and much of academic analysis. Weak employment will remain the core predicament of the German economy. While domestically traded services will stagnate, job losses in Germany's traditionally strong sector, high-quality manufacturing, will accelerate, not least due to the high German social insurance contributions. High spending on social welfare transfers will continue, to a large extent in compensation for low employment. Very likely, this will increasingly be accompanied by protest from those whose benefits must be cut in order to keep total expenditure constant or, more realistically, prevent it from rising by more than the small increments that can be presented to the public as conjunctural fluctuations.[68] And, given the tightening constraints on taxation of all sorts, the transfer-heavy welfare state, which at best mollifies the impact of low employment but cannot create employment itself, will continue to leave little if any space for public investment in the sort of infrastructure required to maintain the international competitiveness of a high-wage economy like Germany.

What prevents a fundamental restructuring – and nothing else would probably do – of a welfare state that is now widely recognised as strangling the labour market? At first glance it appears nothing short of astonishing that shifting the funding base of social insurance from contributions to general taxes should be politically difficult at all. Not only is there no reason in principle why such a shift should imply lower benefits, or why it should raise the total level of taxation including social insurance contributions. Also, a tax-based welfare state would be more redistributive and egalitarian than a contribution-based one, if only because contributions are usually paid only up to a specified income ceiling while income taxes, apart from a country like Slovakia, tend to be more or less progressive under democratic government.

A range of factors may be listed that have in the past decade stood in the way of meaningful welfare state reform in Germany, and will very likely continue to do so in the coming decade.

1. As has been shown, the pension and unemployment insurance funds are already heavily subsidised by the Federal Government, and subsidies have increased in recent years. Calls from the social policy community for tax support are not unknown to the Finance Minister, who from past experience tends to regard them as attempts to avoid cuts in benefits. Afraid of pouring fresh money into what invariably seemed to them a bottomless pit, all recent Finance Ministers have tried to make further subsidies conditional on structural reforms. The fact that they have rarely succeeded does not make them more amenable to proposals to shift the funding of the welfare state even further towards general taxes.
2. In any case, the first priority for the Federal Government is *balancing* its budget, not *expanding* it. The main criterion by which the performance of the Finance Minister

is judged year by year is whether his budget meets the targets of the Maastricht Stability Pact. These oblige him to reduce, not unemployment, but public borrowing. For some time now, German governments have in addition been under relentless pressure from business and the general public to lower corporate and individual taxes. Balancing the budget while cutting taxes leaves little space for refinancing social insurance.[69] This was experienced most dramatically by the CDU which, at its Leipzig party convention in late 2003, came out with great fanfare for both deep tax cuts and a complete de-coupling of public health insurance from wage and employment. The new system (a flat rate contribution called *Kopfpauschale*) implied that households with a low income were given tax subsidies. As was to be expected, the two projects turned out to be incompatible. Also unsurprisingly, the CDU later stuck to its tax cuts and abandoned the *Kopfpauschale*.

3. The trade unions, and in part also the employers, insist on separate parafiscal budgeting of social insurance, and on its being funded in principle by independent sources of revenue. Of course, unions in particular have no objections to social insurance being subsidised by the state, if this helps sustain or even expand benefits. An entirely tax-funded welfare state, however, is considered to be at the mercy of party politics and of government fiscal consolidation efforts, more than parafiscal institutions collecting contributions from workers and employers and operating under the 'self-government' of the 'social partners'. Employment concerns remain secondary as long as benefits for the non-employed can be defended, not least by pressuring the government to cover possible deficits in social insurance budgets. Employers, on their part, while certainly not averse to lower contributions, prefer lower taxes if they must choose, probably because a tax-based welfare state would be much more redistributive. Moreover, while German employers have become adroit at shifting employment to countries with lower labour costs, they may still have to pay income and corporate taxes in Germany. Finally, both union and employer associations cherish the many opportunities for patronage offered especially by the unemployment insurance system and the Bundesagentur für Arbeit that administers it.
4. The deadlock in German welfare state reform is not, however, exclusively caused by the undoubtedly impressive number of veto points and veto players in Germany's political system. The conservative welfare state and the *Äquivalenzprinzip* by which it is largely governed (the principle that benefits have to be basically proportionate to contributions, which in turn are proportionate to earned income) are popular with German voters, far into the middle class. The idea that status-securing social insurance entitlements are something like private property, rather than the outflow of a public right to social citizenship, is deeply rooted and is reinforced by German legal doctrine, which tends to impose narrow limits on political discretion with respect to earned entitlements. This corresponds to the fact that flat-rate benefits are widely considered incompatible with social justice.

In recent years, Germans have become wary of anything introduced to them as 'reform', which they probably rightly expect to end up in a reduction or levelling of their benefits. Resistance to change has assumed traits that an outside observer might easily be tempted to consider nothing short of irrational. In a representative survey conducted in 2004, 50 per cent of the German adult population agreed that the social insurance systems faced 'significant problems' and another 44 per cent believed that they were 'about to collapse'. Still, 50 per cent stated that they were unwilling to retire later; 80 per cent did not find it necessary to lower the level of pensions; 68 per cent believed there was no need for employees to pay higher social insurance contributions; 69 per cent rejected the idea that health insurance funds might have to cut benefits; and no less than 80 per cent disagreed with increasing the legal age of retirement gradually to 67 years.[70]

Thus by the end of 2004, welfare state reform is taking more 'time out'. Faced with public protest against Hartz IV, the government concluded already in the middle of its term that voters had had enough of change for the time being. Now the strategy is essentially a return to the 'policy of a calm hand' (*Politik der ruhigen Hand*) of the summer of 2001, in the hope of some sort of spin-off from global economic recovery carrying the coalition over the September 2006 election. An important political side benefit of government inactivity is that it might tempt the opposition to make even more unpopular reforms a centrepiece of its election platform, predictably accompanied by two years of publicly displayed internal disagreement over how far such reforms may have to go. New serious attempts to break the stranglehold of the German welfare state on the German labour market will not be made until 2007 at the earliest, and are unlikely to come into force before 2008. In the meantime the governing parties hope that the continuing structural disintegration of the German social market economy can be covered up by a little fresh paint on its façade, like forcing the health insurance funds by law to put off repaying their debt and instead keep contribution rates constant or even lower them by a symbolic fraction. Once again it would appear that, according to an old German political adage, *Wahltag* will be *Zahltag*.

NOTES

1. See Herbert Kitschelt and Wolfgang Streeck, 'From Stability to Stagnation: Germany at the Beginning of the Twenty-First Century', in Herbert Kitschelt and Wolfgang Streeck (eds.), *Germany: Beyond the Stable State* (London: Frank Cass, 2004), pp.1–34.
2. Ibid., Table 3, p.15.
3. See AmCham Germany and Boston Consulting Group, *AmCham Business Questionnaire 2003* (Berlin: AmCham Germany and Boston Consulting Group Deutschland, 2003), http://www.dialogzukunft.de/de/data/pdf/amcham_wirtschaftsstandort_deutschland.pdf (accessed 6 Dec. 2004); Sigurt Vitols, *Unternehmensführung und Arbeitsbeziehungen in deutschen Tochtergesellschaften großer ausländischer Unternehmen.* Studie des Forums Mitbestimmung im Auftrag der Bertelsmann Stiftung und der Hans-Böckler-Stiftung (Gütersloh: Bertelsmann Stiftung, 2001).
4. See Jörn Kleinert, Axel Schimmelpfennig, Klaus Schrader and Jürgen Stehn, *Globalisierung, Strukturwandel und Beschäftigung*, Kieler Studie 308 (Kiel: Mohr Siebeck, 2000), pp.71–7; for an overview of the effects of globalisation on the German economy and labour market, see Deutscher Bundestag, *Schlussbericht der Enquete-Kommission 'Globalisierung der Weltwirtschaft – Herausforderungen und Antworten'*, BT-Drks. 14/9200, http://www.dip.bundestag.de/btd/14/092/1409200.pdf (accessed 6 Dec. 2004).
5. Fritz W. Scharpf, 'Employment and the Welfare State: A Continental Dilemma', *MPIfG Working Paper 97/7* (Köln: MPI für Gesellschaftsforschung, 1997), pp.9–10; Fritz W. Scharpf and Vivien A. Schmidt, 'Conclusions', in Fritz W. Scharpf and Vivien A. Schmidt, *Welfare and Work in the Open Economy. Volume I. From Vulnerability to Competitiveness* (Oxford: Oxford University Press, 2000), pp.310–15.
6. Bernhard Ebbinghaus, 'Any Way Out of "Exit from Work"? Reversing the Entrenched Pathways of Early Retirement', in Fritz W. Scharpf and Vivien A. Schmidt (eds.), *Welfare and Work in the Open Economy. Volume II. Diverse Responses to Common Challenges* (Oxford: Oxford University Press,

2000), pp.511–53; Bernhard Ebbinghaus, *Reforming Early Retirement in Europe, Japan, and the USA* (Oxford: Oxford University Press, forthcoming in 2006).
7. Statistisches Bundesamt, *Durchschnittsalter der deutschen Studienanfänger und Absolventen nach Geschlecht 1980 bis 2000* (Wiesbaden, 2004), http://www.destatis.de/download/hoch/bild12_1.xls (accessed 6 Dec. 2004).
8. For a collection of comparative data on the German economy see Werner Eichhorst, Eric Thode and Frank Winter, *Benchmarking Deutschland 2004: Arbeitsmarkt und Beschäftigung*. Bericht der Bertelsmann Stiftung (Berlin etc.: Springer, 2004).
9. See Wolfgang Strengmann-Kuhn, *Armut trotz Erwerbstätigkeit. Analysen und sozialpolitische Konsequenzen* (Frankfurt am Main: Campus, 2003).
10. See Kitschelt and Streeck, 'From Stability to Stagnation', Table 1, p.11.
11. Ibid. For a comparative overview of the development of employment rates, social expenditures and non-wage labour costs, see Table 4, p.15.
12. Bernhard Ebbinghaus and Anke Hassel, 'Striking Deals: Concertation in the Reform of Continental European Welfare States', *Journal of European Public Policy* 7/1 (2000), p.46, Table 1.
13. Wolfgang Streeck, 'From State Weakness as Strength to State Weakness as Weakness: Welfare Corporatism and the Private Use of the Public Interest', *MPIfG Working Paper 03/2* (Köln: MPI für Gesellschaftsforschung, 2002), p.8; also in Simon Green and William E. Paterson (eds.), *Governance in Contemporary Germany. The Semisovereign State Revisited* (Cambridge: Cambridge University Press, 2005).
14. Philip Manow and Eric Seils, 'Adjusting Badly. The German Welfare State, Structural Change, and the Open Economy', in Fritz W. Scharpf and Vivien A. Schmidt (eds.), *Welfare and Work in the Open Economy. Volume II. Diverse Responses to Common Challenges* (Oxford: Oxford University Press, 2000), p.265.
15. Karl Hinrichs, 'Reforming the Public Sector Pension Scheme in Germany: The End of the Traditional Consensus'. Paper presented at the XIVth World Congress of Sociology, International Sociological Association, Research Committee 19, Session 3: 'Reforming Public Pensions Schemes (I)', Montreal, Canada, 26 July–1 August 1998, p.13; quoted in Steven Ney, 'Pension Reform in Germany', ICCR, The Interdisciplinary Centre for Comparative Research in the Social Sciences, 2001, http://www.iccr-international.org/publications/researchreports-spa.html (accessed 12 Dec. 2004), p.26.
16. Wolfgang Streeck and Anke Hassel, 'The Crumbling Pillars of Social Partnership', in Kitschelt and Streeck (eds.), *Germany: Beyond the Stable State*, pp.107–13.
17. Streeck, 'From State Weakness', p.13.
18. Anke Hassel, 'Negotiating Wage Restraint: Europe's Response to a New Economic Environment', Habilitationsschrift (Bochum: Sozialwissenschaftliche Fakultät der Ruhr-Universität Bochum, 2003), pp.216–18, http://imperia.iu-bremen.de/hss/ahassel/36168/index.shtml.
19. See Christine Trampusch, 'Institutional Resettlement: The Case of Early Retirement in Germany', in Wolfgang Streeck and Kathleen Thelen (eds.), *Beyond Continuity: Explorations in the Dynamics of Advanced Political Economies* (Oxford: Oxford University Press, 2005), pp.203–28.
20. Martin Kohli, Martin Rein, Anne-Marie Guillemard and Herman van Gunsteren (eds.), *Time for Retirement. Comparative Studies of Early Exit from the Labour Force* (Cambridge: Cambridge University Press, 1991), p.190.
21. Rainer George, *Beschäftigung älterer Arbeitnehmer aus betrieblicher Sicht: Frühverrentung als Personalanpassungsstrategie in internen Arbeitsmärkten* (München: Hampp, 2000); Isabela Mares, *The Politics of Social Risk: Business and Welfare State Development* (Cambridge: Cambridge University Press, 2003).
22. Christine Trampusch, 'Ein Bündnis für die nachhaltige Finanzierung der Sozialversicherungssysteme: Interessenvermittlung in der deutschen Arbeitsmarkt- und Rentenpolitik', *MPIfG Discussion Paper 03/1* (Köln: Max-Planck-Institut für Gesellschaftsforschung, 2003), Table 5.
23. Martin Schludi, 'The Reform of Bismarckian Pension Systems. A Comparison of Pension Politics in Austria, France, Germany, Italy and Sweden', (Amsterdam: Amsterdam University Press, 2005), pp.141–143.
24. Stephan Leibfried and Herbert Obinger, 'The State of the Welfare State: German Social Policy between Macroeconomic Retrenchment and Microeconomic Recalibration', in Streeck and Kitschelt (eds.), *Germany. Beyond the Stable State*, p.200.
25. Schludi, *The Reform*, pp.143–144.
26. Stephen J. Silvia, 'The Fall and Rise of Unemployment in Germany: Is the Red–Green Government Responsible?', *German Politics* 11/1(2002), p.15.
27. Bertelsmann (Bertelsmann Stiftung), *International Reform Monitor. Social Policy, Labour Market Policy and Industrial Relations. Today's Survey, April 2004, Government Proposal on a 'Pension Reform 2000'*, http://www.reformmonitor.org (accessed 18 April 2004), p.5.

28. Frank Bönker and Hellmut Wollmann, 'Stumbling towards Reform', in Peter Taylor-Gooby (ed.), *Welfare States under Pressure* (London: Sage, 2001), p.87.
29. Ibid., p.87.
30. FORSA, 'Meinungen der Bürger zur Rentendiskussion', 1999 (unpublished).
31. Leibfried and Obinger, 'The State of the Welfare State', p.213.
32. Streeck and Hassel, 'The Crumbling Pillars of Social Partnership', p.118.
33. German Council of Economic Experts, *Consolidate Public Finances – Reform the Tax System. Annual Report 2003/2004*, First Chapter (2003), p.31.
34. *German News*, 28 May 2003.
35. See Bundesministerium für Gesundheit und Soziale Sicherung, *Nachhaltigkeit in der Finanzierung der sozialen Sicherungssysteme* (Bundesministerium für Gesundheit und Soziale Sicherung: Berlin, 2003), http://www.arbeitnehmerkammer.de/sozialpolitik/doku/05_soziales/sgb_vi/berichte/2003_08_28_ruerup_lang.pdf (accessed 7 Dec. 2004).
36. Streeck, 'From State Weakness', pp.7–8.
37. Manow and Seils, 'Adjusting Badly', p.293.
38. Streeck, 'From State Weakness', p.8.
39. Wolfgang Streeck, 'No Longer the Century of Corporatism. Das Ende des "Bündnisses für Arbeit"', *MPIfG Working Paper 03/4, Mai 2003* (Köln: MPI für Gesellschaftsforschung, 2003).
40. By law, any deficit in the unemployment insurance fund must be automatically covered by the federal government.
41. Streeck and Hassel, 'The Crumbling Pillars', p.119.
42. In 2004, this was enacted by the so-called 'Hartz IV reform', which we will discuss later. Until the reform, German unemployment assistance consisted of 'unemployment benefit' (*Arbeitslosengeld*), financed by contributions from workers and employers, and the means-tested 'unemployment assistance' (*Arbeitslosenhilfe*), which was financed by the federal budget. Unemployed workers generally drew *Arbeitslosengeld* first and only moved to *Arbeitslosenhilfe* if they continued to be unemployed after their eligibility for *Arbeitslosengeld* had expired (the so-called long-term unemployed). *Arbeitslosengeld* was paid for a period of up to 32 months, whereas *Arbeitslosenhilfe* was offered for an unlimited period. Unemployed persons who were not eligible for *Arbeitslosengeld* or *Arbeitslosenhilfe* could apply for social assistance (*Sozialhilfe*). Whereas *Arbeitslosengeld* and *Arbeitslosenhilfe* were administered by the Bundesagentur für Arbeit, *Sozialhilfe* was administered by the municipalities (*Kommunen*) and mainly financed by them.
43. *Financial Times*, 23 May 2003, p.8.
44. Ibid.
45. Ibid.
46. Bertelsmann Stiftung, *International Reform Monitor. Social Policy, Labour Market Policy and Industrial Relations. Today's Survey, April 2004, Agenda 2010*, http://www.reformmonitor.org (accessed 18 April 2004), p.3.
47. This is because of a transition period of 25 months. The shorter period of entitlement will fully apply to all those claiming unemployment benefit from February 2006 onwards.
48. Unlike social assistance (*Sozialhilfe*), unemployment assistance (*Arbeitslosenhilfe*) was income-related. *Arbeitslosengeld II* is no longer tied to a recipient's former income, but will be set approximately at the (flat-rate) level of what used to be social assistance (€345 per month in West Germany and €311 per month in East Germany). *Arbeitslosengeld II* is financed out of the federal budget.
49. *German News*, 17 Oct. 2003.
50. German Council of Economic Advisers, *Annual Report 2004/05* 'External Success – Internal Challenges', Press Release, 17 Nov. 2004, http://www.sachverstaendigenrat-wirtschaft.de (accessed 22 Nov. 2004), p.2.
51. *Frankfurter Allgemeine Zeitung*, 16 Nov. 2004, p.12.
52. Ibid., 13 Nov. 2004, p.14.
53. Ibid., 11 Nov. 2004, p.15.
54. Ibid., 11 Nov. 2004, p.13.
55. *Financial Times*, 30 Jan. 2003, p.17.
56. OECD, *Economic Surveys Germany*, Vol.2002, Supplement No.4 – January 2003 (Paris, 2003), p.92.
57. Ibid., p. 92.
58. Ibid., p. 93.
59. *Deutsches Ärzteblatt* 101, 2 Feb. 2004, p.A-313.
60. OECD, *Economic Surveys*, p.96.
61. Leibfried and Obinger, 'The State of the Welfare State', p.212.
62. Unlike the other branches of the German social insurance system, the health insurance funds do not receive regular subsidies from the federal government. To cover a shortfall in their revenues, they are allowed within limits to incur debts.

63. Anja K. Hartmann, 'Patientennah, leistungsstark, finanzbewusst? Die Gesundheitspolitik der rot-grünen Bundesregierung', in Tobias Ostheim Christoph Egle and Reimut Zohlnhöfer (eds.), *Das rot–grüne Projekt: Eine Bilanz der Regierung Schröder 1998–2002* (Wiesbaden: Westdeutscher Verlag, 2003), p.273.
64. OECD, *Economic Surveys*, p.93.
65. Hartmann, 'Patientennah', p.276.
66. German Council of Economic Experts, *Consolidate Public Finances*, p.30.
67. Bertelsmann Stiftung, *International Reform Monitor. Social Policy, Labour Market Policy and Industrial Relations. Today's Survey, April 2004, Comprehensive Health Care Reform*, http://www.reformmonitor.org (accessed 18 April 2004), p.3.
68. Upward pressure on contribution rates comes also from economic activity moving underground, depriving the social insurance system of revenue, and from the current rapid displacement of conventional employment by so-called 'mini jobs'. Mini jobs are low-wage jobs with significantly reduced social insurance contributions, introduced in the course of the Hartz reforms to facilitate employment especially in the service sector. They are an example of how a supposed solution to a problem can in fact aggravate it.
69. Thus taking effect at the beginning of 2004, the top income tax rate was once more lowered while co-insurance payments for low-income patients were raised.
70. Bundesverband Deutscher Banken, *Inter/esse: Informationen, Daten, Hintergründe* 11/2004, http://www.bankenverband.de/pic/artikelpic/112004/IE112004.pdf (accessed 13 Dec. 2004), pp.2, 6. Another example of how bizarre the German debate has become is the story of the CDU *Kopfpauschale.* The proposal was immediately attacked by the government as unfair as it would make 'the *Generaldirektor* and his secretary' pay the same monthly insurance premium. The attack was much in line with public sentiment, which almost immediately rejected the *Kopfpauschale* as 'neo-liberal'. This was regardless of the fact that the tax subsidy for low income earners that was part of the proposal would have significantly *increased* the effective contribution of high income earners – indeed to an extent that appeared outright shocking to the traditional CDU clientele, which at the time was rallying behind demands for tax relief. The *Kopfpauschale* was finally killed by the CSU, which managed to adopt the government position, according to which the proposal was 'unfair' to the *Generaldirektor*'s secretary, while at the same time arguing that it was inconsistent with CDU and CSU remaining 'the parties of tax relief', including a significant lowering of the maximum rate of income tax.

Old Bottles – New Wine: The New Dynamics of Industrial Relations

GEORG MENZ

> There are occasionally measures that have to be taken and that do not cause any enthusiasm. Not with me, either, by the way. However, they are necessary. That is why we will implement them. (Gerhard Schröder, Speech to the Bundestag, 14 March 2003)

> We never felt that we were looking eye to eye with Siemens during the talks. It always seemed like Siemens was standing on the table, and we were cowering in the basement. But current market conditions don't allow us to voice our side of the story. (Michael Stahl, head of works council at Siemens Bocholt phone factory, cited *Pittsburgh Post-Gazette*, 11 Aug. 2004)

Notwithstanding predictions to the contrary, Germany has not as yet experienced a Thatcherite revolution. Despite pressures towards convergence the 'coordinated' Rhineland 'varieties of capitalism'[1] remain distinct from their more liberal Anglo-American cousins. The literature contains three distinct analytical approaches to evaluating developments in the German political economy. First, it is argued that divergent 'varieties of capitalism' persist, and that business actors remain committed to patterns of high-wage, high-quality production, embedded in institutionalised coordination mechanisms.[2] A second argument is the 'Cologne decline thesis', which maintains that in the face of European Union (EU) liberalisation, the burden of unification, mass unemployment, and the competitive pressures on quality production, the German model may already be in the process of disintegration.[3] Finally, a third approach acknowledges the common external pressures on national economies, but emphasises the persistence of different adjustment strategies, suggesting 'hybridisation' or 'convergence within diversity'.[4]

The institutionalist perspective that dominates the debate, however, may obscure the view of significant changes in *behaviour* and policy *outcomes*. This article adopts a functionalist approach to persistence and change in German political economy. Instead of taking *institutional* persistence or change as the yardstick of convergence, it explores the negotiations that occur within those institutions and the outcome they produce. Despite the relative stability of the established Rhineland model, its institutions may well serve differently defined goals and produce very different – and more liberal – policy outcomes. Thus, rather than abandoning the established system of industrial relations, German employers have used their power to push for decentralisation and flexibility within established (and some new) institutions. A second distinctive feature of the study is its focus on the role of domestic actors, rather than amorphous forces of Europeanisation and globalisation, as the drivers of change.

COMPARATIVE POLITICAL ECONOMY AND THE RHINELAND MODEL: 'VARIETIES OF CAPITALISM' OR VARIETIES OF NEO-LIBERALISM?

Drawing on earlier work on divergent systems of capitalism, the 1990s witnessed a vivid debate over the future of European capitalism. Would the twin pressures of globalisation and accelerating European economic integration cause the demise of Rhineland-style organised capitalism? Is the Anglo-American model the only game in town? Is convergence occurring? Was neo-corporatism disintegrating?[5] Early work was pessimistic. The 'declinist' literature identified a number of challenges: increasing global competition in the high-quality product markets that German producers used to dominate, unrestrained and more ruthless capital either fleeing high-wage high-regulation production sites or using the threat to do so as a bargaining chip, market liberalisation and privatisation, induced and justified by pointing to the EU, an inability to attract significant foreign direct investment, and not least the awesome costs associated with transferring the West German welfare state eastwards.

This pessimistic analysis of Rhineland-style capitalism seemed to be borne out by lacklustre German economic performance which contrasted sharply with that of the liberal Anglo-American model with its deregulated labour markets, minimal welfare states and weakened unions. Despite its superior performance in sustaining low inflation and employment in the 1970s, the prospects for Rhineland capitalism in the 2000s appeared grim. Economic liberals claimed that a lack of reforms (*Reformstau*) was impeding growth, causing persistent unemployment, and blocking a deregulation of labour market and social policy.[6] In 1997, President Herzog famously demanded a fundamental shift (*Ruck*). The head of the major business organisation BDI Hundt encapsulated this sentiment when he quipped: 'Societal consensus has cost us millions of jobs'.[7]

At least one branch of scholarship, however, has resisted this neo-liberal logic. The varieties of capitalism literature[8] points to the benefits to companies of 'non-market coordination': cooperative industrial relations, collective provision of vocational training and long-term oriented financial systems.[9] Far from seeking low wages and low regulation environments, companies find it advantageous to remain embedded in the high-wage, high-regulation and high-trust environment of Rhineland-style industrial relations.[10] Different systems of political-economic governance, it is argued, develop different strategies to cope with the challenges of increased international competition. Recent empirical evidence, however, pointing to the abandonment of German industrial relations institutions,[11] casts serious doubts on one of the central pillars of the coordinated market economy.

Rather than taking sides in this debate, I argue that the institutional resilience of the German model has obscured a far-reaching liberalisation in industrial relations and labour market policy. The process is a complex one with conflicting forces operating at different levels. *Employer associations* seek to implement favourable wage levels and working conditions within the existing system, advocating decentralisation, but not the individualisation of industrial relations. *Employers* themselves are divided along the lines of sector, region and size. In the export-oriented metal-processing sector, employers seek flexibility in wages and working hours within the existing framework of institutions. In the east, employers have virtually abandoned their associations. Smaller companies are concerned about excessive wage levels, while larger companies use their bargaining power to persuade trade unions to accept micro-level agreements. For their part, the *trade unions* are divided between those like the chemical and energy workers' union, IGCBE, that embrace liberal reforms and others like the construction workers' union that are implacably opposed to reform. The pivotal metal workers' union IG Metall is divided internally by this fault line. Weaker eastern unions often find themselves tacitly accepting wildcat substandard agreements with local employers.

Amongst the major *political parties*, the post-war consensus on a social market economy has given way to a neo-liberal agenda justified rhetorically by invoking globalisation and competitiveness. The *government*, after years of reticence, is re-emerging as an important actor in industrial relations and labour market policy. Initially it sought union acquiescence to its reform measures by reviving neo-corporatism in the form of the Alliance for Jobs. With the failure of this strategy, it has now turned to a 'workfarist' social policy that impinges on the autonomy of labour market interest associations (*Tarifautonomie*) and arguably undermines union bargaining power.

The emphasis of the 'varieties of capitalism' literature on the persistence of traditional Rhineland institutions is therefore misleading. Institutional persistence should not be equated with policy continuity. The debate over the future of neo-corporatism, whilst initially helpful, obscures changes in the underlying distribution of power and the interests that these institutions serve. With the exception of some, but not all, trade union leaders, the key actors in industrial relations and labour market policy are now oriented towards neo-liberalism. Of course, German neo-corporatism has *always* helped secure labour acquiescence and wage moderation. However, what sets the neo-corporatism of the 2000s apart from its predecessors is that it no longer places a priority on 'negotiating a secure status for workers and unions, insulating these from economic fluctuations'.[12]

CHANGING DYNAMICS IN GERMAN INDUSTRIAL RELATIONS

The traditional model of German industrial relations relied on four key strands that made it somewhat similar to neo-corporatist Austria and Sweden, yet contains enough particularities to render it unique: first, the absence of state intervention into wage-setting (*Tarifautonomie*); second, sectoral-level wage bargaining, with regional associations often taking the lead in 'pattern agreements'; third, high-membership employer associations concluding wage agreements that were legally binding for members and that constituted a benchmark for non-members; finally, ideologically cohesive trade unions that were encouraged to contribute both to micro-management through co-determination and to macro-steering of the economy.

Labour market policy was shaped partly by a reaction against state interventionism in the Third Reich. It also emerged out of the neo-corporatist nexus between trade unions and SPD on the one hand, and employers and CDU on the other (the latter also had a more tenuous link with the unions). The role of the 'social partners', however, never extended to that of a 'shadow government' as in Austria. Thus, prior to the early 1980s, criticism of labour market policy came more from the left than the right, highlighting the inadequacies of a 'male breadwinner' model that discouraged female participation in the labour market and linked welfare benefits to employment status.

The political impetus for labour market reform derived from an emerging neo-liberal consensus that extended across the spectrum of party elites. This shift was accelerated by the so-called *Standortdebatte*, instigated by the confederation of German industry (BDI). Its rhetoric was designed to de-legitimise the post-war consensus, questioning labour market regulation, the scope of the welfare state, and tax levels in light of the purported need to render the country an attractive site for investment and production.[13] This debate was mainly conducted and supported by the neo-liberal newspapers (*Die Welt, Die Zeit, FAZ*) and the business press (*Handelsblatt, Wirtschaftswoche, Capital*), and was supported by economic liberals in academia. The key assertion was that inflated wage levels and employer contributions to social insurance imposed an intolerable burden on business and discouraged inward investment. A second important strand of this debate was the search for models from which Germany could learn lessons of labour market and welfare state reform. Attention focused on neo-liberal 'models' like New Zealand and the US, the 'Dutch miracle' and more recently Denmark, despite the fact that none of these countries was truly comparable to Germany in terms of size or economic structure. The BDI along with the employer association BDA has lost its faith in the Rhineland model.

The second factor in the emergence of the neo-liberal consensus was a shift to the right in the SPD. The re-branding of the party was signalled by Gerhard Schröder's *Neue Mitte* (New Centre) programme and his joint policy paper with Tony Blair in June 1999.[14] The purge of the party's neo-Keynesian left-wing figurehead, Oskar Lafontaine, from office as Finance Minister in March 1999 consolidated the internalisation of the *Standortdebatte* agenda. Crucially, the Schröder/Blair paper announced that 'recipients of transfer payments ... are to be examined regarding the extent to which they can earn their own income' and that 'the labour market needs a sector with low wages to afford low qualified with jobs'.[15]

The Greens' shift to the right was even more surprising. Having purged itself of its left-wing 'fundi' fraction in the internal battles of the late 1980s, the party's economic policy in the 1990s was dominated by staunch neo-liberals like Oswald Metzger. An anti-statist tradition easily translated into neo-liberal advocacy of a lean state, a stance supported by an affluent clientele of 'alternative' entrepreneurs. Green initiatives to introduce a low-wage sector and to merge unemployment insurance with welfare benefits at 'basic subsidence' levels[16] resemble those of the liberal Free Democrats.

EMPLOYERS DRIVING CHANGE

While the *Standortdebatte* was articulated by export-oriented larger businesses, the employer camp was divided internally along regional, organisational and sectoral fault lines between 'exit' (abandoning employers' association), 'voice' (calling for a decentralisation of bargaining) and 'loyalty'. Within the last category, differences emerged between those employers largely content with the status quo and those seeking to use existing or newly created institutions such as the Alliance for Jobs to help administer a radical overhaul of social and labour market policy.

The role of employers as policy entrepreneurs continued with the formation of the so-called New Social Market Initiative in 2000. With a budget of €100 million over ten years, and supported by the metal sector employer association, this platform advocates the decentralisation of wage bargaining, labour market deregulation, and 'workfare'-type social policy. It is a bipartisan advocacy group, seeking to manipulate public opinion through articles and opinion pieces in the media, thereby undermining key components of Germany's founding myth of a social market economy. Bombarding the press with articles stressing the need to learn from abroad in restructuring the German political economy, the initiative has been very effective in securing public acquiescence to the Agenda 2010 programme in the face of trade union protests.[17]

THE EAST–WEST DIVIDE AND *VERBANDSFLUCHT*

German unification proved pivotal for social and labour market policy. Between 1991 and 1998 alone, a total of DM 1.37 billion was transferred to the east for social security, state aids, investment, and infrastructure programmes. The combination of a politically motivated conversion rate between the two currencies, the collapse of its eastern markets, and shock therapy-style privatisation led to the effective de-industrialisation of the east. Between 1989 and 1998, the registered number of employees in the east decreased from 9.858 million to 7.757 million, while unemployment increased accordingly. The subsequent drain on the welfare systems was enormous, social security payments in the east increasing from DM 56 million to DM 84 million between 1991 and 1998.[18]

Unemployment contributed to the disintegration of the established system of industrial relations in the east, strengthening the bargaining position of business in relation to the unions, thereby facilitating company exit from the employer associations. According to surveys conducted by economic research institute DIW, 79 per cent of East German employers were no longer members of an employer association in 1998, up from 64 per cent in 1994. Companies founded after 1989 are even less likely to be members. Since membership implies obligation to pay standard wages, exiting the association (*Verbandsflucht*) is a way to avoid doing so. More disconcertingly, even among members only 67 per cent actually adhere to these standard wages, down from 83 per cent in 1994.[19] The East German metal sector employers' associations responded by offering members the terms of the wage clauses signed off by conciliatory Christian union CGM. But much more significant is the trend for businesses either to enter alternative employer associations that do not impose legal obligation to standard wages or, most recently, to adopt a special status *within* the existing employer associations that does not imply such requirement either (*ohne Tarifbindung*). The low wage environment in the east is characterised by wildcat agreements in violation of standard wage agreements between workers anxious to avoid unemployment and management keen to exploit its bargaining power.

Moreover, *Verbandsflucht* is not an exclusively eastern phenomenon. Membership in the German metalworking industry employer association Gesamtmetall has dropped from 57.9 per cent of all companies in 1980 to 31.8 per cent in 1998. In the east, coverage can be as low as 8 per cent.[20] IBM is one prominent example of a company simply quitting the association. But even medium-sized companies are abandoning Gesamtmetall, choosing instead to enter an alternative interest association for metal sector employers (Arbeitgeberverband der Metall- und Elektroindustrie), which acts as a lobby group and legal and information service provider without requiring its members to respect sectoral wage agreements.

THE DECLINING COVERAGE OF SECTORAL AGREEMENTS

An alternative means of exit from collective wage bargaining is corporate restructuring to create subdivisions that are no longer easily classifiable within existing sectoral subdivisions and thus not covered by any collective agreement. This trend is particularly prevalent in the German metalworking industry, where in the 1990s newly founded companies – often the product of corporate restructuring – simply did not join employer associations. Thus, while the total number of companies in the Western German metal sector *increased* from 15,333 to 18,348 between 1985 and 1992, the total number of employees in the metal sector covered by clauses negotiated by Gesamtmetall *declined* from 73.8 to 70.3 per cent and by 1998 had dropped to an average of 62.2 per cent in united Germany, but only 32.2 per cent for the east.[21]

Simply not joining an employer association is thus an attractive option. Still better for business, newly emerging sectors often do not have an association at all. Sectoral subdivisions in German industrial relations are not very dynamic and newly emerging professional fields are difficult to categorise. German employers are particularly keen to avoid being classified within the metalworking sector given the powerful sectoral union there. Tellingly, in new economic sectors such as 'general services' and 'business-related services' 52.7 (76.3) and 82.9 (82.7) per cent of all companies in the west (east) were not covered by sectoral agreements in 2000. By contrast, coverage is considerably higher in traditional sectors, such as banking/insurance, mining/energy and investment goods industry.[22]

Once again, the situation is even more dramatic in the east. Employer organisations attract even fewer of their potential constituents. According to a recent study, the percentage of employees covered by a sectoral agreement based on organisational membership of their employer stood at 70.1 per cent in the west, but only 55.4 per cent in the east in 2000. A combination of variables of political culture (distrust) and hard-nosed economics (a dismal economic situation, high unemployment giving employers leverage) are responsible for low coverage in new sectors, but also in traditional sectors such as construction, basic material processing and trade, where 60.9, 72.4 and 77.6 per cent respectively of all companies are not covered.[23] The east is also experiencing a greater growth of company-level agreements – often 'wildcat' agreements without approval from above. Illegal undercutting of standard wage levels is common, though statistics on this trend are difficult to assemble. According to a 1996 survey among medium-sized manufacturing companies in the west, only 78 per cent of organised employers actually paid standard wages, though legally obliged to do so.[24] This 'wild east' climate explains why German car manufacturers are so ready to invest there. Eastern Germany offers a familiar language, legal system, political stability and current EU membership in combination with a climate of low unionisation, high unemployment and a workforce thus willing to accept longer hours, lower pay and extra shifts.

DECENTRALISATION IN INDUSTRIAL RELATIONS AND THE NEW ROLE OF WORKS COUNCILS

A decentralisation of industrial relations is already underway. The number of companies with such company-level agreements rose from 2,550 in 1990 to 6,415 in December 2000, according to the Ministry of Labour. This trend is particularly prevalent within the mining/energy and transport/media sector where 16.3 (13.3) and 17.2 (32.5) per cent of all employees in the west (east) are covered by company agreements, with the figure continuing to increase. Research shows further instances in which micro-corporatism, combined with constant threats to relocate production, have extracted significant concessions from unions. Some 56 per cent of larger German enterprises have already signed plant-level agreements that permit undercutting standard wage levels.[25]

Encouraged by the shifting balance of power, employers are keen to modify the structure of industrial relations. The employers' association BDA seeks to undermine sectoral bargaining and universal wage agreements (*Flächentarifverträge*), advocating a downward shift to company bargaining. At the same time, it has said it will no longer follow the lead role of the metal industry in the south-western state of Baden-Württemberg, which traditionally sets the tone for subsequent wage bargaining rounds throughout the economy. Gesamtmetall continues to lobby for proposals first issued in 1996–97, for a two-tier wage agreement, the first tier setting a basic standard wage rate, general working time, and holidays, with substantial room for manoeuvre in a second tier of negotiations at company level. Alternatively, whole parts of the framework agreement could be substituted by agreements at the company level. This apparent imitation of the Swedish employers' strategy is appealing because trade unions never have had as strong a grip on work councils in Germany as in Austria where union coverage among work councillors approaches 100 per cent. In this bargaining arena, German unions are thus somewhat feeble and have in fact lost further ground. Between 1981 and 1994 the percentage of shop stewards being DGB members decreased from 77.5 to 75.2 per cent in the private sector, according to the DGB itself.[26] Not only are unions weaker within works councils, but in smaller companies there may not even be one at all. Thus in 1995, 54.8 (29.1) of all employees in companies with (9) 4 or fewer employees were not covered by any agreement.[27] Even where union members are among the works councils, they may feel more loyal to the company than the union, especially if management offers at least medium-term job security in return for concessions on issues like overtime pay and working hours. Micro-corporatism thus emerges on terms favourable to the employers.

Decentralisation works in the favour of employers because at this level the 'exit' threat possesses great credibility. When Siemens frankly threatened to relocate some of its production to Hungary during the summer of 2004, IG Metall felt unable to avoid conceding to wage and benefit cuts, as well as a re-introduction of the 40-hour working week. DaimlerChrysler followed suit shortly thereafter and extracted similar concessions, also including the abandonment of the 35-hour week.[28] Volkswagen, while always exempt from sectoral wage agreements, introduced a two-tier wage model as early as 2001. In 2001, the company concluded a deal with IG Metall launching the '5,000 * 5,000 model'. It entails hiring 5,000 new employees to build VW's minivan at a monthly salary of DM 5,000 (€2,550). Chancellor Schröder heralded this as an innovative example of modern wage policy. In fact, while still within the wage limits for the car industry, the agreement significantly undercuts standard VW wages. It also permits the introduction of flexible work hours with no overtime pay, including work on Saturdays. Originally, the company wished to link pay to performance rather than working time. Conceding to union pressure, VW accepted not falling below the standard wage for the car industry. This compromise still permits a 20 per cent cut in wages. After management had publicly contemplated moving production abroad, it announced that 'Germany can compete with low wage countries' given the terms of this agreement.[29]

DIVISIONS WITHIN THE UNIONS

While internal fault lines have undoubtedly emerged within the employer camp, this observation is even more accurate for the unions. While the unions were united in rejecting concessions sought from them in the original Alliance for Jobs, since then internal divisions over whether to reject labour market reform altogether or demonstrate willingness in administering such reform have pitched 'modernisers' notably within the mining, chemical and energy union IG BCE and some sections of IG Metall, against 'traditionalists' within the construction union IG BAU as well as fractions of IG Metall, rallying around Jürgen Peters. The former head of IG Metall Zwickel made headlines in 2000 by suggesting that maybe the time had come to endorse more flexible and differentiated wage agreements. The conflict within IG Metall that eventually led to Zwickel stepping down from his post erupted into the open in the course of the union's unsuccessful campaign for a reduction of the working week in Eastern Germany. This so-called 'time is ripe' campaign not only encountered an unprecedented level of resistance on the part of the employers.[30] It also exposed rifts within IG Metall, with western union officials openly questioning the rationale behind this campaign.

GOVERNMENT AS A NEWLY ASSERTIVE ACTOR: FROM THE ALLIANCE FOR JOBS TO HARTZ

In line with Schröder's campaign pledge to reduce unemployment, the Red–Green government wasted no time in reviving the Alliance for Jobs and Education in autumn 1998. Thematic working committees were set up. A group of *Neue Mitte* social scientists, partially funded by media conglomerate Bertelsmann, was commissioned to draw up reform proposals. It advocates New Democrat-style active labour market policy[31] such as the proposed establishment of a low-wage sector in which the state would cover employers' social contributions. In contrast to other European countries, however, the unions refused to make significant concessions in the framework of the alliance.

This did not discourage the government from proactively asserting itself in labour market policy. In August 2002, a 15-member commission led by VW personnel manager Peter Hartz proposed a variety of measures aimed at labour market deregulation, inspired by US-style workfarism. It promised to reduce unemployment by 50 per cent over three years by reforming the management of unemployment and, more crucially, significantly increase the pressure on individuals to secure employment, despite the dismal current situation of the German labour market. In rhetorically setting the stage for further cuts in social expenditure and higher demands on job seekers, Schröder announced that there is 'no such thing as a right to sloth', adding that '[we] expect this assistance to be responded to with personal efforts'. This aggressive rhetoric of *fördern und fordern* ('support and demand') found its first expression in the 'Job Aktiv' Law of 2001.[32] In the autumn of 2002, Schröder merged the 'red' Ministry of Labour with the staunchly economically liberal Ministry of Economic Affairs, replacing ex-union official Walter Riester with Wolfgang Clemens, a self-proclaimed admirer of Thatcher's reforms.

In 2003, Schröder also launched Agenda 2010, a wide-ranging legislative proposal that seeks to deregulate the labour market, decrease welfare spending, and partially privatise health insurance. This package is based on the Hartz proposals, but also contains significant cuts in personal tax for both the highest income earners and more modest reductions at the bottom end. Approved in the Bundestag with the support of the SPD and the Greens, as well as the opposition CDU, the law was briefly blocked by the opposition in the Bundesrat, successfully demanding that certain limits on 'acceptability' (*Zumutbarkeit*) of jobs for the unemployed be abolished. Agenda 2010 is a clear indication of the extent to which business and employers' associations have been successful in colouring the political agenda with their *Standortdebatte*. Indeed, the BDI enthusiastically welcomed this package, while the unions were unable to formulate a coherent policy position.[33]

The four Hartz measures implemented so far are a dramatic illustration of choosing US-style workfare policies over traditional social democratic solutions and preferring punitive supply-side policy to constructive demand-side stimulus. Their actual performance record is mixed. The first part of Hartz, implemented in January 2003, permitted private labour agencies temporarily to hire unemployed individuals and despatch them to third parties. Only one-third of the 44,732 individuals involved have found permanent employment as a result. The second part, effective as of April 2003, created a tax-exempt status for low-income earners and promoted entrepreneurialism. Critics highlight the conversion of standard jobs into multiple 'mini jobs' and question just how sustainable the 142,000 newly created one-man companies will turn out to be. The third section of Hartz has renamed and sought to restructure the unemployment offices, starting in January 2004. The fourth component has caused the most controversy and opposition. It abolishes the second tier of German unemployment assistance and limits eligibility for the more generous upper tier of unemployment benefits to 12 months. Critics point out that the new level of the lower tier in many cases lies below the official poverty line.[34] Mass demonstrations, especially in the east, have highlighted the danger in imposing workfarism on regions in which the labour market cannot accommodate most job seekers. Individuals refusing 'reasonable job offers', 'employability' training measures, and making no constant efforts to actively seek employment face punitive measures in the form of benefit cuts by up to 100 per cent in the case of youngsters under 25. Most menacing from the perspective of unions is the imposed duty for recipients to accept jobs that are remunerated at up to 30 per cent below standard wages. Regional and communal governments are exempted from this requirement and may remunerate their employees at even lower rates.

CONCLUSION

This article shows that *both* the early predictions of convergence on an Anglo-American model *and* more recent studies emphasising continued divergence of distinct 'organised variety of capitalism' need to be amended. While the institutions of economic governance in Germany continue to diverge from the liberal Anglo-Saxon model, the *policy output* produced by these institutions varies dramatically from earlier decades. While traditional Rhineland institutions may survive, they serve fundamentally different goals. While no neo-liberal 'revolution' has occurred as in Britain and New Zealand, actual policy output has assumed a distinctly neo-liberal direction.

Analysis of recent trends in German labour market policy shows that even where traditional aspects of the German model persist, they serve new goals. Thus, decentralisation and individualisation of wage bargaining has led to the micro-level of industrial relations assuming new importance, a trend almost universally to the detriment of unions, as they are unable to counter a particularly potent and credible exit threat. Micro-level 'pacts for employment' are bargaining arenas in which the unions pack almost no punch, command little control, and are faced with individuals desperate to secure their own employment above all. The government has taken a proactive stance in implementing 'activating' and punitive welfare state reform that has pivotal repercussions for the future structure of the labour market and the power of trade unions. Influenced by business-led lobbying, a bipartisan consensus on the purported need for 'reform' has emerged. The union's cooperation may be requested, but, if it refuses and resists, policy measures may be implemented against its will.

NOTES

1. Michel Albert, *Capitalisme contre capitalisme* (Paris: Le Seuil, 1991); Wolfgang Streeck, 'Le Capitalisme Allemande: Existe-t-il? Peut-il Survivre?', in Colin Crouch and Wolfgang Streeck (eds.), *Les capitalismes en Europe* (Paris: La Découverte, 1996), pp.33–55; David Coates, *Models of Capitalism: Growth and Stagnation in the Modern Era* (Cambridge: Polity Press, 2000); Vivien A. Schmidt, *The Futures of European Capitalism* (Oxford/New York: Oxford University Press, 2002); Kozo Yamamura and Wolfgang Streeck (eds.), *The End of Diversity? Prospects for German and Japanese Capitalism* (Ithaca: Cornell University Press, 2003).
2. Peter A. Hall and David Soskice (eds.), *Varieties of Capitalism: The Institutional Foundations of Comparative Advantage* (Oxford: Oxford University Press, 2001); Kathleen Thelen, 'Varieties of

Labor Politics in the Developed Democracies', in Hall and Soskice (eds.), *Varieties of Capitalism*, pp.72–103.

3. Streeck, *Les capitalismes en Europe*; Anke Hassel and Wolfgang Streeck, 'The Crumbling Pillars of Social Partnership', in Herbert Kitschelt and Wolfgang Streeck (eds.), *Germany: Beyond the Stable State* (London: Frank Cass, 2004, Special Issue of *West European Politics* 26/4), pp.101–24; Jürgen Bayer and Martin Höpner, 'The Disintegration of Organised Capitalism: German Corporate Governance in the 1990s', in Kitschelt and Streeck (eds.), *Germany: Beyond the Stable State*, pp.180–97.
4. Yamamura and Streeck, *The End of Diversity*; Susanne Lütz, 'Convergence within National Diversity: A Comparative Perspective on the Regulatory State in Finance (Cologne, MPIfG Discussion Paper 07/03, 2003).
5. Karl Polanyi, *The Great Transformation* (Boston: Beacon Press, 1957); Andrew Shonfield, *Modern Capitalism* (New York: Oxford University Press, 1969); Peter Katzenstein, *Small States in World Markets: Industrial Policy in Europe* (Ithaca, NY: Cornell University Press 1985); Fritz W. Scharpf, *Crisis and Choice in European Social Democracy* (Ithaca, NY: Cornell University Press, 1991); Suzanne Berger and Ronald Dore (eds.), *National Diversity and Global Capitalism* (Ithaca, NY: Cornell University Press, 1996); Herbert Kitschelt, Peter Lange, Gary Marks and John D. Stephens, 'Convergence and Divergence in Advanced Capitalist Democracies', in Herbert Kitschelt, Peter Lange, Gary Marks and John D. Stephens (eds.), *Continuity and Change in Contemporary Capitalism* (Cambridge: Cambridge University Pres, 1999), pp.427–60; David Soskice, 'Divergent Production Regimes: Coordinated and Uncoordinated Market Economies in the 1980s and 1990s', in Kitschelt *et al.* (eds.), *Continuity and Change in Contemporary Capitalism*, pp.101–35.
6. Rudi Dornbusch, 'The End of the German Miracle', *Journal of Economic Literature* 31/3 (1993), pp.881–5; *Berliner Zeitung*, 15 April 1997; 15 July 1996; Horst Siebert, 'Labor Market Rigidities: At the Root of Unemployment in Europe', *Journal of Economic Perspectives* 11 (Summer 1997), pp.37–54; BDI, 'Internationale Wettbewerbsfähigkeit – Benchmarking' [International Competitiveness – Benchmarking] (2002). Available at http://www.bdi-online.de (accessed 5 June 2003); Bertelsmann Stiftung, *Internationales Beschäftigungs-Ranking* (Gütersloh, 2002).
7. *Berliner Zeitung*, 20 Sept. 1997; *Berliner Zeitung*, 26 Nov. 1996.
8. Berger and Dore, *National Diversity*; Kitschelt *et al.*, 'Convergence and Divergence'; Fritz W. Scharpf and Vivien A. Schmidt (eds.), *Welfare and Work in the Open Economy: From Vulnerability to Competitiveness* (Oxford: Oxford University Press, 2000); Fritz W. Scharpf and Vivien A. Schmidt (eds.), *Welfare and Work in the Open Economy: Diverse Responses to Common Challenges* (Oxford: Oxford University Press, 2000); Hall and Soskice, *Varieties of Capitalism*; Vivien A. Schmidt, *The Futures of European Capitalism* (Oxford/New York: Oxford University Press, 2002). For a sceptical view see Mark Blyth, 'Same as it Never Was: Temporality and Typology in the Varieties of Capitalism', *Comparative European Politics* 1/1 (2003), pp.215–25.
9. Hall and Soskice, *Varieties of Capitalism*, p.103.
10. Thelen, 'Varieties of Labor Politics', pp.75ff.
11. Anke Hassel 'The Erosion of the German System of Industrial Relations', *British Journal of Industrial Relations* 37/3 (1999), pp.484–505; DIW – Deutsches Institut für Wirtschaftsforschung Berlin, in cooperation with Institut für Weltwirtschaft an der Universität Kiel and Institut für Wirtschaftsforschung Halle (1999), Gesamtwirtschaftliche und unternehmerische Anpassungsfortschritte in Ostdeutschland [Macroeconomic and enterprise-level progress in adaptation in Eastern Germany]. Available at http://www.diw.de/deutsch/publikationen/wochenberichte/docs/99-23-1.html#FN11 (accessed on 5 June 2004); Hassel and Streeck, 'The Crumbling Pillars'; Damian Raess, '"Time is Ripe" Bargaining Round: Globalisation, Employers and the German System of Industrial Relations', paper prepared for delivery at the ECPR Workshop 'Changing Industrial Relations in Contemporary Capitalism', Uppsala, Sweden, 13–18 April 2004.
12. Wolfgang Streeck, 'The Internationalization of Industrial Relations in Europe: Prospects and Problems' (Cologne: MPIfG Discussion Paper 98/2, 1998), p.15.
13. See for example: *Berliner Zeitung* 15 July 1996, 20 September 1997.
14. Gerhard Schröder and Anthony Blair, 'Der Weg nach vorne für Europas Sozialdemokraten' [The Way Forward for Europe's Social Democrats], *Blätter für deutsche und internationale Politik* 7 (1999). The paper emphasises that 'competitiveness' is best secured by reducing taxes on corporations and high-income earners and capping public expenditure, while reducing labour and social protection. It advocates 'competition in the product markets and free trade [which] are of pivotal importance for the stimulation of productivity and growth' (p.2). Government's role is to do 'all it can to support enterprise but never believes it is a substitute for enterprise' since 'the essential function of markets must be complimented and improved by political action, not hampered by it'. Similarly, 'corporate taxes should be simplified and the income tax reduced' while to 'make the European economy more dynamic, we have to make it more flexible as well' (p.4). In rhetoric plainly reminiscent of the US

New Democrats, the authors 'expect ... that everyone accepts the [job] opportunities afforded to him' since 'part-time work and seasonal work is better than no work'.

15. Schröder and Blair, 'Der Weg nach Vorne', pp.6–7.
16. Financial Times Deutschland, 29 May 2002.
17. Daniel Kinderman, 'Pressure from Without, Subversion from Within: The Two-Pronged German Employer Offensive', paper prepared for delivery at the American Political Science Association Annual Conference, Chicago, Sept. 2004.
18. DIW, Gesamtwirtschaftliche Anpassungsfortschritte, 1999.
19. DIW, Gesamtwirtschaftliche Anpassungsfortschritte, 1999.
20. Figures provided by the association, quoted in Hassel and Streeck, 'The Crumbling Pillars', p.23 and Raess, 'Time is Ripe', p.30.
21. Figures cited in Hassel, 'The Erosion of the German System of Industrial Relations', p.495; Hassel and Streeck, 'The Crumbling Pillars', p.23.
22. EIRO, Collective Bargaining Coverage in Western Germany (2002).
23. Ibid.
24. Cited in: Hassel, 'The Erosion of the German System of Industrial Relations', p.500.
25. Kinderman, 'Pressure from Without'; EIRO, Collective Bargaining Coverage in Western Germany (2002); EIRO, Collective Bargaining System under Pressure (2003).
26. Figures cited in Hassel, 'The Erosion of the German System of Industrial Relations', p.500.
27. S. Kohaut and L. Bellmann, 'Betriebliche Determinanten der Tarifbindung: Eine empirische Analyse auf der Basis des IAB-Betriebspanels 1995', *Industrielle Beziehungen* 4 (1997), p.323.
28. EIRO, Siemens Deal Launches Debate on Longer Working Hours (2004).
29. *Der Standard*, 28 June 2001, 29 Aug. 2001.
30. *Frankfurter Rundschau*, 23 July 2003; Raess, 'Time is Ripe'.
31. Bertelsmann Stiftung, Internationales Beschäftigungs-Ranking, 2002
32. *Frankfurter Rundschau*, 27 June 2002; 9 Sept. 2004; 15 Sept. 2004.
33. *Berliner Zeitung*, 2 June 2003; 3 June 2003; *Frankfurter Rundschau*, 16 June 2003; *Berliner Zeitung*, 30 May 2003; 2 June 2003.
34. According to calculations by Peter Wahl of NGO attac, cited in 'Bundesregierung sagt die Unwahrheit', press release 16 Sept. 2004.

Economic Reform at the Länder Level: New Life for Regional Interventionism

ROLAND STURM

POWERLESS LÄNDER?

Globalisation of industrial competition, as well as the Europeanisation of its rules, affects the Länder as much as every nation-state. In contrast to nation-states, however, they are much less equipped with the range of policy instruments and scale of resources that would allow them to react to an economic crisis situation autonomously. Their power to influence their economic fortunes is limited. Still, the Länder are more than victims of adverse circumstances, and they are not all in the same boat. Size and economic performance vary considerably and so does the mixture of policies chosen to improve regional competitiveness.

From a policy perspective the educational policies of the Länder and their efforts to create regional innovation systems are two sides of the same coin. In practice, however, because of the separation of policy making (education is predominantly a Land responsibility, whereas regional economic development policies are a typical example of multi-level government in the EU) only a fairly abstract connection is made between the two. All the Länder agree that better education has to be a priority if the German economy wants to secure its future competitiveness. Whether national educational standards, as proposed by the federal government, can be helpful in this context is under dispute.

The characteristics of economic reform at the Länder level can be detected in regionalised strategies of economic adaptation. These strategies have notable features in common, not least because they are embedded in a relatively inflexible institutional strait-jacket. Where economic strategies differ, they profit from regional political initiatives and the processes of policy-learning which federalism provokes. None of the German Länder governments has ever had ideological problems with interventions to promote economic competitiveness.[1] What we observe today, as in the past, is a search for efficient strategies to steer economic development, but now in a new and geographically wider economic and political environment.

This article maps out the restrictions under which Länder governments operate in the field of economic policy making. It then examines their room for manoeuvre, how and why their responses to the challenge of Germany's economic downturn differ, and what are the more general strategic problems of the Länder. The discussion sheds light on Länder policies to fight unemployment and the unhealed rift between the East and the West German Länder. Finally, some concluding thoughts are offered about the policy options available to the Länder in economic reform, especially in the context of a changing international economic environment.

RESTRICTIONS ON LÄNDER STRATEGIES

Economic strategies of the Länder only make a difference if they influence the preconditions for regional economic success (infrastructure investments, investments in research and technology and in education) and/or if they target partners whose preferences can be influenced by the input the Länder can provide.[2] The latter means that in practical terms the Länder can only hope to steer economic reform efficiently when they offer incentives to small and medium-sized enterprises (SMEs). The success of Länder programmes is even more likely when, for its own special reasons, the SME in question is attached to the German region where it is situated. Regional flagship companies, such as DaimlerChrysler in Baden-Württemberg, VW in Lower Saxony, or BASF in Rhineland-Palatinate, are in the role of principals vis-à-vis Land governments, which can confront Land decision makers with their demands and can even blackmail them.

Institutionalised restrictions on autonomous economic decision making of the Länder originate from the European and the federal political levels. Decisions on the most important sources of income for the Länder – on direct and indirect taxes – have to be made jointly with the federal government. No Land can avoid compromise with the other Länder and the federal government. Taxation controlled by the Länder amounts to less than one-third of their total tax income. But the income of the Länder is also determined by a complicated system of financial equalisation transfers both between the Länder and between the federal government and the Länder. A report of the Bertelsmann Foundation[3] on the economic competitiveness of the Länder sees in the consequences of the financial equalisation mechanism a heavy burden for the economically more successful Länder, such as Bavaria, Baden-Württemberg, Hesse or Hamburg, which reduces their economic options.

Notwithstanding financial equalisation there remain important economic differences between the Länder. Most of the Länder have budgetary problems – or

TABLE 1
DEBT QUOTAS* OF THE LÄNDER (2002) (LÄNDER AVERAGE: 18.3%)

Land	Debt quota (%)	Land	Debt quota (%)
Baden-Württemberg	10.9	Bavaria	5.2
Berlin	57.9	Brandenburg	33.2
Bremen	41.7	Hamburg	24.2
Hesse	13.0	Mecklenburg-West Pomerania	29.3
Lower Saxony	21.8	North Rhine-Westphalia	19.1
Rhineland-Palatinate	22.4	Saarland	25.7
Saxony	14.1	Saxony-Anhalt	36.2
Schleswig-Holstein	26.3	Thuringia	29.9

*Total debt in % of GDP.
Source: Deutscher Bundestag, *Jahresgutachten 2003/04 des Sachverständigenrates zur Begutachtung der gesamtwirtschaftlichen Entwicklung* (Berlin: Bundestagsdrucksache 15/2000), 14 Nov. 2003, p.180.

worse – are in a deep budgetary crisis, but not all of them. As a comparison of Länder debt quotas demonstrates (Table 1) there is a wide range of difference between the relatively solid budgetary situation in Bavaria, Baden-Württemberg or Saxony and the budget catastrophes in Berlin or Bremen. The income situation of many Länder is an obvious restriction for economic reform initiatives. For them it is more than a temptation to prefer the tutelage exercised through transfer payments by the federal government to political autonomy in economic affairs.

Not only do Länder have limited sovereignty over the financial resources that are needed to stimulate the economy or to implement strategies for structural economic change. Also, a number of important tasks of the Länder with wide-ranging economic implications are co-financed by the federal government (see Table 2). Here again there is little a single Land can do on its own to tailor these expenditures to its specific needs.

In addition to national restrictions to Länder economic policy making the EU's subsidy controls limit the alternatives Land governments have when they try to intervene in their regional economies.[4] Since 1996 there has been a *de minimis* clause which exempts small subsidies from these controls, and since 1998 the possibility for exemptions also exists for the support of SMEs. These decisions were followed by further possible exemptions for research and development, environmental protection, restructuring of companies, employment and training, financial guarantees and venture capital. Traditional regional development policies are, however, no longer the sole

TABLE 2
FEDERAL TRANSFER PAYMENTS TO THE LÄNDER (2002 IN €M)

Common tasks (Art. 91a, b Basic Law)		Federal aid (Art. 104a Basic Law)	
Construction of universities	1,074	Transport and local streets	8,421
Regional development	1,001	Housing	678
Agriculture and the coast	933	Housing improvement	6
Education and research	556	Spatial planning	399
Total	3,564	Total	9,502

Source: OECD, *Wirtschaftsberichte Deutschland* (Paris: OECD, 2003), p.82.

responsibility of the EU member state or sub-national regions, such as the Länder. This is the logical consequence of European integration. The European Commission protects competition in the Single Market and therefore tries to provide a level playing field for all companies operating in Europe.

For the Länder the European context is of limited advantage when it comes to the transfer of funds. East Germany certainly profits considerably from regional aid. EU subsidy controls are, however, much less welcome. And this is true for all the Länder. The Länder see subsidies as an instrument to rearrange regional competitive strength in their favour. When regional aid, outside the framework accepted by the EU Commission, became illegal, the Länder started to look for strategic alternatives. They found alternative justifications for using funds in order to stimulate their economies.[5] Land subsidies are now paid to support SMEs, and to develop research and technology (see Table 3) or infrastructure. The more prosperous a Land is, the more it can invest in such strategies and has done so in the past.

LÄNDER STRATEGIES

It would be wrong to assume that economic strategies of the Länder are, because of the restrictions mentioned, mostly inflexible and reactive, i.e. driven by the need to help out whenever a regional crisis situation develops. Poorer Länder certainly find it more difficult to search for strategies of regional economic innovation. They are very much occupied with the problems of managing industrial decline. But, as we will see, even they try to develop forward strategies (see Table 4).

In the 1980s the Länder began for the first time to situate themselves in a more global context. Both the Asian challenge and the preparation for the European Single Market project forced them to reflect on their new competitors both worldwide and in Europe. In Europe for a short time even the vision of a Europe of the Regions, which was believed to be able to sideline the nation-states, found support. The Länder interpreted the new European challenge realistically as a new form of regional competition in Europe, namely the competition between regions. The economic well-being of regions in a Europe with a Single Market was no longer in the hands of nation-states alone. The regions, too, had to find plausible economic strategies to attract investments.

TABLE 3
LAND EXPENDITURES ON RESEARCH AND DEVELOPMENT 1999, IN €M (% OF LÄNDER TOTAL)

Land	Expenditures	Land	Expenditures
Baden-Württemberg	1,000 (13.3)	Bavaria	1,183 (15.7)
Berlin	556 (7.4)	Brandenburg	198 (2.6)
Bremen	96 (1.3)	Hamburg	229 (3.0)
Hesse	478 (6.4)	Mecklenburg-West Pomerania	165 (2.2)
Lower Saxony	559 (8.0)	North Rhine-Westphalia	1,442 (19.2)
Rhineland-Palatinate	262 (3.5)	Saarland	101 (1.3)
Saxony	524 (7.0)	Saxony-Anhalt	232 (3.1)
Schleswig-Holstein	190 (2.5)	Thuringia	266 (3.5)

Source: Deutscher Bundestag, *Faktenbericht 2002 zum Bundesbericht Forschung 2000* (Berlin: Bundestagsdrucksache 14/8040), 21 Jan. 2002, p.346.

TABLE 4
ECONOMIC STRATEGIES OF THE LÄNDER (1999–2001)

Land	**Structural characteristics of the Land economy**	**Industrial policies of special importance**	**Budgetary policies**	**Economic success (Bertelsmann ranking*)**
Baden-Württemberg	mix of small and medium-sized enterprises (SMEs) and global players (car industry/IT and telecommunication)	high spending on research (Land leads in patents); reform of public administration	privatisation (*Landesstiftung*); budgetary discipline	3 (1996–98: 3) no change (1991–95: 3)
Bavaria	highly competitive; attracts direct investments, especially advanced technologies (many patents); inward migration of labour	corporatism (*Beschäftigungspakt Bayern*); efficient public administration; support for start-ups	strong on investments; relatively small deficit; privatisation	2 (1996–98: 2) no change (1991–95: 2)
Berlin	economy stagnant; not competitive; decoupled from the world market; some movement in the service sector; well-trained workforce	support for SMEs; Business Location Centre to attract investments; hope to initiate clusters of innovation	permanent budgetary crisis (unconstitutional budgets)	13 (1996–98: 14) +1 (1991–95: 13)
Brandenburg	lowest economic growth rate; de-industrialisation; agrarian		budgetary problems (especially above average financial burden of social policies and interests on debt); lowest share of expenditures for research and development	15 (1996–98: 11) −4 (1991–95: 14)
Bremen	end of ship-building crisis; car industry and service sector growth; low share of self-employed	human capital investment (especially universities); development of industrial sites; support for start-ups (*BEGIN* initiative)	budgetary crisis; investment in road transport infrastructure	5 (1996–98: 5) no change (1991–95: 5)

(*continued*)

TABLE 4
(cont'd)

Land	Structural characteristics of the Land economy	Industrial policies of special importance	Budgetary policies	Economic success (Bertelsmann ranking*)
Hamburg	efficient regional centre and international harbour; growing service sector; highest percentage of self-employed; weak industrial base and loss of FDI	labour market policies to reduce unemployment; strategies; support for SMEs; cluster: air and space technologies; IT and life sciences; transport infrastructure development	lack of financial options; public–private partnerships and cut-backs	1 (1996–98: 1) no change (1991–95: 1)
Hesse	two-thirds of all jobs in the service sector; regional divide between the prosperous south and the poorer north; attractive for FDI	reform of public administration	lack of financial options (large share of payments on interest rates); investment in human capital and transport infrastructure; privatisation (*Zukunftsoffensive Hessen*)	4 (1996–98: 4) no change (1991–95: 4)
Mecklenburg-West Pomerania	competitive agriculture; ship-building and tourism	support for biotechnology; support for start-ups and SMEs; reform of public administration	budgetary crisis	14 (1996–98: 15) +1 (1991–95: 16)
Lower Saxony	ship building (but also ongoing crisis) and tourism; weak in innovation (patents) and investments in industry; low number of SMEs and self-employed	support for SMEs and research and technology (*Technologieagentur*)	budgetary crisis (large share of budget for interest rates)	10 (1996–98: 7) −3 (1991–95: 8)
North Rhine-Westphalia	Change to service economy, but important legacy of heavy industry; highest number of international companies	support for SMEs (move initiative) and start-ups (Go! initiative); cluster	budgetary problems	8 (1996–98: 8) no change (1991–95: 7)

(continued)

TABLE 4
(*cont'd*)

Land	Structural characteristics of the Land economy	Industrial policies of special importance	Budgetary policies	Economic success (Bertelsmann ranking*)
Rhineland-Palatinate	agrarian; conversion of military installations	policies against unemployment; reform of public administration; support for SMEs; venture capital	budgetary problems (large share of budget for interests)	7 (1996–98: 7) −1 (1991–95: 6)
Saarland	service sector replaces heavy industry	support for start ups (*Saarland Offensive für Gründer*), bio-technology and IT (*Sondervermögen Zukunftsinitiatim-ve*); tax subsidies	budgetary crisis, privatisation	6 (1996–98: 10) +4 (1991–95: 12)
Saxony	underdeveloped service sector; industrial investment and research; regional growth poles	investment in human capital	stable public investment, on the brink of budgetary crisis	11 (1996–98: 13) +2 (1991–95: 10)
Saxony-Anhalt	breakdown of industries; lack of exports and innovation (patents); lack of SMEs and self-employed	cluster (*Chemiepark Sachsen-Anhalt*)	budgetary crisis	16 (1996–98: 16) no change (1991–95: 15)
Schleswig-Holstein	dependent on Hamburg; crisis of maritime employment; tourism, few jobs in industry, but industrial growth	support for SMEs and advanced technologies (cluster: health)	budgetary problems	9 (1996–98: 9) no change (1991–95: 9)
Thuringia	competitive industries; industrial investment; lack of innovation (patents)	policies against unemployment; cluster: *Technologiedreieck Erfurt-Jena-Ilmenau*; Land investment in research; support for SMEs	budgetary problems; public investment	12 (1996–98: 12) no change (1991–95: 11)

*The Bertelsmann Index measures employment, income and security (i.e. social security as well as public safety).

Sources: Information rearranged as provided by Bertelsmann Stiftung (ed.), *Die Bundesländer im Standortwettbewerb 2003* (Gütersloh: Verlag Bertelsmann Stiftung, 2003) and Bertelsmann Stiftung (ed.), *Die Bundesländer im Standortwettbewerb* (Gütersloh: Verlag Bertelsmann Stiftung, 2001).

The global challenge and regional competition in the EU have continued to confront the Länder. However, the major new change was in Germany itself. Unification added five new and poor Länder to the 11 old ones, and affected general approaches to regional economic policy making. It is difficult, however, to match new approaches with the party political composition of regional governments. Research has shown, for example, that the degree of economic interventionism which goes with unemployment policies of the Länder depends mainly on regional socio-economic pressures and problems and not on party political preferences.[6]

New Ideas

Industrial policy as a concept of state interventionism to support regional economies was discovered in the 1980s by Baden-Württemberg, soon to be followed by a similar *idée directrice* in North Rhine-Westphalia and Bavaria. What then started was a process of policy learning which led to the wide range of industrial policies that is to be found in all of the Länder today. After unification these economic strategies travelled with policy advice and the staff of West German Land institutions to the East.

The current policy mix in industrial policies reflects the special strengths of the Land in question and the current 'fashion' of interventionism. When the *Ministerpräsident* (head of government) of Baden-Württemberg, Lothar Späth,[7] who was in office from 1978 to 1991, 'invented' the industrial policy of his Land, he had a kind of amputated 'corporatism' in mind. State interventionism was to be a catalyst to bring together, and to exploit for the economic good of the Land, science, businesses and the Land public administration. Späth also added culture to the list, because he saw a competitive advantage in cultural excellence. The trade unions were, however, excluded from this new kind of corporatist effort. Länder with a social democratic tradition, such as North Rhine-Westphalia, unsurprisingly differed in this respect and included the unions in their modernising coalitions.

The great expectations invested, on the one hand, in culture as an economic factor and, on the other, in numerous technology parks[8] which developed all over Germany, first in the West and after unification rapidly in the East, were, however, soon disappointed. Cultural excellence has not helped Berlin to an economic breakthrough, for example, and the sheer number of technology parks competing for a much smaller number of start-ups has made many of them financial risks. The support for research and development and for technology transfer is still high on the agenda of Länder economic strategies, but proximity to university research and an economic environment that favours applied sciences are indispensable for their success. The lasting legacy of the 1980s was the willingness of Land governments to play an active role in the protection of their individual economic prospects.

Recent Developments

Corporatism was revitalised in the 1990s when the employment situation deteriorated and when it became increasingly difficult to find jobs for the vocational training of school leavers. In the field of employment and vocational training the most efficient Land proved to be one in which the conservative Christian Social Union (CSU) has had an absolute majority since 1966. Bavaria organised – parallel to a similar, but not identical effort on the federal level[9] – an 'alliance for jobs'. But, generally speaking, the trade unions in all of the Länder have lost influence over economic strategies. Supply-side politics has become accepted as the influential guideline for interventionism.

In addition, greater stress is laid on the mobilisation of social capital by means of decentralisation than on top-down corporatism. Forms of decentralised regional participation intended to stimulate regional social capital have been practised especially in North Rhine-Westphalia,[10] the first Land to implement such programmes in 1987, later in Brandenburg as the first Land in the East, and – with a different idea of regionalisation – Hesse and Baden-Württemberg.[11] In North Rhine-Westphalia regional representatives on the sub-Land level were supposed to act as programme planners and as those responsible for the implementation of programmes to develop the regional economy. These structures are still in place, but Land economic policies have remained much more centralised than expected. Efforts are now made (and co-financed by the federal government[12]) to develop a more professional approach to regional management. This approach includes its outsourcing.

Today many Länder define a central problem as the deficits in their administration, which is perceived as being too big, too distant from the real problems, too intrusive, and therefore burdensome for economic development. Reform of public administration has become of central importance for economic innovation. Reform efforts are by no means only fashionable among the richer Länder, such as Baden-Württemberg or Bavaria. One of the poorest, Mecklenburg-West Pomerania has declared its intention of becoming the German Land with the most modern public administration. Hesse plans for 2005 as an additional step of public sector reform the reorganisation of its infrastructure for regional development policies. The formerly separate institutions responsible for banking, technology transfer, research and development, and tourism will be merged into one agency, the Hessenagentur GmbH, and financial aid will in future be the task of the investment bank Hesse.[13]

There is consensus among the Länder that they should concentrate their efforts on the support of SMEs and new technologies. In addition there is widespread support for activities which mobilise venture capital, and some of the Länder, like Baden-Württemberg, have organised a number of funds for this purpose. Corporatism in its traditional form may be dead, but this does not mean the end of cooperation. All Länder agree that the best possible economic strategy is the support of clusters of innovation,[14] and here the role of the Länder as catalysts for the organisation of clusters becomes crucial again. In a way this mirrors their former efforts to organise regional cooperation with the help of the Land administration. But now firms, start-ups and science are the nuclei for economic networks.

For some Länder, privatisation strategies have provided additional funds to support research and development and technology transfer. As the *Treuhand*, under the control of the Federal Finance Ministry, managed the privatisation of the East German economy centrally, none of the East German Länder was in a position to sell Land assets in a big way. The major beneficiaries of privatisation were the richer Länder, for example Bavaria with €4.2 billion additional income, Baden-Württemberg and Hesse. They have used their additional resources for economic development strategies.

When it comes to economic deregulation, most of the Länder are still way behind international standards. Although cross-border leasing arrangements have been allowed by the Länder on the local level, they are still very hesitant to mobilise private capital. Recently, the idea of public–private partnership arrangements has, however, gained ground. Hamburg and Baden-Württemberg are the Länder with the greatest willingness to use public–private partnerships. In addition, in Baden-Württemberg, because of a Liberal (FDP) economics minister who tried to please the supporters of his party, the law on SMEs was reformed. It now allows the definition of the learned professions as SMEs and their support by public funds, and it forces local governments to accept the bidding of small firms when they offer contracts for public works.

Labour Market Policies

An analysis of Länder labour market policies[15] has found evidence for different strategies to cope with the challenge of growing unemployment (see Table 5). A majority of the Länder favours 'push strategies', which combine innovation, far-reaching interventionism to steer the labour market, in close cooperation with industry, and government spending. Subsidies provide incentives for companies to employ the long-term unemployed. The training of the unemployed is seen as a precondition for new employment opportunities. Part of this strategy is the support of technology transfer, especially to SMEs, which are seen as playing a crucial role in new employment. Push strategies also include corporatist arrangements with regional employers to steer labour market policies.

'Pull strategies' invest less in these fields of activities. They target, above all, special problems in the labour market, such as youth unemployment. Labour market policies are not seen as an integral part of economic policies. The Länder that favour 'pull strategies' are more likely than the majority of the Länder to rely on market mechanisms to solve problems on the labour market. The third and smallest group of Länder opts for 'stay' strategies. They are as reluctant as the Länder that

TABLE 5
LABOUR MARKET POLICIES OF THE LÄNDER (1989–97)

Push strategies	Pull strategies	Stay strategies
Hamburg	Hesse	Schleswig-Holstein
Bremen	Rhineland-Palatinate	Saarland
Lower Saxony	Baden-Württemberg	
North Rhine-Westphalia	Bavaria	
Berlin		
Mecklenburg-West Pomerania		
Brandenburg		
Saxony-Anhalt		
Thuringia		
Saxony		

Source: Josef Schmid and Susanne Blancke, *Arbeitsmarktpolitik der Bundesländer. Chancen und Restriktionen einer aktiven Arbeitsmarkt- und Strukturpolitik im Föderalismus* (Berlin: edition sigma, 2001), p.222.

favour pull strategies when it comes to political interventions, but invest more money in traditional labour market policies.

This grouping of the Länder refers to a time period up to 1997, and it does not imply that Länder cannot change their labour market strategies. By 2005, for instance, Rhineland-Palatinate would be included in the group of modernising Länder that pursued 'push' strategies. It invented a wage subsidy model in 2000 (*Mainzer Modell*), which was later adopted as a national labour market strategy by the federal government.

The East–West Divide

Though from the point of view of budgetary stability it can disputed whether West and East German Länder are still in different boats, there is no doubt that they are clearly divided with regard to economic capabilities (see Table 6).[16] The Bertelsmann Index locates the East German Länder (including Berlin) at the bottom of the Länder league table. Brandenburg, Mecklenburg-West Pomerania and Berlin have the worst prospects for their economic future, and Saxony-Anhalt struggles to move up from last place. Another ranking by the Institut der Deutschen Wirtschaft, which measured economic potential, gave Berlin the worst marks. It was classified 25 per cent below the German average.[17]

Brandenburg has a particularly dismal history of failed gigantic projects such as the 'cargolifter' (a cargo Zeppelin which never overcame its technical problems), the Lausitzring (for Formula 1 races that were not held there) or a micro-chip factory that did

TABLE 6

THE ECONOMY OF THE EAST AND THE WEST GERMAN LÄNDER IN COMPARISON (2002)

Land	Unemployment (%)	BIP (€bn)	Turnover by industry (€bn)
Mecklenburg-West Pomerania	18.6	29.6	8.0
Brandenburg	17.5	44.1	16.6
Saxony-Anhalt	19.6	43.3	21.2
Thuringia	15.9	40.7	20.0
Saxony	17.8	75.8	34.9
East Berlin	–	–	3.4
East German Länder total	*18.0*	*233.5*	*104.1*
Schleswig-Holstein	8.7	65.6	27.9
Hamburg	9.0	75.2	66.0
Lower Saxony	9.2	183.1	135.3
Bremen	12.5	23.0	21.1
North Rhine-Westphalia	9.2	464.0	287.3
Hesse	6.9	191.6	82.2
Rhineland-Palatinate	7.2	93.3	62.2
Baden-Württemberg	5.4	307.4	238.0
Bavaria	6.0	368.9	255.8
Saarland	9.0	25.4	19.9
West Berlin	–	–	26.6
West German Länder total	*7.9*	*1,797.6*	*1,222.3*
Berlin	16.9	77.1	30.0

Source: Deutscher Bundestag, *Jahresbericht der Bundesregierung zum Stand der Deutschen Einheit 2003* (Berlin: Bundestagsdrucksache 15/1550), 17 Sep. 2003, p.90.

not start production.[18] The East German Länder are also still behind the West German Länder in international technological competitiveness.[19] The days when German politicians could announce (and believe in) a rapid process of catching up of the East German economy are definitely over. A new realism of political perceptions has started a process of rethinking and has produced fresh ideas with regard to the available options for Land economic policies in the East.[20]

All the East German Länder are heavily dependent on outside transfers from the federal government (DM 89.4 billion in 1999), from the West German Länder and their local governments (DM 11.6 billion in 1999), from the social security system (DM 36 billion in 1999), and from the European Union (DM 7.0 billion in 1999). To protect their EU subsidy levels after enlargement, the East German Länder demanded that Objective 1 payments be no longer dependent exclusively on the regional GDP, but also on unemployment levels.

Whereas the budgets of the five new Länder were on average 42.8 per cent (2002) financed by tax income, the average for the West German Länder was 69.4 per cent. Berlin, not included in this comparison, is a special and extreme case with only 36.0 per cent of its expenditures financed by Land tax income.[21] The lion's share of transfers is, however, not used for the stimulation of the East German economy, but goes into consumption. The development of industrial infrastructure and subsidies to companies made up only18.4 per cent of the 1999 transfer payments (see Table 7).

In 2004 a group of experts[22] under the chairmanship of the Social Democrat Klaus von Dohnanyi published a report that questioned the logic of industrial development policies for the East German Länder that had come to be accepted after unification.[23] This report echoed the sceptical findings of the second progress report that the five economic think-tanks[24] had prepared for the federal government in November 2003. All experts agreed that the effects of financial transfers were minimal, and that their volume tended to have a negative impact on economic growth in the West.

For a short time in April 2004 the idea of making East Germany more attractive for investments by means of a big enterprise zone (characterised by lower taxes, deregulation and subsidised wages) was at the core of a new public debate about economic strategy options.[25] The West German Länder reacted with demands that all economically less well-off regions in Germany should be given the same opportunities.[26] Soon the bottom-line of the debate was that the wage levels in East Germany were too high and should be brought into line with labour productivity. Measured against productivity the average wage level in East Germany is still 10 per cent higher than in West

TABLE 7
WHAT DO TRANSFER PAYMENTS TO THE EAST GERMAN LÄNDER FINANCE? (%)

	1991	1992	1993	1994	1995	1996	1997	1998	1999
Industrial infrastructure	12.4	9.9	8.6	10.1	13.0	13.3	13.2	12.9	12.6
Subsidies to companies	2.5	4.7	7.6	7.5	8.0	7.0	6.3	6.4	5.8
Social expenditures	45.4	54.1	54.3	54.4	49.5	49.7	49.7	49.1	51.4
Financial transfers	28.0	22.3	20.0	19.5	23.5	24.6	25.0	25.8	24.5
Categorical financial transfers	11.7	9.0	9.3	8.4	6.0	5.4	5.8	5.8	5.7

Source: OECD, *Wirtschaftsberichte Deutschland* (Paris: OECD, 2001), p.136.

Germany. The proposal to reduce wage levels caused the predictable resistance of the representatives of the East German Länder. The federal government tried to avoid the issue of an enterprise zone solution altogether. Until 2019 the volume of federal subsidies is determined by the Solidarity Pact II. Innovation is, in the government's view, only possible, if at all, in the context of the decisions made for 2007 when the EU starts its new financial programme.[27] In the end no decisions were made. The support for the enterprise zone idea was, in other words, weak because of conflicting interests and lack of political support. In addition, it would have violated EU subsidy rules.

Agreement could, however, be found on a strategic change in the subsidisation of the East German economy. Instead of indiscriminate financial support for all regions of the East German Länder, even East German *Ministerpräsidenten* now favoured the idea of financing economic growth poles. Though this is one of the traditional approaches that development theories have been offering for some time, the support that it found in the East German Länder is remarkable for at least two reasons. East German politicians are for the first time prepared to accept uneven development in their Länder, with all the attendant social and political consequences. Secondly, they are ready to face globalisation pressures with these new flagship projects even if this means reduced social consumption for the less well-off regions of their Länder. In short, the freedom to differ and to deregulate[28] and to set Land priorities is valued higher than formal equality when it comes to the distribution of resources. In this respect change has, however, just begun. The federal government has started negotiations with the East German Länder governments to set priorities for federal subsidies accordingly. It plans 'partnerships for growth and innovation' (*Partnerschaften für Wachstum und Innovation*) from which it expects to learn from the Länder on which projects the federal government should focus its financial support.[29]

This new emphasis on economic growth poles may also help to bring more transparency into subsidisation. There are still several hundred mostly uncoordinated programmes. About 90 per cent of all subsidies are, however, spent on the following four instruments: subsidies for investments, jointly financed by the federal government and the Länder; premiums on investments for equipment and the development of industrial sites; cheap credit for SMEs and start-ups, financed by federal banks; and support for research and technology (financial and staff) for SMEs and for research networks.[30] With regard to the latter East Germany is also part of the national SME programme: *PROgramm INNOvationskompetenz mittelständischer Unternehmen* (PROINNO). Sixty per cent of the PRO INNO funds went to East Germany. Of the 71 networks of competency, 14 were situated in East Germany in the regions Berlin-Brandenburg, Dresden-Chemnitz, Halle-Merseburg and Jena-Ilmenau-Erfurt.[31] PROINNO II, which started in 2004, has fully embraced the growth pole concept and the idea that regional clusters are crucial for economic success.[32]

THE ECONOMIC STRATEGIES OF THE LÄNDER IN A NEW INTERNATIONAL CONTEXT

Economic policy reforms of the Länder have to cope with a dilemma. It took them more than 20 years to develop their competencies in regional cooperation. Now they try with some success to mobilise their social capital and to develop their endogenous growth potentials. The Länder have also accumulated practical experience with growth poles. But what sounds like a success story is in danger of becoming mostly irrelevant. The global information society erodes this kind of internal regionalism. Outsourcing on a world-wide scale even affects the service sector and makes strong inroads into the economic sectors that are dominated by SMEs. Regional production systems fall apart.

This development has at least three consequences for the Länder. When they want to protect their economies, they should do all they can – which is precious little – to convince those of their firms that are global players to keep a foot in the respective Land. As the federal government is more important than the Länder when it comes to the attractiveness of Germany for direct investments, and because the Länder have no exclusive control over important investment incentives, they can only hope that Germany as a whole will overcome its economic problems.

One strategic option is for the Länder to look for partners, especially regional partners, to improve the economic attractiveness and the competitiveness of their regions. In addition to Land efforts to market their economic strengths on the global stage, the Länder *Ministerpräsidenten* can travel around the world as ambassadors of their regional industries.[33] Here they are becoming increasingly active. Another strategic option is to seize the opportunities that are available to cross-border regions, which are better placed internationally, especially in the context of the Single Market, than German regions would be on their own. Cross-border regions can now be found on all German borders. They are supported by the EU-INTERREG programme.

The Länder do not agree on whether a redrawing of Länder boundaries might also contribute to their competitiveness. The obvious candidates for integration into larger territorial units would be the city states of Berlin, Bremen and Hamburg, and the very small states, such as the Saarland. The Social Democrats in Saxony-Anhalt[34] suggested a merger of Saxony-Anhalt, Thuringia and Saxony. At the moment, however, no powerful political coalition for a territorial reform is in sight.[35]

An additional strategy is to adapt regional economies better to the world-wide information society and to transform the Länder into knowledge-based societies. The problem seems to be that the Länder need access to the information society more than the information society needs the cooperation and support of the Länder.[36] Some of the German Länder, especially Baden-Württemberg[37] and Bavaria, were quick to develop genuine regional programmes for developing into knowledge-based societies. Both Länder embraced the idea of data highways in the early 1990s. In Baden-Württemberg this idea was boiled down in 1996 to the initiative Baden-Württemberg medi@. Its aim was industrial networking and the marketing of product innovation. In 1999 the Land developed a programme to facilitate the introduction of e-commerce.[38]

There was from the start a certain tension between the global character of information technology and the idea that it could be tamed for regional purposes. The vision of a regional information society has been reduced to mostly infrastructure policies, support for increased knowledge transfer into the universities, and priority to improvement of the access of SMEs to the information society as they are seen as central to regional economic development. National e-government strategies have to involve the Länder, because they are responsible for most of Germany's public administration. In summer 2003 the federal government, the Länder and local government agreed on the strategy *DeutschlandOnline*. The idea is to allow internet access to 50 per cent of the public administration services that all levels of government offer. Public works shall be advertised in the internet (*eVergabe*). And it will be possible to bid for them electronically and to enter into electronic contracts.[39]

CONCLUSION

Economic reform at the Länder level moves slowly. However, one should not forget that the autonomous decision-making powers of Land governments are restricted. In view of the unitary character of Germany's federalism and the Europeanisation of Germany's political system, it is surprising how active and innovative the Länder have been when confronted with new economic challenges, such as the Single Market and globalisation. Regional corporatism lives on and has found new expressions. The poorer and the richer Länder may have more or less to contribute to regional economic growth, but they do not differ in principle with regard to their economic strategies. Slowly the role of the market has become more prominent. What remains a dilemma for the economic policy making of the Länder is that German federalism in its present form is too cooperative to allow the degree of competition between the Länder that the forces of globalisation and the European Single Market make indispensable.

NOTES

1. Roland Sturm, 'The Industrial Policy Debate in the Federal Republic of Germany', in Simon Bulmer (ed.), *The Changing Agenda of West German Public Policy* (Dartmouth: Gower, 1989), pp.155–74.
2. Roland Sturm with Edmund Ortwein, 'Neben Brüssel und Berlin: Wirtschaftspolitik in Baden-Württemberg', in Hilde Cost and Margot Körber-Weik (eds.), *Die Wirtschaft von Baden-Württemberg im Umbruch* (Stuttgart: Kohlhammer, 2002), pp.280ff.
3. Bertelsmann Stiftung (ed.), *Die Bundesländer im Standortwettbewerb 2003* (Gütersloh: Verlag Bertelsmann Stiftung, 2003).
4. Franz Nägele, 'Die "graue Eminenz" der regionalen Wirtschaftspolitik. Zur regionalpolitischen Bedeutung der EG-Beihilfenkontrolle in der Bundesrepublik Deutschland', *Staatswissenschaft und Staatspraxis* 8/1 (1997), pp.109–30.
5. Roland Sturm, *Die Industriepolitik der Bundesländer und die europäische Integration. Unternehmen und Verwaltungen im erweiterten Binnenmarkt* (Baden-Baden: Nomos, 1991).
6. Josef Schmid and Susanne Blancke, *Arbeitsmarktpolitik der Bundesländer. Chancen und Restriktionen einer aktiven Arbeitsmarkt- und Strukturpolitik im Föderalismus* (Berlin: edition sigma, 2001), p.245.
7. Lothar Späth, *Wende in die Zukunft* (Reinbek: rororo, 1985). Sturm with Ortwein, 'Neben Brüssel und Berlin', p.287.
8. Nicolai Dose and Alexander Drexler (eds.), *Technologieparks. Voraussetzungen, Bestandsaufnahme und Kritik* (Opladen: Westdeutscher Verlag, 1988).
9. For more information see for example Rolf G. Heinze, *Die Berliner Räterepublik. Viel Rat – wenig Tat?* (Wiesbaden: Westdeutscher Verlag, 2002).
10. On the concept see Heinz Kruse, *Reform durch Regionalisierung. Eine politische Antwort auf die Umstrukturierung der Wirtschaft* (Frankfurt and New York: Campus, 1990); Helmut Voelzkow, *Mehr Technik in die Region. Neue Ansätze zur regionalen Technikförderung in Nordrhein-Westfalen* (Wiesbaden: DUV, 1990); and Thomas Köller, 'Die Entwicklungslinien der NRW-Strukturpolitik seit 1966 und ihre staats- und globalisierungstheoretischen Implikationen', in Edgar Grande and Rainer Prätorius (eds.), *Politische Steuerung und neue Staatlichkeit* (Baden-Baden: Nomos, 2003), pp.211–34. For a comparison with Lower Saxony see Alexander Krafft and Günter Ulrich, *Chancen und Risiken regionaler Selbstorganisation* (Opladen: Leske + Budrich, 1993).
11. For greater detail see Bernd Steinbacher, 'Der Verband Region Stuttgart', *Bürger im Staat* 48/4 (1998), pp.220–23.

12. Deutscher Bundestag, *Dreiunddreißigster Rahmenplan der Gemeinschaftsaufgabe 'Verbesserung der regionalen Wirtschaftsstruktur' (GA) für den Zeitraum 2004 bis 2007* (Berlin: Bundestagsdrucksache 15/2961), 22 April p.49.
13. Matthias Bartsch, 'Die Wirtschaft einfacher födern. Finanzielle Hilfe und Beratung sollen getrennt werden', *Frankfurter Rundschau*, 24 April 2004, p.13.
14. Josef Hilbert, Michael Kleinaltenkamp, Jürgen Nordhause-Janz and Brigitta Widmaier, *Neue Kooperationsformen in der Wirtschaft. Können Konkurrenten Partner werden?* (Opladen: Leske + Budrich, 1991).
15. Schmid and Blancke, *Arbeitsmarktpolitik der Bundesländer*, pp.218ff.
16. Roland Sturm, 'Wirtschaftsförderung und Industriepolitik in Ostdeutschland – eine Zwischenbilanz nach 10 Jahren', in Konrad Löw (ed.), *Zehn Jahre deutsche Einheit* (Berlin: Duncker & Humblot), pp.147–63.
17. Christoph Seils, 'Berlin hofft auf Unterhaltungsbranche als Stimmungsmacher', *Frankfurter Rundschau*, 19/20 May 2004, p.12.
18. For background information see *Der Spiegel*, 16 Dec. 2002, pp.38–42.
19. Deutscher Bundestag, *Bericht zur technologischen Leistungsfähigkeit Deutschlands 2002 und Stellungnahme der Bundesregierung* (Berlin: Bundestagsdrucksache 15/788), 3 April 2003, p.167.
20. See among others the contributions by the East German Social Democrats Wolfgang Thierse, *Zukunft Ost. Perspektiven für Ostdeutschland in der Mitte Europas* (Berlin: Rowohlt Berlin Verlag, 2001), and Jens Bullerjahn, *Sachsen-Anhalt 2020. Einsichten und Perspektiven* (Magdeburg: SPD Landesverband Sachsen-Anhalt, 2004), or the East German Christian Democrats Kurt Biedenkopf and Georg Milbradt, 'Zukunft Ost – Chance für Deutschland', *Frankfurter Rundschau*, 7 April 2004, p.8.
21. Deutscher Bundestag, *Jahresbericht der Bundesregierung zum Stand der Deutschen Einheit 2003* (Berlin: Bundestagsdrucksache 15/1550), 17 September 2003, p.90.
22. Members of the *Praktiker-Kreis* or *Gesprächskreis Ost* are Edgar Most (Deutsche Bank), Heinz Putzhammer (Migration Commission of the Federal Government), Karl-Ulrich Meyn (University of Jena), Klaus Weise (Immergut-Dauermilch GmbH), Dietrich Lehmann (Me-Le Holding), Bart J. Groot (Dow Olefinverbund), Helmut Seitz (European University Viadrina, Frankfurt (Oder)), Klaus Hieckmann (Chamber of Commerce, Magdeburg), Horst Klinkmann (BioCon Valley, Greifswald), Hilmar Fuchs (Association of Innovative Companies), Karl Döring (Eko Stahl GmbH, Eisenhüttenstadt).
23. On this debate see, for example 'Tabuzone Ost', *Der Spiegel*, 5 April 2004, pp.24–41.
24. DIW (Berlin), IAB (Nürnberg), IfW (Kiel), IWH (Halle) and ZEW (Mannheim).
25. Klaus-Peter Schmid, 'Frei und erfolglos. Experten rufen nach einer Sonderwirtschaftszone für die neuen Bundesländer. Dabei existiert sie schon', *Die Zeit*, 15 April 2004, p.27.
26. 'Politiker warnen vor Sonderweg im Osten', *Frankfurter Rundschau*, 13 April 2004, p.5.
27. Christopher Seils, 'Schröder plant Zäsur im Osten erst 2007', *Frankfurter Rundschau*, 20 April 2004, p.5.
28. The former Federal Chancellor Helmut Schmidt has also advocated deregulation as the core of an economic reform strategy for East Germany (Helmut Schmidt, 'Lichtet den Dschungel der Paragraphen!', *Die Zeit*, 4 Oct. 2001, p.13).
29. Deutscher Bundestag, *Pläne der Bundesregierung zur Änderung der Förderpolitik in Ostdeutschland*, (Berlin: Bundestagsdrucksache 15/2914), 13 April 2004.
30. OECD, *Wirtschaftsberichte Deutschland* (Paris: OECD, 2001), pp.143f.
31. Deutscher Bundestag, *Jahresbericht*, p.32.
32. Deutscher Bundestag, *Innovationen und Zukunftstechnologien im Mittelstand – High-Tech-Masterplan* (Berlin: Bundestagsdrucksache 15/2551), 1 February 2004, pp.8f.
33. A full account for Brandenburg (1990–94), for example, is to be found in Raimund Krämer, *Im internationalen Netzwerk. Brandenburg und seine auswärtigen Beziehungen* (Potsdam: Brandenburgische Landeszentrale für Politische Bildung, 1995).
34. Bullerjahn, *Sachsen-Anhalt 2020*, p.7.
35. Roland Sturm, 'Länderneugliederung – kein Thema mehr?', *WiSt* 33/3 (2004), pp.133 and 152.
36. On this debate see Roland Sturm and Georg Weinmann (eds.), *The Information Society and the Regions in Europe. A British–German Comparison* (Baden-Baden: Nomos, 2000).
37. Hans-Dieter Köder, 'Die baden-württembergische Multimedia-Enquete als Instrument gesellschaftlicher Konsensbildung', in Jörg Tauss, Johannes Kollbeck and Jan Mönikes (eds.), *Deutschlands Weg in die Informationsgesellschaft. Herausforderungen und Perspektiven für Wirtschaft, Wissenschaft, Recht und Politik* (Baden-Baden: Nomos, 1996), pp.802–23.
38. Sturm with Ortwein, 'Neben Brüssel und Berlin', p.291.
39. Deutscher Bundestag, *Unterrichtung durch die Bundesregierung: Aktionsprogramm Informationsgesellschaft Deutschland 2006* (Berlin: Bundestagsdrucksache 15/2315), 23 December 2003, pp.16f.

Binding Hands as a Strategy for Economic Reform: Government by Commission

KENNETH DYSON

This essay addresses one type of strategy of economic reform that has proved very appealing to German political leaders. Its appeal rests on the search for a strategy for reform that reconciles mounting economic policy problems with systemic constraints on policy change. These constraints mean that direct chancellor majority action and even the ultimate threat of the use of such action lacks credibility. In this systemic context binding hands through government by commission provides a potential source of leadership power over economic reform. The essay does not explore more general (and more frequently addressed) questions about how formal institutions affect the autonomy and leadership capacity of German federal governments or about the range of formal powers available to federal chancellors and the implications of these resources. It is concerned with how leaders are induced to rely on and use mechanisms of binding hands, often unsuccessfully, to build credibility. Government by commission provides a source of power in a highly differentiated political system that offers numerous veto points on change and in an age of increasing electoral volatility in which leaders seek to increase their autonomy of action by focusing on the median voter. These two phenomena act as an incentive to opt for a strategy of binding hands. At the same time government by commission remains embedded in party political competition for electoral profile and policy influence as well as in disputes between ordo-liberals, advocates of cooperative capitalism and Keynesians about the most appropriate ways in which to bind hands. Government by commission has played a central role in the politics of economic reform under the Schröder governments (the so-called *Räterepublik*). By 'process chasing' its economic reforms it is possible reflect on the strategy of binding hands as a technique for economic policy reform and on the conditions that shape its effectiveness.

CREDIBILITY, BINDING HANDS AND THE PROBLEMS OF COMMITMENT

At the heart of the politics of economic policy reform is the problem of collective action. The credibility of commitments is central if such action is to be made possible, to be sustained over time, and reputation built so that the future costs of reform can be reduced. The problem of credible commitment manifests itself in different ways across political systems according to the institutional setting and the specific and varying opportunities for, and constraints on, collective action that particular settings offer. In the German case, majoritarian features, based on party and chancellor-led government, co-exist with the features of a consensual democracy, especially with the dual majorities of Bundestag and Bundesrat and the prospects that they throw up for informal grand coalition (notably through the arbitration committee between the two chambers).[1] However much political parties may seek to define preferences and lead in programmatic activity, the politics of economic reform soon take on the characteristics of a 'negotiation' model of democracy.[2] They express the strong incremental bias of a 'semi-sovereign' polity, especially of a system of 'interlocking politics'.[3] A complex overlapping of jurisdictions, accompanied by the interpenetration of political parties and federalism, and by powerful organised groups, weakens the expression of state power and places a high premium on forms of consensus-seeking.

Recent scholarship has traced how semi-sovereignty and consensus have ceased to be seen as assets for German economic policy by focusing on the opportunities that are offered for powerful, entrenched interests to act as veto players so that inertia and gridlock dominate.[4] Policy is seen as in danger of being caught up in a 'catastrophic equilibrium' of *Reformstau*, consequent on intractable problems of collective action. These problems remain serious, but are made more tractable because of the capacity of policy leaders to design and make creative use of two key institutional venues – the European Union and government by commission – to bind hands and thereby make commitments to reform more credible. Europeanisation as a mechanism for economic policy reform has been examined elsewhere by the author.[5]

Reliance on, and use of, these techniques is hedged with serious qualifications. There is, for instance, a contest about legitimacy. To those – like the president of the Federal Constitutional Court – who are attached to the primacy of parliamentary and party democracy, the EU and government by commission represent threats of disempowerment of democratic processes.[6] To others, not least in the Schröder governments, they are attractive because useful in opening up opportunities for policy leadership in the German institutional context of fragmented and overlapping jurisdictions and of intra-party conflict as well as party competition. They provide a dual legitimation of expertise and consensus and the basis for an authoritative critique of the lack of ambition in policy reform. Government by commission – and Europeanisation – offer mechanisms to circumvent party and parliamentary obstacles to reform by binding in potential opponents within larger processes that have their own dynamics.

Government by commission and Europeanisation have proved attractive to domestic economic reformers because they promise to provide external disciplines that bind the hands of German governments, change expectations of elites, publics and markets about what needs to be done, and will be done, better enable governments to resist the claims of powerful domestic interests, and help to reduce the costs of carrying through reforms by shifting expectations. They strengthen the constraints on how governments, the political parties on which they rest, and even opposition parties and organised interests can behave in the future. To the extent that German traditions of broad permissive consensus about European integration and of respect for the role of expertise (*Sachverstand* and *Sachlichkeit*) in the policy process are retained, these mechanisms offer domestic levers with which to strengthen the argument for reforms and political leadership of the process. Reforms can be legitimated by reference to shared national interest in meeting European commitments and strengthening the European project or to commitments based on a combination of science-based policy with broad representation in the design of policy. Above all, Europeanisation and government by commission provide opportunities to break the grip of the political business cycle, which leads economic policy to be driven by short-term domestic electoral incentives to retain power: whether by stimulating economies before elections (or failing to take corrective action) and then pursuing contraction in their wake, or keeping sensitive issues in labour market or social policy reforms off the agenda.[7] By binding hands, government by commission and Europeanisation can be seen as consistent with a more stable pattern of sustainable growth and employment creation and as better promoting inter-generational equity in managing labour market policy, financing social policy and public debt management.

Credibility is central to economic reform. For policies to be credible they must be time-consistent: that is, incorporate no future incentive to renege.[8] The problem of time inconsistency is addressed by limiting one's own future freedom of action, strategic sequencing, honouring the commitments into which one has entered, and building reputation with elites, publics and market participants for credible commitments.[9] Incentives to renege can be reduced, and credibility enhanced, by various forms of pre-commitment that involve binding hands. In turn, pre-commitments can be used as resources to induce agreements from other actors in the future by building up a momentum of support for policy reform – the tactic of strategic sequencing.[10] Policy makers fear that loss of reputation from reneging on one commitment will be translated into diminished influence over other and later issues. Chancellor Gerhard Schröder engaged in a tight form of binding hands when he committed to 'one-to-one' implementation of the Hartz report after the 2002 elections, before the commission had finished its work.

However, government by commission is fraught with hazards to governments, which find themselves caught anxiously between the attractions of binding in potential opposition and constraining behaviour and the risks from pre-commitment that they will not be able to deliver on promises, suffer a consequent loss of reputation and forfeit future leadership of economic reform. Three main sources of risk arise. Firstly, the obligations that a government enters into by binding hands may clash with powerful ideological commitments of one or more political parties that support the government. Most strikingly, economic modernisers in the Social Democratic Party (SPD) – who were keen to bind hands in these two ways – clashed with those who saw the SPD as first and foremost a party historically wedded to social justice. The depth of this ideological commitment to social justice raised in turn doubts about the SPD's credibility as a party that was able to abide by the constraints of government by commission – and Europeanisation.

Secondly, the risks from pre-commitment are increased when detailed and firm pre-commitments tie the hands of economic policy makers too tightly and prevent an effective response to unforeseen contingencies and the changes of preference to which they may give rise. For instance, key German policy makers came to view the Stability and Growth Pact, which many in the Bundesbank and the Finance Ministry had seen in 1997 as not tight enough, as limiting the scope for effective counter-cyclical policy after 2001. They sought to make it less constraining by proposing a more evolutionary, flexible approach.

Thirdly, the risks are increased when the costs of reform are experienced in the short to medium term (for instance, social benefit cuts, cuts in insured health services, large falls in popular approval, exit of party members, and electoral setbacks), whereas the benefits in more jobs, higher growth and increased incomes are long term (at least beyond the next federal and major state elections). From this perspective what is optimal at a certain time for economic reform ('act now or it will be too late') may prove sub-optimal as the passage of time reveals the severity of political costs. In these circumstances a government is trapped between the costs to its reputation from reneging on reform commitments and the costs of sticking with commitments. Faced with this situation in 2004, the Schröder government deferred bold reforms to care insurance and to the long-term financing of the health system beyond the 2006 elections.

The problem of compliance is exacerbated by domestic electoral timetables, which mean that the potential political costs of imposing time-consistency by binding hands are high, not least in intra-party disaffection and conflict. It is compounded in a federal state like Germany, in which state elections directly affect the distribution of federal political power, and in fiscal policy, where EU rules affect the room for political manoeuvre to distribute resources in order to maximise domestic electoral support. Credible commitments are especially problematic in structural reforms to promote growth and employment and to secure fiscal consolidation. Here the announcement of future reforms to labour markets and to social policies raises questions about whether the federal government will renege in face of the problems of securing the support of state governments, of opposition from powerful organised interests, and of domestic problems of adjusting underlying macro-economic policies like fiscal policy to the requirements of reform. In order to minimise the potential political costs to their reputation from reneging, federal governments have an incentive to avoid making the sort of meaningful, specific commitments to future action that effective binding hands in structural economic reforms requires. For these reasons German federal governments recognise the value of binding hands as a strategy for reform but are disposed to do so in a hesitant and cautious manner, especially in fiscal and structural reforms.

GOVERNMENT BY COMMISSION: CREDIBILITY LOST, CREDIBILITY REGAINED?

Government by commission has been a defining characteristic of the Schröder governments and highlights its strengths and weaknesses as a mechanism for domestic economic reform. Between 1998 and 2002 they appointed 32 commissions at a cost of over €8 million, and an additional €4.5 million was budgeted for 2003 (€1 million for the Rürup Commission).[11] Their use was by no means original to the Schröder governments: the Kohl governments had, for instance, appointed commissions on pensions and tax reforms, as well as flirted briefly in early 1996 with the trade union-inspired idea of an Alliance for Jobs. However, with Schröder they became central to his governing style. This style reflected a response to the complex policy making structures of Germany and the manifold veto points that they offered to powerful organised interests. Reform by consensus offered a means of subtly binding in political opponents; creating a new dynamics of policy reflection and learning that could break down ideologically fixed modes of thinking about policy; and, not least, testing how far reform could be pushed.

The Schröder governments illustrate both the potential strengths and the difficulties of this approach, not least the rather restricted conditions under which it produces useful short-term results. Agenda 2010 has an ambivalent relationship to government by commission. On the one hand, it was a response to the collapse of the Alliance for Jobs, and the subsequent sense of a vacuum that the Chancellor had to fill by seizing a personal leadership role on economic reform and making it his own historical project and legacy. In this respect Agenda 2010 involved a new governing style in which Schröder presented himself as a 'motor' of reform; there was no alternative on the table. On the other hand, the content of Agenda 2010 owed much to the work of the Hartz and the Rürup commissions. On issues that went beyond these two reports – like statutory reforms to open up area-wide collective bargaining and to relax redundancy provisions – Agenda 2010 made much less progress.

Schröder's predilection for government by commission reflected a combination of motives: his commitment to economic modernisation, his acute sense of the complex problems of power in economic reform and of the reluctance of Germans to embrace reform, his belief in 'social balance' as the German way, his lack of firm and clear ideas about the content of reform, his underlying pragmatism in economic policy and opportunistic approach to reform, his ambivalent attitudes to the SPD whose capacity to agree on effective reform policies he doubted, and his preference for presenting himself as a pragmatist of power who stood above party.[12] Frank-Walter Steinmeier, head of the Federal Chancellor's Office from 1999 and close colleague from Lower Saxony, acted as chief theorist of government by commission. By 2000–01 he legitimated this practice as the 'innovative power of consensus' that Schröder had developed in Lower Saxony and whose value had been demonstrated in the negotiations about the phased withdrawal from atomic power.[13] It had, however, deeper and more complex roots in Schröder's conception of chancellor leadership and his notion of how reform could be expedited in the German institutional setting. His conception of chancellor leadership mirrored his view that the SPD was a hindrance rather than source of economic reform ideas and that it had a long-term public image problem of governing competence. Credibility depended on binding in the SPD to policy ideas that were external in origin. However, because of complex intra-party tensions and conflicts between 'modernisers' and 'traditionalists', the process of credibility building was necessarily fraught with difficulties. One key source of credibility was a conception of chancellor leadership that was not principally party-based but media-centred and rooted on his direct relationship to, and support from, the German public as a source of power over policy. Schröder sought out opportunities to present himself as *Moderator*, pushing forward and orchestrating the process of economic reform rather than acting as the source of, or conduit for, SPD ideas. Government by commission expressed his core policy belief, which was in social balance in economic reform as the main means of getting reluctant Germans to accept reforms. It also reflected his deep distrust of the SPD and protracted concern to bind it in to his reform agenda.

Important examples of this strategy in economic reform include the commission on withdrawal from atomic energy, the commission on immigration, the national ethics council on genetic technology, and the commission on local authority financial reform. Each has helped in its own way to reframe public debate and to bind in opponents. For instance, the appointment of Rita Süssmuth – Christian Democratic Union (CDU) – to chair the commission on immigration, along with the managing director of the Federation of German Industry, helped to constrain opposition and give greater credibility to a policy paradigm of immigration that was economic rather than cultural in inspiration. Similarly, the national ethics council contributed to a better informed debate on the use of genetic technology, freed from the shackles of party discipline. In these two highly sensitive areas Schröder was able to highlight the gap between economic modernisers and cultural conservatives within the CDU/ Christian Social Union (CSU) opposition. This paper deals with the three most prominent cases of economic policy reform through government by commission in order to highlight the conditions under which it is effective – the Alliance for Jobs, the Hartz Commission, and the Rürup Commission.

THE ALLIANCE FOR JOBS, TRAINING AND COMPETITIVENESS: CREDIBILITY LOST

In 1998 the Alliance for Jobs was given the central role in the core project of the new SPD/Green government under Schröder – structural economic reform to reduce unemployment by means of consensus, especially by seeking out new strategic alliances on behalf of new policy ideas.[14] Its launch was accompanied by high expectations of an ambitious agenda that would be supported across federal ministries and by the employer organisations and the trade unions.[15] Its organisation and working methods appeared to reflect these expectations. Schröder chaired the top-level meetings; Bodo Hombach, head of the Federal Chancellor's Office, assumed responsibility for its development; and a complex structure was developed under a steering group and including various working groups on particular issues, as well as the Benchmarking Group to inject new thinking. Even so, it had an improvised character from the outset. Before the election little thought had been given to the Alliance or to the ideas that might inspire its work.

Initially the Alliance for Jobs had considerable credibility as a mechanism for reform. The personal reputation of the new Chancellor as a *Macher* was at stake. It stood as a symbol of his electoral commitment to 'modernisation with social justice' and to embody *die neue Mitte*. The Alliance could also count on support from the trade unions and the left of the SPD. The original idea had come from the new head of IG Metall, Klaus Zwickel, in 1995 as a means of securing a more pro-active role for the trade unions in economic reform: commitment to moderate wage agreements was promised in return for specific promises on job creation. Following the failure of this initiative, and subsequent confrontation with the Kohl government over sickness pay, redundancy and pension reforms, the Alliance offered a new opportunity to the trade unions to help shape the agenda. They were given further incentives by the appointment of Walter Riester from IG Metall as Federal Minister for Labour and Social Affairs, by the new government's reversal of the Kohl reforms, and by the new tax and contribution requirements on the low-wage sector and those working in so-called self-employment for firms. In turn, the employers saw the Alliance as an instrument to strengthen the position of Schröder as moderniser against the left of the SPD and to offset the power of Lafontaine as both Federal Finance Minister (with new powers) and SPD chair. They saw in 'benchmarking' best European and international practice a technique for making the debate about economic reform more technocratic and thereby challenging conventional wisdom. Hombach and officials in the political planning division of the Federal Chancellor's Office sought to use the Alliance for Jobs to escape the policy preferences of Lafontaine and the SPD left, to project the Chancellor directly to the public and the notion of the median voter, and to force a debate about the nature and implications of modernisation and of the commitment to embody *die neue Mitte*. The Blair–Schröder paper of 1999 served the same purpose. Its angry reception in the SPD also demonstrated the risks of alienating party activists. Finally, reformers on the centre-right of the SPD, led by Wolfgang Clement, saw the Alliance as the expression of the SPD's traditional commitment to Rhineland or cooperative capitalism. It had widespread support in the biggest and most powerful SPD region, North Rhine-Westphalia, which through Hombach had a strong presence in the Federal Chancellor's Office and in the Benchmarking Group.

This early promise of the Alliance had evaporated by 2001. Its eighth and final pre-election meeting in January 2002 was embittered and unproductive (Schröder had difficulty getting its members to attend); and its only post-election meeting in March 2003 had neither a formal agenda nor an agreed declaration at its close. Some reforms were credited to it: the JUMP employment and training programme of 1999 for young unemployed people; the Job-AQTIV law of January 2002 that strengthened job placement; the 1999 guidelines agreed by the Federation of German Employers (BDA) and the German Trade Union Federation (DGB) on a longer-term, productivity-based wage policy (in return for a reduction in working time); and the paradigm change at the March 2001 meeting away from the early retirement of older workers. However, these reforms were not part of a process of exchanging binding commitments in the Alliance, from which it might have emerged stronger. Schröder's attempts to strike deals – as for instance in March 2003 between trade union acceptance of relaxation of dismissal protection and training commitments by employers – met with rebuff. The strategy under Steinmeier was to keep the Alliance alive by using its steering group as a testing ground for ideas and keeping controversy away from its agenda. The result was that major reforms that might have served as parts of a package deal to bind hands were kept on the margins or away from the Alliance, notably the reform of the work constitution law, the pension reform and the law on part-time work. Eichel's budget consolidation and tax reforms were not negotiated there. Later, in autumn 2001, Eichel refused to contemplate a public investment programme as a means of extracting renewed concessions on wages from the trade unions. Schröder's Green Card initiative and the proposals of the Süssmuth Commission on immigration were presented but not used to activate the Alliance. Steinmeier and the Federal Chancellor's Office pursued a tactics of strategic sequencing that did not work principally through the Alliance.

The trade unions argued with growing bitterness that they had traded wage concessions in 2000–01 in return for an employer-friendly tax reform that had not been negotiated in the Alliance, a pension reform in which the Alliance had been marginalised and that struck at the basic principle of parity financing and solidarity in social policy, and failure of the employers to deliver on new training places and jobs and on limitation of overtime. Zwickel referred to the Alliance as 'an unsafe building site'. In return for continuing cooperation, the trade unions demanded the reform of the work constitution law to extend and strengthen the rights of works councils and vetoed its discussion in the Alliance. They also refused to discuss wage policy without the willingness of employers to enter into clear and binding commitments on training and jobs (which the employer organisations said that they could not do). The works constitution law and the refusal of the trade unions to discuss wages in the Alliance led the employers to see the discussions as futile. By 2002 mutual trust and confidence had collapsed.

Underlying this development was an intractable problem of credible commitment in structural economic reform through the Alliance for Jobs. Firstly, credible commitment was difficult because of the absence of a shared set of policy beliefs about unemployment and social policies. In their absence it was impossible to gain agreement on appropriate policies. In one view, which was dominant within key trade unions and the left of the SPD, the cause of unemployment was inadequate demand; higher wages and increased public expenditure would help close the 'output gap'. In another view, the problems were structural, but here again there was no agreement. For some – notably within the Federal Ministry of Labour and Social Affairs and again the trade unions and the left of the SPD – the problem was the distribution of available work, and the solution in a reduced working week, lower overtime, longer holidays, job rotation, more part-time work and early retirement (the IG Metall idea of retirement at 60). Policies needed to focus on the management of working time. For others – for instance, in the Benchmarking Group – the problem was the lack of new jobs in the labour-intensive service sector and the excessive length of unemployment, and the solution was public policies to create a 'low-wage' sector and to develop job placement services, along with greater differentiation in wages.[16] Labour market policies privileged 'insiders' (mainly qualified, middle-aged males in large firms) and neglected 'outsiders'.

A similar lack of shared policy beliefs jeopardised credible commitment in social policy reform. Classically, social policy views – especially within the SPD and the trade unions – were conditioned by the presumption that economic and population growth would provide the resources for a redistributive politics of solidarity. This paradigm of social policy was increasingly challenged by those who saw its increasing expense – worsened by early retirement, the financing of unification, and an ageing population – as a major cause of competitiveness problems and hence of slowing growth, rising unemployment and increasingly acute financing problems in social policy. Social policy was uneasily poised between a 'traditional' paradigm of solidarity through redistribution (financed from economic growth) and a 'modern' paradigm of competitiveness through economic incentives to participate in the labour market.

Secondly, the Alliance proved to be a highly imperfect structure for giving credibility to a paradigm shift in policies towards unemployment and social policy, partly because of its composition and the lack of opportunity for science-based ideas to enter into and inform debate, and partly because of Schröder's reluctance to go beyond a role as *Moderator*. The Alliance represented leading figures in the federal government, the employer organisations and the trade unions rather than a collection of economic modernisers from these groups and outside experts. Hence, if Schröder wished to build strategic alliances with modernisers in the trade unions, he had to go outside the Alliance. Crucially, the trade union leadership made it clear that certain issues were of such symbolic importance that they were off the agenda, especially in labour market policy (notably area-wide collective bargaining or bold steps to create a low-wage sector). The science-based policy advice available to the Alliance used comparative research to show that willingness of trade unions to commit to long-term moderate wages policy has been at the heart of successful social pacts in Europe.[17] However, this message fell on deaf ears, as did other recommendations from the Benchmarking Group (see above). Hence the Alliance seemed doomed to fail. Science-based advice was not internal to the Alliance but a structural appendage that could be ignored.[18] The influence of the Benchmarking Group was also dependent on the reputation that Hombach – its creator – enjoyed within the Alliance. Hombach's lack of a disciplined approach diminished the credibility of the science-based advice that he had put in place, and his departure in summer 1999 pushed it into the margins. His successor as coordinator of the Alliance, Steinmeier, paid little attention to the Benchmarking Group, used the steering group as a testing board for ideas, and adopted a very flexible approach to whether, when and how proposals might be routed through its structures.

Faced by these problems in the composition and structure of the Alliance, Schröder decided, for electoral reasons, to defer labour market and social reforms to a second term. The first term's achievements were to be fiscal consolidation, tax reform and pension reform. This deferral meant that the Alliance had little relevance. Schröder was unwilling to use the Alliance to champion paradigm change in policies towards unemployment and social policy because he saw it as offering him little room for political manoeuvre. The complex division of views about unemployment within the Alliance, and the use of its structures to keep issues off the agenda, led Schröder to conclude that it served more to bind him in than to bind in employers and trade unions, or indeed ministerial colleagues who were reluctant to embrace reform, notably Riester in the Labour and Social Affairs Ministry. The Alliance was not a structure that provided external discipline but a part of the broad problem of credible commitment to structural reform. He became increasingly disillusioned with its composition, the myopic attitudes of the employers and trade unions, and the lack of evidence of any collective policy learning about unemployment. Hence he sought out political room for manoeuvre outside the Alliance. One example was working with modernisers in key trade unions like IG Bergbau, Chemie und Energie to promote ideas of longer-term, productivity-based wage bargaining and a more differentiated approach to wage bargaining within sectors. However, Schröder tried to avoid any notion of a *Machtwort* over wages and labour market policy.

Thirdly, there were problems of credible commitment facing both employers and trade unions. Both were suffering a loss of legitimacy and of negotiating power from falling membership. Membership of the unions in the German Trade Union Federation fell from 8.8 million in 1998 to 7.7 million in 2002. In 1992 some 40 per cent of the work force were trade union members; this fell to under 20 per cent in 2002. This threat to legitimacy increased the sensitivity of employer organisations and trade unions and the incentive to cultivate their clienteles by taking up tough, mobilising positions on key issues that assumed a highly symbolic significance. The credibility of the Alliance as a motor for structural reforms was further and seriously jeopardised by internal structural problems within employer and trade union organisations. The leaders of powerful trade unions like IG Metall and ver.di could not bind in their powerful regional wage negotiators; they lacked internal authority to make agreements credible.[19] The employer organisations could not make credible commitments on job creation and training places when firms take these decisions in response to market conditions. In short, the Alliance was a highly imperfect external discipline because its key participants could not make credible commitments.

This problems of credible commitment extended into the federal government. Federal ministries defended their prerogatives by reference to the principle of departmental responsibility in Article 65 of the Basic Law. The Finance Ministry stood aloof from the Alliance. This aloofness amounted to contemptuous indifference under Lafontaine. Eichel supported structural economic reform – principally to assist fiscal consolidation – but stressed the special position of budgetary law and used the constraints of the EU fiscal rules to avert commitments to new public investment programmes in favour of using extra revenue to defray debt costs. The Federal Ministry for Labour and Social Affairs under Riester – as earlier under the CDU's Norbert Blum – represented the ascendancy of the 'lump' theory of labour and of the paradigm of social policy as solidarity. Hence Schröder lacked powerful ministerial allies who were committed to the Alliance as an instrument of structural economic reform. Key federal ministries avoided having their hands bound by the Alliance. In addition, the Green Party lacked a powerful economic portfolio and any opportunity to profile itself within the Alliance. Hence Schröder's coalition partner had no real incentive to see the Alliance develop into a powerful external discipline on the work of the coalition government.

Finally, the Alliance ran into the hard rocks of the electoral timetable, a tough federal election campaign, and the coincidence of the collapse of Schröder's reputation with the employers and mounting expectation by January 2002 that the government would lose the autumn elections. In this situation the employers had no incentive to make commitments in the Alliance that might offer political advantages to Schröder. The Alliance was being drawn into a political timetable. Schröder was seeking success by calling a top-level meeting; the employers were able to deny him success with low expectations that they would be punished; whilst the trade unions were left infuriated by what they saw as the politically motivated disloyalty of the employers.

This experience left long-term scars on Schröder's conception of the value of the Alliance and made its successful revival after the federal elections highly unlikely, at least in its current form.

THE HARTZ COMMISSION ON MODERN SERVICES IN THE LABOUR MARKET: CREDIBILITY REGAINED

Paradoxically, the lost credibility of the Alliance for Jobs did not deter Schröder from a strategy of binding hands through government by commission. It produced a rethink of how best to use this mechanism for economic policy reform. The humiliations and failures of the Alliance in January 2002 and March 2003 were linked respectively to Schröder's appointment of the Hartz Commission in February 2002 and to his Agenda 2010 speech and acceleration of the work of the Rürup Commission in March 2003. Both failures signalled a serious loss of reputation as an economic moderniser, and the need to regain the initiative. A redesigned form of government by commission was seen as providing a new external discipline – 'creating facts' – and finding new ways to bind in potential opposition.

The Hartz Commission represents the most successful example of government by commission in economic reform. It produced a unanimous report that went further in advocating labour market reforms than Schröder and his officials had expected at the outset. The reasons are to be found in the circumstances of its origin; the powerful discipline of the tight electoral timetable in enabling Schröder to bind in the SPD and the trade unions; the qualities and skills of its chair, not least in negotiating his way around sensitive political symbolism; and its departure from the tripartite composition of the Alliance for Jobs. Few of these conditions are easily transferable to other settings, as the Rürup Commission showed.

The origins of the Hartz Commission were provided by the manifest failure of the job placement policies of the Bundesanstalt für Arbeit, the crisis of the labour market administration brought on by the Federal Audit Court's discovery of false statistics on job placements, and the subsequent resignation of the head of the Bundesanstalt. This crisis – which came alongside the poisonous Alliance meeting in January 2002 – represented both a threat and an opportunity to Schröder. A crisis of this type in a context of higher unemployment than when he took office, and of an imminent federal election, spelt major political danger. It also offered an opportunity to take the issue out of the hands of the traditionalists in the Federal Labour and Social Affairs Ministry. An economic moderniser from the SPD – Florian Gerster – was brought in as new head of the Bundesanstalt to implement immediate reforms, and Peter Hartz – personnel manager at Volkswagen – was asked to lead a commission to report on 'modern services for the labour market' by August 2002. In consultation with the Federal Chancellor's Office, Hartz was given the freedom to choose his own commission and a strong influence over the definition of the agenda. This crisis atmosphere placed the trade unionists and employer representatives who were committed to tripartite administration of labour market policy on the defensive. Such a context had been missing in the work of the Alliance, which lacked a similar sense of urgency to agree on essential reforms. Agenda setting was taken out of the hands of Riester, IG Metall and the DGB.

This binding in of potential opposition from the left of the SPD and the trade unions was tightened by the electoral timetable and by Schröder's commitment during the campaign to implement the Hartz report '1:1'. The labour market crisis and the uphill task facing the SPD in the federal elections in September were used by Schröder to tie the hands of traditionalists. Hartz was careful to consult with the leadership of the SPD parliamentary party and of the federal executive, and especially with Schröder in order to ensure that the commission was sensitive to overall political constraints. These consultations led the commission to avoid making specific proposals on reductions of entitlement to unemployment benefits and social assistance, though its basic principle of creating incentives to take up work rather than stay in unemployment pointed in this direction. In turn Hartz used the electoral timetable to enforce a strict discipline of confidential teamwork within the commission and to insist on the principle of unanimity in its conclusions. Indiscreet leaks to the media were avoided. The only exception was an agreed testing of ideas by Hartz in July.

The commission's effectiveness owed a great deal to the qualities of its chair and the nature of its composition. Peter Hartz brought a great deal of personal authority and practical experience to the commission, had won widespread respect for his innovative ideas as head of personnel at Volkswagen, enjoyed very close personal relations with Schröder that went back to his period as head of government in Lower Saxony, and – not least – had the trust of Schröder. His first success was in securing a relatively small commission of 15 that avoided the tripartite principle of the Alliance. It included modernisers from the SPD (like Harald Schartau) and the trade unions, management consultants, and academic experts on labour market policy. The DGB, IG Metall and ver.di leaderships – as well as Riester's ministry – were excluded from membership. Above all, Hartz was a hands-on chair, with clear ideas that derived from his own work as personnel director for Volkswagen in Wolfsburg and with a strong preference for developing these ideas with the management consultants and academic experts on the commission. Commission members were kept busy in working groups, and the Federal Ministry of Labour and Social Affairs at a distance, whilst the main work was done elsewhere under the close control of Hartz and his own team. Hartz was the motor of reform, not *Moderator* like Süssmuth in the Commission on Immigration or Schröder in the Alliance.

The key basis of his success in producing a relatively ambitious and unanimous report was gaining initial agreement on core principles that would drive the work and proposals of the commission. The main principles were that a structure of incentives was needed to encourage people into work and out of unemployment; that the core problem was the lengthening average period of unemployment (from less than 10 weeks in the 1970s to 33 weeks and above the EU and OECD averages); that a modern customer-oriented and efficient labour market administration was required; and that policy should seek to draw on both comparative knowledge of labour market policy and examples of best practice. These principles gave unity and an underlying logic to the various proposals.

The Hartz report represented a major shock to many in the SPD and the trade unions.[20] It weakened the tripartite principle in labour market administration in favour of a more managerial, customer-focused and decentralised approach to job placement based around new job centres. It created the instruments for developing a subsidised 'low-wage' sector in personal services through 'mini-jobs' (Hartz would have preferred to extend its coverage, as happened during the legislative process); encouraged self-employment and discouraged 'black market' work through the 'Ich-AG' (personal or family firms); and proposed personal service agencies (PSAs) as temporary employment agencies, from which firms could hire workers at preferential rates. Even more controversially it signalled that the burden of proof about whether someone was genuinely seeking work would shift from the labour market administration to the unemployed person; that the length of period for drawing unemployment benefit should be reduced to 12 months; and that unemployment assistance and social benefit should be integrated into a single payment at a level that would encourage active job search.

Despite this success in producing a bold, unanimous report, the credibility of the Hartz report was challenged on three fronts. First, ordo-liberal economists attacked as highly unrealistic its goal of halving unemployment by 2005 through costly measures like PSAs and through measures like the Ich-AG that were likely to involve displacement and substitution effects in the labour market rather than new jobs. Effective job placement presupposed that there were jobs, an assumption that was highly problematic where unemployment was highest – in the east. Moreover, job creation depended on lowering wage costs and non-wage labour costs through appropriate flexibility in wage bargaining and social policies that uncoupled financing of benefits from work. Hartz did not tackle these issues.[21] Secondly, politicians in the east – CDU as well as SPD and PDS – argued that Hartz's emphasis on job placement was not just irrelevant to the east but that the integration of unemployment assistance with social benefits would especially disadvantage the east. The effects of Hartz would be felt through loss of income rather than access to new jobs. Thirdly, traditionalists in the SPD and in the trade unions sought to turn the debate back to the principle of social justice and solidarity, for instance 'equal pay for equal work'. The very narrow majority of the SPD/Green coalition after the 2002 federal elections suggested potentially increased difficulties in implementing Hartz.

Schröder's determination to realise his campaign commitment of '1:1' implementation was symbolised by the dismantlement of the Federal Ministry of Labour and Social Affairs, the creation of a new Federal Ministry of Economics and Labour, and the appointment of an energetic arch-SPD economic moderniser, Wolfgang Clement' as its new 'super' minister. Clement was to champion the four complex Hartz laws through parliament. To provide political cover for Clement in the tough negotiations ahead, and to bind in Hartz himself, a top-level steering group on implementation was created under Schröder and including Clement, Hartz and Steinmeier. However, this device did not stop Hartz and other commission members going public with their criticisms of emasculation of the report in November 2002. Hartz condemned the lack of political courage in dealing with the trade unions' insistence on the principle of equal pay for equal work, with the result that the incentive for firms to take on temporary workers from the PSAs was being reduced. He also argued that implementation had been undermined by the unwillingness of the Finance Ministry to grant sufficiently generous tax and contribution concessions to stimulate the 'low-wage' sector.[22] Others argued that the emergency higher pension and health contributions agreed by the government were 'poison' for Hartz because they increased non-wage costs.[23]

Against this background, implementation was not completely '1:1' in part because some compromises were made to placate opposition (notably over wage levels in temporary employment), and in part because some proposals proved impractical or unpromising (like the 'capital for work' scheme, training vouchers and employment audits for firms). In other respects, however, implementation proved bolder, especially in relation to the scope of 'mini-jobs', which were extended beyond personal services. Changes to unemployment benefit and the flat-rate, means-tested payment for the new unemployment benefit II (which replaced unemployment assistance and social assistance and was lower than the earlier unemployment assistance) were also radical.

This boldness in implementation owed much to the use of another mechanism for tying the hands of opposition within the SPD – the need to achieve agreement in the arbitration committee (*Vermittlungsausschuss*) where measures – like the new unemployment benefit II – affected the administrative, financial or territorial interests of the states and could be vetoed in the Bundesrat. Just as the coalition government's majority in the Bundestag was weakened, so in February 2003 the loss of Lower Saxony and a CDU majority government in Hesse following state elections strengthened the CDU/CSU majority in the Bundesrat. This majority could be used to extract further concessions in labour market reform. Furthermore, the credibility of this threat was increased by the way in which under Angela Merkel's leadership – and strongly influenced by Friedrich Merz in the parliamentary party and by Roland Koch, head of government in Hesse – the CDU had moved sharply in an ordo-liberal direction. This ideological shift within the CDU – and the greater affinities between modernisers like Clement and Merz than between Clement and traditionalists in the SPD like Ottmar Schreiner – meant that the credibility of the arbitration committee as an external discipline on the SPD grew.

The strategy of binding hands by the Hartz Commission – complemented by the use of the arbitration committee in the subsequent legislative process – served to focus and expedite a long-term process of paradigm change in labour market policy towards a greater emphasis on individual responsibility (*aktivierende Arbeitsmarktpolitik*). More broadly, it opened up a debate within the SPD about redefining solidarity as a two-way and conditional process between the individual and the state. Despite its limitations as an approach to reducing unemployment, the Hartz Commission forced traditionalists to re-examine their core beliefs in relation to new evidence about how labour markets functions. Its value was in structuring debate in a particular direction.

THE RÜRUP COMMISSION ON THE SUSTAINABLE FINANCING OF THE SOCIAL INSURANCE SYSTEMS: CREDIBILITY SALVAGED?

In contrast to Hartz, the Rürup Commission on reform of care, health and pension policies was less successful in providing Schröder with a means to bind in potential opposition to radical reform. The agenda was much more difficult to manage because of it scope, complexity and the conflicts that it generated; its chair proved highly controversial; its working methods were more chaotic; its members prone to public conflicts that excited media attention; its chair locked in a duel with the adviser of the Federal Health and Social Affairs minister; and its final report of August 2003 notable for various minority votes. Above all, the commission failed to achieve either unanimity or even a majority behind a basic policy model that would drive bold health reforms, let alone a timetable for decisions. Rürup sought to make the connection between the two commissions by stressing their complementary roles in bringing down unemployment: Rürup by reducing the high non-wage labour costs caused by the way in which social insurance was financed through employment and the vicious circle to which they gave rise (see the contribution by Streeck and Trampusch to this volume). However, from the outset he sought to manage expectations by stressing the differences in scope and nature of the subject matter. Hartz had focused on practical issues of labour market organisation; Rürup was concerned with big issues of distribution of resources across generations and social groups and access to fundamentally important services for all. In particular, because pensions involved accumulated property rights, step-by-step reform was the only feasible approach. The Rürup Commission was also limited in how bold it could be on health reform, because of the combination of formidable organised interests (doctors, hospitals, chemists, pharmaceutical companies, health insurers) with the conflicting political values that lay behind different long-term financing models. By emphasising the risks of failure at the outset, and the differences from Hartz, Rürup sought to reduce the problem of credibility that he faced.[24]

The long-term influence of the Rürup Commission stemmed from asking systemic questions about the future of German social policy, focusing public debate on the prime requirement of reforms to social policies that reduce non-wage labour costs, and identifying the need for political choice between the two main policy models in health (citizens' insurance versus per capita premium). Along with the consolidation policy of Eichel, it helped to stimulate a debate within – as well as outside – the SPD about social justice in the context of demographic developments (an ageing population) and of competitiveness pressures from globalisation and Europeanisation. The SPD was confronted with a new public debate about inter-generational justice, notably in pensions, and about financing social policies so that they promoted employment that challenged cherished beliefs and symbols.

More specifically, the Rürup Commission promoted the ideas – highly controversial within the SPD and a policy reversal – of pensions at 67 (its introduction in a step-by-step process from 2011 to 2035) and of a sustainability factor in the formula for calculating pensions – so that, by 2030, pensions would fall from 48 to 40.1 per cent of the average wage. Though a political consensus for pensions at 67 could not be found, debate had shifted to agreement on the need to stop costly early retirement and raise the *de facto* pension age above 60. In addition, the Rürup Commission provided the rationale and support for taking some health services (like sickness pay) out of tripartite financing, for new charges for visiting the doctor and increased charges for medicines, and for greater competition in provision of health services. The effects on employers' costs from the health reforms were real, but modest because little had been done to tackle the basic issue of uncoupling the financing of social policies from employment. The importance of this issue was underlined in the widely accepted formula that a one percentage point reduction in non-wage labour costs creates around 100,000 new full-time jobs. By 2006 the health reforms of the Rürup Commission are estimated (by Rürup) to deliver a reduction of some 0.7 per cent.[25] The target of reducing non-wage labour costs to

40 per cent (from 41.3) was used to give focus and coherence to the work of the commission.

The Rürup Commission was marked by its origins in the chaotic and confusing conditions of the SPD/Green coalition after the September 2002 elections: the sense of economic and financial crisis; Eichel's insistence on an immediate package of tax rises and increased social contributions; the lack of a convincing strategy for handling the crisis or for making sense of increasing non-wage labour costs and reducing consumer spending power at this time; and mounting criticisms of Schröder's lack of leadership within the SPD. The Rürup Commission was part of the coalition agreement, promoted by Schröder as a symbol of the will to reform, and argued for strongly by the Greens as a device for binding the government more firmly into making reductions in non-wage labour costs the central objective of economic reform. Its agenda was extended beyond health to pensions as the Greens' price for accepting the pension contribution increase and, above all, as a means of restoring the credibility lost so quickly after the election by giving new momentum and coherence to economic reform. The association of the Rürup Commission with political profiling by the Green Party as the reform motor of the coalition irritated Ulla Schmidt and many in the SPD.

The commission was appointed in November 2002, well before Agenda 2010 was launched. However, there were two links to Agenda 2010. Firstly, under Steinmeier the Federal Chancellor's Office worked in November–December 2002 to produce a major reform strategy paper that prioritised reduction of non-wage costs (the mandate of Rürup) and that laid the basis for the launch of 'Schröder II' in contrast to the Chancellor as *Moderator* ('Schröder I'). The Rürup Commission was identified as central to providing the ideas on reducing non-wage labour costs that would complement the ideas from Hartz, and it was asked to give a new centrality to pension reform as the largest expenditure item for the federal government. The Steinmeier paper, the Hartz report and the ongoing work of the Rürup Commission provided the substance of Agenda 2010, on the basis of which Schröder could redefine his role as *Motor* of reform. The strategy paper offered powerful new support to Rürup, not least in being bolder on pension reform especially in revising the pension formula.

Secondly, the launch of Agenda 2010 led Steinmeier to argue the case for an acceleration of the work of the Rürup Commission on health policy, the close coordination of its ideas on long-term financial sustainability with the proposals of Ulla Schmidt, Federal Minister for Health and Social Policy, on structural reform, and the value of using the Rürup Commission to bind in Schmidt to a more ambitious reform programme. Rürup and Schmidt were being pressed to work together to produce a comprehensive reform concept as part of Agenda 2010. This fast-evolving and complex political context confused rather than clarified the early work of the commission and diminished rather than strengthened its credibility.

In contrast to Hartz, the Rürup Commission lacked the external discipline of a tight electoral timetable. Established in November 2002, it was scheduled to report in August 2003. This period was seen as consistent with its large work load (care, health and pensions) and the complexities and controversies of the issues as well as with Rürup's insistence on a quality product. However, by February 2003 the Federal Chancellor's Office was pressing on Rürup the discipline of having health reform legislation in place during 2003 in good time to produce discernible results in time for major state elections in 2005 and state and federal elections in 2006. For this reason the working party on health was expected to produce its main recommendations, in close coordination with Ulla Schmidt, by May 2003. This external disciplining by Steinmeier was also a response to a perception of chaos in the work of the commission, with Schröder threatening to dissolve it unless it showed greater cohesion. The Hartz Commission began its work in a context of a tight electoral timetable; the Rürup Commission had discipline enforced on it belatedly by an angry Schröder. Part of the problem was that the real pain from the financial problems of the health and pension systems lay in the period from 2010. The solution was for Rürup to focus on the urgent need to tackle a problem of non-wage labour costs that was already inflicting pain on the labour market.

Partly because of political circumstances, partly because of the composition of the commission, and partly because of his own qualities, Rürup proved a less effective chair than Hartz. First and foremost, Schmidt was a very reluctant supporter of the commission and of Rürup's appointment, their different styles (she integrative, he provocative) led to a difficult relationship, whilst Rürup – unlike Hartz – was not close to Schröder's inner circle. Hence he operated without the clear structure of political support that Hartz had enjoyed. Also, unlike Riester, Schmidt was one of the two new 'super' ministers and enjoyed strong support within the SPD parliamentary party. Rürup's one advantage was that key officials in Schmidt's ministry were less opposed to the ideas circulating in the Rürup Commission than officials in the labour market divisions of the former Federal Ministry of Labour and Social Affairs had been to the Hartz Commission. However, Schmidt was resistant to what she perceived as the clear efforts of the Federal Chancellor's Office to bind her hands through the Rürup Commission and discredit her image as a reformer. She sensed that the commission had been imposed on her. Hence she aimed to undermine its capacity to bind her in by an active role in appointing the members of the commission (unlike Riester with Hartz, and getting two of her key people in its ranks); encouraged her adviser on the committee – Karl Lauterbach – to act as a strong counterweight to Rürup; stressed the division of labour between her work on the expenditure side of social policy and Rürup's on long-term financing; got the principles for her reform concept into the coalition agreement; and sought to align herself closely with the SPD parliamentary party to increase her freedom of manoeuvre. Crucially, backed by Franz Müntefering, chair of the SPD parliamentary party, Schmidt ruled out any pre-commitment to '1:1' implementation on the Hartz model: 'Hartz is Hartz and Schmidt is Schmidt'.[26] She was intent on asserting her ministerial autonomy on social policy and her role as a cautious balancer between modernisers and traditionalists, sensitive to the need for reforms to be consistent with sustaining 'welfare and social justice at a high level'. To a greater extent than with Hartz, the Federal Chancellor's Office was kept at a distance from the work of the Rürup Commission, and Schröder induced to declare that the Rürup report was 'keine Bibel'.

Secondly, Schmidt ensured that the commission was much more broadly representative of opinion than the Hartz Commission and consequently – with 26 members – much larger in size. It was an unwieldy commission consisting in part of modernisers, in part of traditionalists (like Ursula Engelen-Kefer from the DGB); in part, academic experts, in part representatives from key organised interests in social policy; in part, management consultants and industrial representatives, in part public officials. However, the representative bodies of the doctors, hospitals, pharmaceutical industry and chemists were excluded. There was no wish to repeat the experience of the so-called *Runder Tisch* on reform of the health system at the end of the previous legislative period under Schmidt. It had achieved little more than a declaration on the advantages of preventive medicine. Despite this attempt to learn from the lessons of past efforts at government by commission in health, the diversity and size of the Rürup Commission suggested from the outset that unanimity on a single policy model for health policy reform would be difficult, if not impossible to achieve. In addition, Rürup's potential to shape the work of the commission was reduced by the appointment of Heinrich Tiemann, Schmidt's State Secretary (and formerly working on the Alliance for Jobs in the Federal Chancellery), and Karl Lauterbach, an academic adviser of Schmidt and member of the Advisory Council on Health, as members. Lauterbach was known to have an opposed view about the basic model for social policy model to that of Rürup. Hence the Rürup Commission started life with a much greater problem of credibility than the Hartz Commission. Its complexity – allied to its wide and potentially unwieldy agenda – suggested to many that it was destined to fail. Its credibility as a mechanism to bind in the SPD and the trade unions was compromised by the way in which its composition replicated the wider problems in public debate about social policy rather than offered a way of recasting the debate.

Rürup had his own credibility problems as chair. He had the advantage of SPD membership, a reputation for a detailed mastery of social policy issues, enormous energy and the image of a 'super' adviser of the federal government who was able to adapt pragmatically to political realities: chair of the Social Policy Advisory Council (*Sozialbeirat*) and of the Advisory Council on Economic Policy (*Sachverstaendigenrat*). He had also played an important advisory role in the so-called 'Riester pension', a supplementary pension outside the framework of statutory social insurance. More problematically, during the Kohl government, he had advised Norbert Blum (CDU) on the introduction of a demographic factor into the pension formula (reversed by the Schröder government on taking office). Rürup had also used speeches, interviews, articles and his numerous advisory roles to speak out forcefully on the need for radical reforms to make social policies both sustainable in the face of demographic developments and consistent with economic competitiveness. In consequence, Rürup had enemies in the SPD parliamentary party, which resolved to appoint its own group of expert advisers to parallel the work of the distrusted Rürup Commission.

His work as chair was made difficult by a reputation for intellectual provocation and vanity and a consequent lack of confidence in his ability to develop teamwork and lead so diverse a commission to produce a unanimous report. This credibility problem was deepened by the forthright way in which Rürup – as designated commission chair – presented controversial ideas (like pensions at 67, excluding certain benefits like sick pay from health insurance, and a per capita premium model for financing health that meant the end of the parity principle of employer and employee financing). These ideas struck at key symbols of SPD thinking; Schmidt supported a flexible pension age depending on years of service (the DGB view), and publicly opposed the premium model. Notably, even Wolfgang Clement offered no support for these ideas of Rürup. Earlier Rürup had sharply criticised the neglect of health and labour market policies by the main political parties in their election programmes, as well as SPD and trade union fixation on 1970s' thinking about 'employee-centred' rather than 'employment-centred' policies. Against this background, Rürup faced an internal credibility problem when he sought to enforce the rule that commission members should avoid public commentary and position taking because these actions undermined internal consensus-building processes and the prospects for unanimity. Tensions within the commission emerged as early as January 2003 (especially between Lauterbach and Bernd Raffelhüschen) and erupted by April 2003, when two members ventilated their fears and frustrations by calling (supported by Seehofer) for its dissolution. Rürup faced four main dissidents who wished to protect the traditional policy model of solidarity and complained about Rürup's inability to stand up to political interference and his disorganised approach. The catalyst was the presentation of the preliminary pension reform concept and anger at the way in which Rürup, Lauterbach and Wagner had agreed the health policy structural reform programme outside the health policy working party of the commission, in the context of strong political intervention on them to compromise.

Rürup was able to reduce the credibility problems of the commission by exploiting the new momentum created by the Federal Chancellor's Office strategy paper of December 2002 (it spoke of 'fundamental reform' of the social security system), by Agenda 2010, and by the EU deadline of May for proposals to consolidate the German budget. The commission's role was redefined as giving substance to Agenda 2010 and its message of courage for fundamental reform and fleshing out Germany's stability programme for the EU. Schröder used a combination of methods to strengthen and give greater discipline to the commission and to bind in Schmidt and the SPD more tightly: he threatened to dissolve the commission unless its public squabbles ceased and it displayed more discipline; he drastically shortened the timetable for its health reform proposals to April; and, in return, he made Schmidt coordinate her forthcoming health expenditure proposals with the Rürup Commission with the aim not just of ensuring overall coherence in health reform but also of using Rürup to put Schmidt under pressure to be bolder. The Federal Chancellor's Office wanted deeper cuts than Schmidt contemplated and trusted Rürup more than Schmidt to deliver on a reduced health contribution rate. In the process Rürup's position was strengthened as the representative of Schröder's mission to achieve a drastic cut in non-wage labour costs. In the Federal Chancellor's Office Schmidt was seen as having an image problem in relation to 'Schroder II': her record as Health Minister since January 2001 suggested someone who was too keen to avoid tough issues and confrontation. Moreover, Schröder was convinced that Schmidt had tried to use the composition of the Rürup Commission to sabotage its prospects.

The limitations of the Rürup Commission as a strategy for binding in were revealed most starkly in the failure in its final report of August 2003 to resolve the central long-term issue of the appropriate health policy model around which to orientate a reduction in non-wage labour costs. This failure was apparent by April 2003, so entrenched were positions. Despite pressure from the Federal Chancellor's Office to provide Schröder with an agreed compromise, it confined itself to outlining the advantages and disadvantages of the main models and leaving the decision to politicians. The conflict was polarised between Rürup, who sought to construct a majority for the per capita or premium model, and Lauterbach, who represented Schmidt's view that this outcome must be prevented. Lauterbach – backed by Frank Nullmeier – promoted the citizens insurance (*Buergerversicherung*) model, which had support from the Greens, key social policy figures in the SPD, the CDU/CSU parliamentary spokesperson on health, Horst Seehofer (CSU), and the consumer protection lobby. This 'solidarity' model offered adaptation of the existing social insurance system and the combination of a reduction of non-wage labour costs (by 2–3 per cent) with redistribution by extending contributors to include the self-employed, professionals and *Beamte* and levying contributions on such sources as rental, dividend and savings income. A key political problem of this model – which led Schröder to distance himself from it – was the implication that private insurance would be phased out. In contrast, Rürup – with support from Gert Wagener and more broadly from economists – advocated the radical solution of a premium model, based on the principle that all adults would pay the same insurance premium, irrespective of income, with those on lower incomes receiving a tax subsidy. This model had the advantage of a complete severance between financing health and work and was justified by Rürup as a paradigm shift from a solidarity system to an 'employment-oriented' system of social policy in which employers' costs would fall by some 7 per cent. Financing health would be uncoupled from employment and the economic cycle, on the Swiss model; whilst the state would use the tax system to compensate lower-income groups. However, it struck at the heart of the principle of parity financing of health insurance that was of high symbolic importance to the trade unions and the left of the SPD. It also raised difficult questions for Eichel about how the federal government would finance the large tax subsidies that the premium system required. Faced with the unwillingness of Schröder to offer clear backing to either reform model (he rejected Rürup's proposal as socially unjust), and the opposition of Eichel, Schmidt, Lauterbach and the trade unionists on the committee, Rürup's fall-back position was to avoid outright rejection of his model in the final report in favour of leaving the decision to politicians. In consequence, unlike with Hartz, Schröder did not get a clear consensual reform concept that could be used to bind the hands of the SPD or a clear timetable for early decisions that he could use as a discipline. The result was procrastination.

The limitations of the Rürup Commission as a device for binding in potential opposition induced the Federal Chancellor's Office to explore early-stage informal 'grand coalition' talks with the CDU/CSU leadership about health reform. These talks had the strategic advantage of simultaneously disciplining debate within the SPD, putting the CDU/CSU under pressure to clarify its position and exploiting its internal power struggles, and offering a distraction from the SPD's internal problems. The incentive to use the device of informal grand coalition was also strengthened by the increased majority of the CDU/CSU in the Bundesrat after the two state elections of February 2003. The tactic of buying off individual CDU/SPD states that Schröder had used in the previous legislative period with the tax reform was no longer viable. In turn, the CDU/CSU could be induced to collaborate in informal grand coalition by the threat of splitting health reform into two bills and of putting key reform provisions in the one that did not require Bundesrat support. This strategy of using informal grand coalition as a discipline was also advocated by Rürup as a means of helping him to push the agenda of radical health policy reform within his commission. He was aware that the CDU was likely to be much more sympathetic to the premium model, which was gaining support in the party's own Herzog Commission on reform of social security (another device for binding in opposition to radical change in the CDU). The combined disciplines of the Rürup Commission and of informal grand coalition served to constrain the potential for Schmidt and the SPD parliamentary party to block change.

CONCLUSION: FROM SCHRÖDER I TO SCHRÖDER II

Economic reform confronted the Schröder governments with the need to make difficult strategic choices in the complex context of the changing pressure and urgency of policy problems and of powerful institutional veto players. These choices were guided by the objective of maximising what was judged to be a limited freedom of manoeuvre to create majorities, above all with respect to intra-party opposition. Though these choices varied over time, especially between Schröder I and Schröder II, this paper has shown that binding the hands of potential opposition has been the most consistent strategic choice. Its choice reflected an awareness of the tight constraints in a semi-sovereign polity of interlocking politics, of limited resources for policy leadership and of dependency on the likely moves of other actors. These constraints made use of the strategy of direct threat of legislative action unattractive – for instance, to introduce greater flexibility and opt-outs into wage bargaining.

Europeanisation and government by commission presented the Schröder governments with different challenges. Europeanisation was a double-edged sword: useful for binding the hands both of domestic opposition and recalcitrant member states, but a threat in case of a misfit that cast into sharp profile the credibility of the federal government for meeting its commitments. In short, Europeanisation could cause as well as help solve problems of credibility. This increasingly overt risk from misfit led the Schröder governments to embrace a strategy of negotiating binding hands that promoted co-evolution of EU and domestic policies rather than conflict. The result was a softening of the Stability and Growth Pact in 2005 and a hesitation about entering into precise commitments within the Lisbon process. The monetary policies and exchange-rate market interventions of the ECB were, by contrast, not amenable to a negotiated binding of hands. The combination of relatively high real interest rates (compared to other Euro Area states) with unwillingness of the ECB to intervene to prevent appreciation of the euro in 2003–04 acted as a potent external discipline that – along with the policy model of structural supply-side reforms promoted by the ECB – strengthened pressures for reforms to labour market and social policies to promote employment.

Government by commission demonstrated an evolution in strategic choices. The Alliance for Jobs represented Schröder I. Recognising the political difficulties and dangers of reform, he opted to move slowly by a careful tactics of strategic sequencing that would build broad support for future reforms: beginning with budget consolidation and tax reform, moving on to pension reform, nurturing trade union support through a new works constitution law – and deferring more difficult labour market and social policy reforms till after the 2002 federal elections. Binding hands in the Alliance was accompanied by Schröder's strategy of acting as honest broker, balancing and mediating between employer and trade union interests. The Hartz Commission, the Rürup Commission and Agenda 2010 represented Schröder II: a response to the perceived depth and urgency of the accumulating problems that had disrupted the tactics of strategic sequencing, and a recognition that Schröder's historical reputation as economic reformer was at stake. Schröder II moved away from the strategic choices of binding hands/honest broker to binding hands/sustained direct and indirect pressure. In short, binding hands by commission was never a stand-alone strategy, but at the same time the most enduring theme and one that gives coherence to the narrative of economic reform under Schröder.

As the Alliance for Jobs, Hartz and Rürup illustrate, government by commission varied enormously in its credibility and produced variegated effects. This essay has identified a range of factors that help explain these differences of success:

- Careful delimitation of the remit and objectives of the commission so that the chair can focus its work
- Whether there is a professional consensus about the basic policy model, in short an existing or emerging epistemic community that shares a body of normative and causal beliefs and a policy project
- Whether the commission is composed in a way that enhances the potential for orchestrating a professional consensus, especially by giving primacy to those backing reform over those appointed because they holding particular positions
- Whether the chair combines ideational leadership with the capabilities of acting as a team builder and the skills to construct package deals
- Whether there is a firm timetable to act as a discipline on the commission's work
- Whether it is backed by a clear, unified political leadership that pre-commits to implementation
- Whether key actors have the instruments under their control to make their commitments credible
- Whether the committee can negotiate its way around sensitive symbolic issues.

Varying with the extent to which it is a majority report or unanimous, commissions represent a powerful indirect pressure. They create facts by setting the agenda in particular ways – whether strengthening incentives to work, lengthening working life, or decoupling financing of social policy from work. It is difficult to for a governing party like the SPD to make policy against a commission.

A larger view of these mechanisms for binding in potential opposition suggests that the top-down, vertical effects of Europeanisation have been less important than the instrumentalisation of Europeanisation and of government by commission by German political leadership to change expectations about the scope, direction, timing and tempo of domestic reforms by forms of pre-commitment. Even in the case of Europeanisation, binding in remains pre-eminently a 'bottom-up' process. The incentive to embrace and use these external disciplines is increased in a polity that is characterised by powerful, entrenched veto players, intra-party conflicts within the SPD, and the domestic inertia of an 'interlocking politics' of political parties and federalism. The problems are defined by the domestic limitations of extra-party and extra-parliamentary consensus building; these problems are not just tactical – what one can get away with – but touch on deeper issues of democratic legitimacy. Hence, for both tactical and democratic reasons, use of the strategy of binding hands is hedged with great political caution.

This analysis of the political management of different commissions shows that problems of credible commitment vary considerably both across space and over time. Credibility is a complex, multi-faceted and on-going problem in the arts of politics, above all in the use of time, timing and tempo in economic reform – when to bind hands, over which issues, and how. As this study illustrates, both the arbitration committee (as with Hartz) and informal grand coalition (as with health reform) have been important accompanying mechanisms for binding hands. However, an elected government needs first and foremost to bring credible proposals to the table. In this sense government by commission, like Europeanisation, has priority as a device for building credibility.

NOTES

This paper draws on extensive interviews conducted as part of a Nuffield Foundation grant and also archival work conducted during a period spent in Berlin with support from the German Academic Exchange Service (DAAD). My thanks are due both to the Nuffield Foundation and to DAAD.

1. A. Lijphart, *Patterns of Democracy: Government Forms and Performance in Thirty-Six Countries* (New Haven: Yale University Press, 1999).
2. E. Holtmann and H. Voelzkow (eds.), *Zwischen Wettbewerbs- und Verhandlungsdemokratie: Analysen zum Regierungssystem der Bundesrepublik Deutschland* (Opladen: Westdeutscher Verlag, 2000).
3. P. Katzenstein, *Policy and Politics in West Germany. The Growth of a Semisovereign State* (Philadelphia: Temple University Press, 1987); F. Scharpf, 'The Joint Decision Trap: Lessons from German Federalism and European Integration', *Public Administration* 66 (1988), pp.239–78.
4. See e.g. S. Green and W. Paterson (eds.), *Governance in Contemporary Germany: The Semi-Sovereign State Revisited* (Cambridge: Cambridge University Press, 2005: K. Dyson and K. Goetz (eds.), *Germany, Europe and the Politics of Constraint* (Oxford: Oxford University Press, Proceedings of the British Academy 119, 2003), chapter 17. Also G. Tsebelis, *Veto Players: How Political Institutions Work* (Princeton: Princeton University Press, 2002).
5. K. Dyson, 'Economic Policies: From Pace-Setter to Beleaguered Player', in Dyson and Goetz (eds.), *Germany, Europe and the Politics of Constraint*, pp.201–30; K. Dyson, 'Germany and the Euro: Redefining EMU, Handling Paradox and Managing Uncertainty and Contingency', in K. Dyson (ed.), *European States and the Euro: Europeanization, Variation, and Convergence* (Oxford: Oxford University Press, 2002), pp.173–211.
6. See H.-J. Papier, 'Reform an Haupt und Gliedern', *Frankfurter Allgemeine Zeitung*, 31 Jan. 2003. Also H. Prantl, 'Schröders Räterepublik', *Süddeutsche Zeitung*, 19 May 2001, p.4.
7. Classically W. Nordhaus, 'The Political Business Cycle', *Review of Economic Studies* 42 (1975), pp.169–90; K. Rogoff, 'Equilibrium Political Budget Cycles', *NBER Working Paper* 2428 (1987); A. Alesina, 'Politics and Business Cycles in Industrial Democracies', *Economic Policy* 8 (1989), pp.55–98.
8. F. Kydland and E. Prescott, 'Rules rather than Discretion: The Inconsistency of Optimal Plans', *Journal of Political Economy* 85 (1977), pp.473–91.
9. R. Barro and D. Gordon, 'Rules, Discretion and Reputation in a Model of Monetary Policy', *Journal of Monetary Economics* 12 (1983), pp.101–22.
10. D. Lax and J. Sebenius, 'Thinking Coalitionally: Party Arithmetic, Process Opportunism, and Strategic Sequencing', in H. Peyton Young (ed.), *Negotiation Analysis* (Ann Arbor: University of Michigan Press, 1991), pp.153–93.
11. See DPA 120956, Jan. 2003.
12. These qualities come out clearly in his long interview 'Am Ende der ersten Halbzeit', *Die Zeit*, 15 Aug. 2002, p.3.

13. See J. Hogrefe, *Gerhard Schröder: Ein Porträt* (Berlin: Siedler, 2002), p.27.
14. Presse- und Informationsamt der Bundesregierung, *Bündnis für Arbeit, Ausbildung und Wettbewerbsfähigkeit. Ziele, Organisation, Arbeitsweise* (Bonn: Schriftenreihe Berichte und Dokumentation, May 1999).
15. For a trade union perspective see H.-J. Arlt and S. Nehls (eds.), *Bündnis für Arbeit* (Opladen: Westdeutscher Verlag, 1999).
16. See e.g. 'Für eine neue Solidarität', in H.-J. Arlt and S. Nehls (eds) *ibid.*
17. A. Hassel, 'Soziale Pakte in Europa', *Gewerkschatfliche Monatshefte* 47 (1998).
18. G. Schmid, 'Gestaltung des Wandels durch wissenschaftliche Beratung', in S. Ramge and G. Schmid (eds.), *Management of Change in der Politik: Reformstrategien am Beispiel der Arbeitsmarkt- und Beschäftigungspolitik* (Münster: Waxmann Verlag, 2003).
19. See A. Hassel, 'Der mühsame Sprung ueber den eigenen Schatten', *Frankfurter Rundschau*, 25 Jan. 2002.
20. Hartz Kommission, *Moderne Dinstleistungen am Arbeitsmarkt* (Berlin: Bundesministerium für Arbeit and Sozialordnung, Aug. 2002).
21. 'Ökonomen halten Hartz-Ziele für unrealistisch', *Frankfurter Allgemeine Zeitung*, 17 Aug. 2002.
22. Spiegel-Gespräch: 'Mein Part ist erfüllt', *Der Spiegel* 48 (2002), pp.31–3.
23. 'Streiten im Konsens', *Der Tagesspiegel*, 8 Nov. 2002, p.4.
24. Spiegel-Gespräch, 'Ich habe Laeuse im Bauch', *Der Spiegel* 47, 18 Nov. 2002, pp.112–17.
25. T. Pache, 'Agenda entlastet Wirtschaft um Milliarden', *Financial Times Deutschland*, 16 Aug. 2004.
26. 'Ideengeber, Minenhund, Rammbock, Prellbock, Blitzableiter, Schiedsrichter', *Frankfurter Allgemeine Zeitung*, 6 Jan. 2003, p.4.

The Party Politics of Economic Reform: Public Opinion, Party Positions and Partisan Cleavages

STEPHEN PADGETT

The electoral backlash against Agenda 2010 and the Hartz IV labour market reform underlines the central role of public opinion in the politics of economic reform. Land elections and opinion polls[1] convey the unequivocal message that, despite the impoverishment of the domestic economy, the German public is unprepared to countenance remedial measures involving reform and retrenchment in the welfare state. Mid-way through its second term, electoral logic prevailed upon the Schröder government to call time-out on the reform process, leaving the structural problems of welfare state finance unresolved.

It is argued in this study that German resistance to welfare retrenchment is attributable in part to a long-term failure of the main German parties to *cultivate* public opinion to accept economic realities. The argument is rooted in the directional variant of Downsian theory that maintains that parties do not merely accommodate or follow public opinion, but that they also have a capacity to shape it, and that 'preference shaping' depends on the intensity of the 'messages' that parties deliver to voters. A cross-national perspective will be used to compare trends in German public opinion to those in other countries, and to test the argument that support for welfare retrenchment is related to the intensity with which parties articulate the reform message.

The essay also investigates the impact of party messages on the *structure* of public opinion. Where parties adopt emphatic and polarised positions on an issue that is important to citizens, we would expect to find a close relationship between issue preferences and voting, reflected in sharp partisan cleavages in public opinion. If, on the other hand, parties play down their differences on issues, voter preferences will make less impact on electoral choice and partisan cleavages in public opinion will be weak. This consensual logic may be self-perpetuating. Parties may be discouraged from embracing reform agendas by the unpredictability of electoral realignments triggered by activating issues that have previously remained dormant in electoral choice.

The strategic choices that parties make between preference *shaping* and preference *accommodation* and between *competition* and *consensus* have been related to party system configuration. It is argued in this article that by accentuating the quest for the median voter, the majoritarian logic of bi-polar party systems favours strategies of preference accommodation. In multi-party systems, the median voter syndrome is relaxed, allowing more scope for directional strategies of preference shaping. German tendencies towards 'reform by stealth' and 'the politics of centrality'[2] may thus reflect a centripetal party system dynamic that revolves around majoritarian competition between the CDU/CSU and the SPD.

PUBLIC OPINION, PARTY POSITION AND PARTISAN CLEAVAGES

The relationship between parties and public opinion is conceptualised in Downsian theories of political competition.[3] Voters, it is assumed, behave like consumers, evaluating the issue positions that parties adopt against their own preferences and interests and voting accordingly. Driven by vote-maximising motives, parties locate themselves in *proximity* to the preferences of the majority of voters. Proximity theory sees voter preferences as exogenous and 'given'. Parties thus have little choice but to accommodate or follow public opinion in a quest for the median voter. This perspective casts the political problem of economic reform in particularly sharp relief. Across most developed countries, *public opinion* is highly supportive of the welfare state and resistant to welfare retrenchment.[4] Vote seeking parties are geared to the accommodation of voter preferences and will therefore be reluctant to embrace welfare state reform.[5]

Whilst *proximity* theory assumes voter preferences to be impervious to party influence, the *directional* variant grants parties the capacity for policy leadership via 'preference shaping'. In directional theory, however, preference shaping is crucially dependent on the *intensity* of the 'messages' that parties convey to voters.[6] Voters respond to parties that offer clear and intense policy alternatives. Thus in contrast to the centre-oriented pattern of political competition postulated by proximity theory, 'directional theory means conflict, if not polarisation, rather than consensus'.[7] The preference shaping effects of political communication[8] offer an escape for the median voter syndrome. By persuading voters that existing welfare state arrangements are unsustainable, parties may thus be able to redefine issues, changing voters' perceptions of the link between policies and their consequences.[9] Centre-right parties have a particular incentive to adopt such a strategy because it offers them the opportunity of shifting the aggregate distribution of preferences closer to their own policy orientation.[10]

Empirical research testing the proximity theory against the directional variant is inconclusive.[11] Mixed models combining preference accommodation and policy leadership tend to produce the best results. Thus 'democratic politics may be best described as an interactive process in which political elites articulate and influence public opinion while the electorate constitutes an emotionally responsive yet critical audience'.[12] Even from this 'mixed' perspective, however, it should be possible to detect the influence of party positions on aggregate levels of public opinion on economic reform.

It should also be possible to detect the influence of party positions on voting behaviour at the *individual level.* Both proximity and directional theories of party–voter relations assume that voting is issue dependent. If voters choose parties whose positions are close to their own issue preferences we would expect to find an association between issue preference and vote, with welfare supporters lining up with left parties and advocates of the market economy supporting parties of the right. This behavioural pattern will result in clearly defined partisan cleavages on welfare state and market economy issues. A strong 'competitive divide' over socio-economic issues has been seen as a precondition for welfare retrenchment. In the absence of economic cleavages, 'party competition is closely entwined and predicated on a broad centrist agreement ... on a mixed economy and a comprehensive welfare state'. Breaking this consensus is a high-risk strategy, since by reactivating latent issue cleavages, the party risks destabilising the social coalition on which its electorate is based.[13]

Empirical research finds quite wide variations in the relationship between partisanship and voter preferences (and consequently the strength of partisan cleavages) on socio-economic issues.[14] From the perspective of directional theory, it should be possible to account for these variations by differences in the intensity with which parties compete on a particular issue.

> If parties adopt very similar issue positions there would be no great incentive to vote for one party rather than another, and ... theoretical variables ... based on party issue positions would not provide much explanatory leverage. Hence other factors ... would tend to become more important for understanding observed patterns of voting.[15]

Weak patterns of issue voting have been explained by 'non-issue bias', originating in voter loyalties rooted in class, religion and party identification, or ... comparisons of the competing party leaders' competence'.[16] Voters motivated by these 'non-issue biases' may be 'issue blind', voting for a party *despite* rather than *because of* its position on particular issues. Thus, instead of reinforcing partisanship, socio-economic issues might cross-cut and divide party electorates. Weak patterns of issue voting and low intensity political competition may indeed be mutually reinforcing. When issues cut across party electorates, it has been found, parties tend to de-emphasise issues and to blur the distinctions between their policies and those of their rivals.[17] Competition remains latent, and parties are unlikely to articulate the issues with the intensity required to reshape voter preferences.

How do party system variables impact on the choices that parties make between directional opinion leadership (preference shaping) and passive response to public opinion (preference accommodation)? The relationship between political competition and party system types is contested.[18] It is argued on one side that the dichotomous character of two-party systems encourages directional strategies, whilst multi-party systems characterised by coalition government offer parties less incentive to adopt strong issue positions.[19] Others have reversed the equation, pointing to the freedom in multi-party systems to pursue preference-shaping strategies. By providing opportunities for representation and influence *without* a plurality of votes, multi-party systems relax the median voter syndrome, allowing parties to adopt strong issue positions designed to differentiate them from their neighbours.[20] Conversely, in two-party systems where the majoritarian principle reinforces vote maximising behaviour and the quest for the median voter, preference accommodation will predominate.

HYPOTHESES AND DATA

The essay contains two hypotheses. Following the directional model, it is hypothesised first that support for the welfare state will be related to the intensity of political competition on market economy/welfare issues. The strongest support for reform will occur where parties (usually those on the centre-right) campaign vigorously on the issues, sending strong messages to voters. The hypothesis is tested by comparative analysis setting Germany against Sweden, Denmark and the Netherlands. The comparators are countries that have experienced significant welfare reforms over the last two decades. Moreover, in contrast to Germany's two-predominant-party system, they have the type of multi-party systems that (as noted above) have been associated with preference shaping strategies. The hypothesis is also tested via longitudinal analysis. Are changes in *public opinion* towards the welfare state associated with shifts in *party positions* on socio-economic issues?

Data on welfare state support is drawn from national election studies for Sweden,[21] Denmark[22] and the Netherlands,[23] and the German *Allgemeine Bevölkerungsumfrage der Sozialwissenschaften* (ALLBUS General Social Survey).[24] The conventional distinction is made between the equality and security dimensions of welfare.[25] Attitudes to *equality* are investigated using questions on income differentiation that occur in broadly the same format in all four national studies. Opinion on the *security* dimension of welfare is plotted using questions relating to appropriate levels of welfare benefits. European Social Survey (ESS) data is used for 'triangulation' purposes.[26]

Three indicators are used to capture the intensity of party message: the *emphasis* placed on market economy/welfare issues, the strength of *centre-right party orientation* towards the market economy, and the extent of *polarisation* in political competition. The indicators are derived from data produced by the Manifesto Research Group at the University of Essex and Wissenschaftszentrum, Berlin.[27] MRG data use content analysis of election programmes to show the selective emphasis on particular issues as a percentage of the programme.[28] My issue category 'market economy' is the sum of three MRG categories: *free enterprise, incentives* and *economic orthodoxy*, whilst 'welfare' comprises the MRG categories *welfare state expansion* and *social justice*. The indicators are designed as follows. E*mphasis* = market economy + welfare as a percentage of programme content. This indicates the extent to which these issues are a focus of political competition. *Orientation* = market economy − welfare and is designed to show party *bias* on socio-economic issues. *Polarisation* = centre-right party orientation − centre-left party orientation, showing the distance between the parties on the market economy/welfare scale. It is not, of course, suggested that election programmes are an effective means of conveying party messages to voters. However, they provide the most readily quantifiable index of party position, and it is assumed that they are representative of wider forms of political communication.

The second hypothesis relates the intensity of political competition on market economy/welfare issues to the strength of partisan cleavages. Vigorous competition, it is hypothesised, will be associated with sharply defined partisan cleavages – an electorate divided into two 'camps' of welfare-oriented left party supporters and market economy advocates on the right. Partisan cleavages in the four countries are evaluated in terms of the correlation between partisanship and voter preference on welfare state issues, with high correlation coefficients indicating sharp differences in issue preference between partisan groups. Cross-national comparison is used to test the association between the intensity of political competition and the strength of partisan cleavages. Data is drawn from national election studies detailed above. Analysis focuses on partisan cleavages between the main centre-right and centre-left parties, with other partisans filtered out.[29]

PUBLIC OPINION

As noted above, it is conventional to distinguish between the equality and security dimensions of welfare. Table 1 shows public opinion on the *equality* dimensions of the welfare state, reporting attitudes to the principle of income differentiation/equalisation.[30] In all four countries, the balance of opinion lies in favour of income equalisation across all of the surveys included in the table. The margin between egalitarians/non-egalitarians, however, is subject to sharp cross-national variation. Sweden exhibits the most pronounced inclination towards equality, with support consistently above 60 per cent against no more than 20 per cent rejecting the principle. Opinion in the Netherlands is also strongly supportive of equality, with egalitarians outnumbering their opponents by an emphatic margin of 20–30 percentage points increasing to over 40 in 1998. Denmark is the least egalitarian of the four countries. Danish support for equality declined over the 1990s. By the end of the decade it fell short of a plurality and egalitarians outnumbered their opponents by only a narrow margin.

German opinion is sharply divided between western and eastern parts of the country. Compared to Sweden and the Netherlands, support for the principle of income equality in *western* Germany is relatively low. In three of the surveys reported in Table 1 there is a bare plurality of support for equality, with only the narrowest of margins (in the range from 1 to 3 percentage points) between egalitarians and their opponents. In the middle to late 1990s the gap widened to 27 percentage points in 1998, only to close again in 2000. Unsurprisingly, East Germans exhibit overwhelming support for income equality, comfortably exceeding even the high levels of support found in Sweden.

Table 2 and Figure 2 show attitudes towards the social protection and security, reporting responses to survey questions about the appropriate level of welfare benefits. Across all four countries, support for the security dimension of welfare exceeds that for equality. Almost without exception, welfare expansionists and advocates of the status quo outnumber those in favour of welfare retrenchment by a considerable margin. Once again, however, opinion is subject to significant cross-national variations. Sweden shows the most readiness to countenance welfare retrenchment, with an average of around 40 per cent of Swedes endorsing benefit reductions across the 1980s and 90s, peaking at 48 per cent in 1982 and again at 46 per cent in 1991. Across all the surveys included in Table 2, these are the only instances in which the advocates of

TABLE 1
PUBLIC OPINION: INCOME EQUALITY

Denmark

A 'differences in incomes are still too high, so people with smaller incomes should have faster improvements'; B The levelling of income has gone far enough. Those income differences that still remain should largely be maintained.

	1990	1994	1998	2001	ESS
Agree A	61.1	51.3	48.7	49.3	42.7
Agree B	33.3	42.0	45.1	44.2	
D/K	5.6	6.7	6.2	6.5	
A-B	27.8	9.3	3.6	5.1	

Sweden

What is your opinion on the following proposal: reduce income differences in society: very good/fairly good/neither good nor bad/bad/very bad?

	1988	1991	1994	1998	ESS
Very good/good	60.3	61.1	61.7	65.9	68.7
Neither good/bad	20.3	18.3	19.0	16.9	
Bad/very bad	19.5	20.7	19.3	17.2	
(V) good – (V) bad	40.8	40.4	42.4	48.7	

Netherlands

Some people consider income differences too high, others too low – where would you place yourself on this scale: % 1–7 on 7 point scale.

	1982	1986	1989	1994	1998	ESS
Differences too high (1–3)	52.4	54.0	53.9	48.8	60.4	59.2
Neither high nor low (4)	14.1	25.4	24.5	24.4	26.6	
Differences too low (5–7)	33.5	20.6	21.6	26.8	16.0	
	18.9	33.4	32.3	22.0	44.4	

Germany

Income differences are fair: strongly agree/agree/disagree/strongly disagree

	1984	1991	1994	1998	2000	ESS
West						
(Strongly) disagree	51.6	50.9	54.5	63.8	50.5	47.2
(Strongly) agree	48.4	49.1	45.5	36.1	49.5	
Disagree – agree	3.2	1.8	9.0	27.7	1.0	
East						
(Strongly) disagree		83.1	87.2	87.6	81.3	76.2
(Strongly agree		16.9	12.8	12.5	18.7	
Disagree – agree		66.2	74.4	75.1	62.6	
All Germany						
(Strongly) disagree	51.6	58.5	61.0	68.0	56.1	58.2
(Strongly) agree	48.4	41.4	39.0	31.9	43.9	
Disagree – agree	3.2	17.1	22.0	36.1	12.2	

retrenchment outnumber expansionists by a clear margin. Relatively high levels of support for welfare retrenchment in Sweden appear to run counter to the strong egalitarian bias in public opinion, underlining the potential for disparity in support for different dimensions of welfare.

FIGURE 1
PUBLIC OPINION: INCREASE INCOME EQUALITY

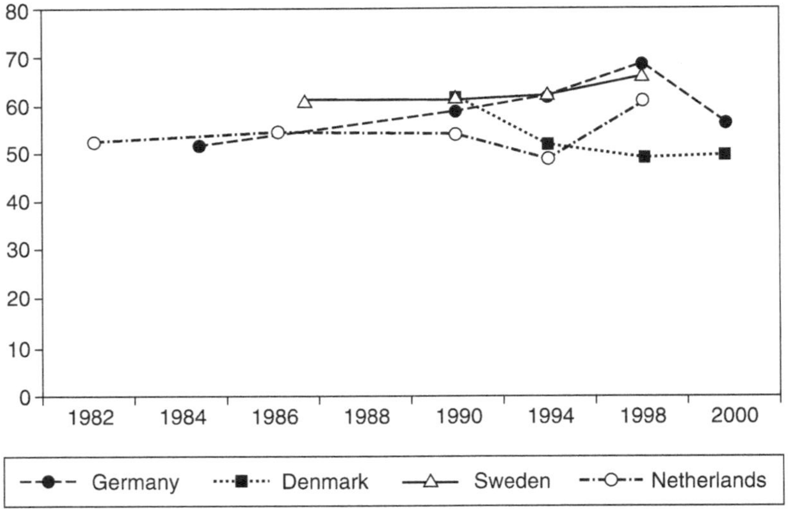

In Denmark there is significantly more resistance to reductions in welfare benefits. Over the 1990s a plurality of Danish opinion was strongly supportive of the status quo in welfare benefits. Support for benefit *reductions was moderate*, in the range from around 25 to 30 per cent. A notable feature of Danish opinion, however, was the low level of support for *increasing* benefits. By the turn of the millennium, barely 10 per cent of Danes advocated expansion, significantly fewer than in the other three countries. The Netherlands displayed a similarly moderate level of support for welfare retrenchment (27–28 per cent). Unlike Denmark, however, support for *increasing* benefits exceeds opinion in favour of *reduction.*

In comparison to the other three countries, German opinion exhibits exceptionally strong resistance to welfare retrenchment. Barely one in ten West Germans sanctioned benefit cuts over the 1980s and 1990s. Welfare *expansionists* predominate over the advocates of welfare *retrenchment* by a significant margin, although there is a marked decline in the proportion of expansionists from the early 1980s. The most notable trend, however, is the sharp increase in support for retrenchment in 2000, coinciding with the deepening of the sense of national economic crisis. This *peak* in West German support for benefit cuts, however, still fails to reach even the *troughs* in retrenchment opinion in the other three countries. Unsurprisingly given socio-economic circumstances, East Germans are united in their reluctance to countenance welfare cuts. Expansionists accounted for around 75 per cent of opinion in 1994, and whilst they had declined by 2000 there was still only a very small minority in favour of benefit reductions.

A striking feature of the West German data is the very *flat* trajectory of opinion across the 1980s and 1990s. Not only is retrenchment opinion very low, it is also very consistent, varying only within a margin of two percentage points. The contrast with the Scandinavian countries is very apparent from Table 3 and Figure 3, which

TABLE 2
PUBLIC OPINION: SOCIAL BENEFITS

Denmark
Do you think the government uses too much money, an appropriate amount or too little money for welfare benefits?

	1990	1994	1998	2001
Too much money	30.4	25.8	31.0	27.7
Appropriate	51.9	61.1	58.7	60.0
Too little money	17.7	13.0	10.3	12.3

Sweden
What is your opinion on the following proposals . . . reduce welfare benefits: very good/fairly good/neither good nor bad/bad/very bad?

	1982	1985	1988	1991	1994	1998
Very good/good	48.2	42.1	35.2	45.7	37.5	30.9
Neither good/bad	8.3	8.4	22.7	21.8	24.5	23.9
Very bad/bad	43.4	49.5	42.1	32.6	38.0	45.2

The Netherlands
Some people think social benefits are too low, others think they are too high; where would you place yourself (1–7)?

	1994	1998
Too low (1–3)	38.4	38.9
4	34.4	32.8
Too high (5–7)	27.1	28.3

Germany
Reduce social benefits: strongly agree/agree/disagree/strongly disagree

	1982	1984	1994	2000–1
West				
Increase benefits	44.5	24.8	27.1	20.5
Maintain benefits	42.5	64.0	60.1	54.9
Reduce benefits	13.0	11.1	12.1	24.5
East				
Increase benefits			70.2	45.0
Maintain benefits			28.9	46.7
Reduce benefits			0.9	8.3
All Germany				
Increase benefits	44.5	24.8	33.0	24.4
Maintain benefits	42.5	64.0	56.2	54.3
Reduce benefits	13.0	11.1	10.8	21.2

report responses to an item in Swedish and Danish election studies suggesting that welfare state development should be curtailed, though without explicitly mentioning benefit reductions.[31] Both Scandinavian countries show significant longitudinal fluctuations in opinion. In Sweden, retrenchment opinion peaks in 1980. A second peak in 1990–91 is followed by a decade of decline. In Denmark support for welfare retrenchment is much lower, but it also follows a fluctuating trajectory. The peak occurs earlier than in Sweden, in 1973. Decline to a low point in 1988 is then followed by a steady

FIGURE 2
PUBLIC OPINION: REDUCE WELFARE BENEFITS

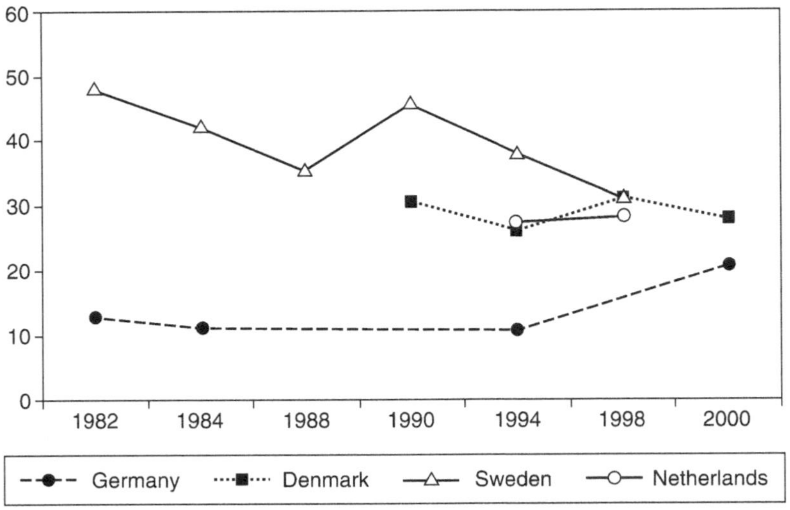

* The absence of values for some elections reflects the omission of the welfare benefits item from national election studies.

increase to a peak in 2001. Fluctuations in opinion in the Scandinavian countries cast the flat trajectory of German opinion in very sharp relief.

There is, however, some evidence suggesting that the shift in German public opinion seen for the first time in 2000 has become more pronounced in 2003–04, coinciding with the politicisation of debate over the *Hartz IV* reform package. The absence of ALLBUS data leaves us reliant on the *Politbarometer* results shown in Table 4.[32] *General* support for the government's reform course increased sharply from 35 per cent to 46 per cent in the first half of 2004. Increases in backing for retrenchment in *specific* areas of welfare are more modest. Support also varies considerably between different welfare functions. It is at its highest in relation to coal subsidies (64 per cent) where the effect of cuts is indirect, and home-owner bonuses (52 per cent) from which there are relatively few beneficiaries. Support for cuts in social assistance and unemployment protection is much lower at 41 per cent and 35 per cent respectively. Even in these core areas of welfare, however, support

TABLE 3
SUPPORT FOR WELFARE STATE RETRENCHMENT: SWEDEN, DENMARK

Social reforms have gone too far, people should manage without social support and benefits from government (% agreeing)

	1964	68/69	1973	1976	79/80	84/85	87/88	90/91	1994	1998	2001
Sweden	63	42	60	61	69	62	61	68	64	56	
Denmark	22	23	58	47	31	24	15	26	28	31	34

FIGURE 3
PUBLIC OPINION: CURTAIL WELFARE STATE EXPANSION (SWEDEN AND DENMARK)

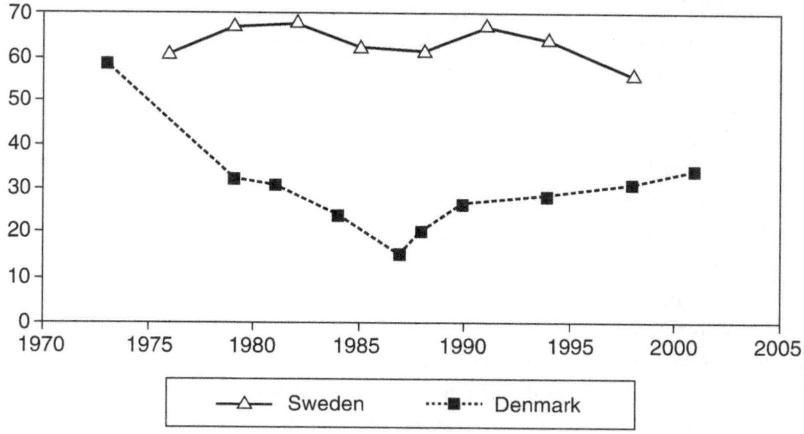

for retrenchment is significantly higher than that registered by the ALLBUS survey of 2000.

Can the cross-national differences and longitudinal trends that have been identified in this section be explained in terms of party system variables? The hypothesis established at the beginning of the study would suggest that they may be related to the positions occupied by the main political parties, and to patterns of political competition between them. In order to test this linkage, however, we first need to plot party positions in relation to market economy and welfare issues, and it is to this that we now turn.

PARTY POSITIONS

In the introduction it was argued that the capacity of political parties to shape voter preferences depends on the intensity with which they articulate their messages, and that preference shaping will be associated with polarised patterns of political competition. This section evaluates the intensity of party messages in the four countries by analysing party programmes on market economy and welfare issues.

TABLE 4
GERMAN PUBLIC OPINION 2003–04

	Reform course % agree	Coal subsidies*	Home-owner bonus*	Job creation*	Commuter tax break*	Social assistance*	Unemployment spt*
Nov 03		61	44	42	41	37	34
Feb 04	35						
May 04		64	52	45	43	41	35
Aug 04	46						

*% agree with benefit reductions.

Three indicators are employed; the *emphasis* parties place on market economy issues (market + welfare as % programme content); the *orientation* of the leading centre-right party on the issues (market–welfare); and party system *polarisation* (the distance between the parties on the market economy–welfare scale). All three indicators are shown in Table 5, in which E = emphasis, O = orientation and P = polarisation.

In Sweden, market economy and welfare issues receive strong emphasis, accounting for around 33 per cent of programme content. The conservative Moderate Coalition Party in particular cranked up the intensity of its message very significantly in the late 1970s and early 1980s, so that by 1985 virtually half its programme focused on the market economy. Danish parties place considerably less emphasis on the issues, averaging 22.6 per cent of programme content, but with high peaks in 1973 and 1981. In comparison with the Scandinavian countries, Germany shows low intensity campaigning, with market economy/welfare issues accounting for only 18.7 per cent of SPD and CDU/CSU programme content. Despite the deepening economic crisis since the mid-1990s, emphasis has actually *declined* since 1994. Only in the Netherlands do socio-economic issues figure less prominently than in Germany,

Scandinavian centre-right parties show a pronounced market orientation. On the market economy – welfare scale, the Danish conservatives and liberals average around 16, and the Swedish conservatives 22.1 percentage points. In both countries, the market orientations of the centre-right parties peak at double this level. By contrast, the CDU fluctuates between welfare and the market, averaging just 1.4 on the market economy–welfare scale. Its strongest market orientation was in the election of 1983, when a return to government was accompanied by a rhetorical commitment to economic liberalism. Even then, however, market advocacy (20 per cent of programme content) was tempered with continued emphasis on welfare (10 per cent). Thereafter the CDU/CSU reverted to a welfare orientation in 1987 and 1990. Whilst reasserting its commitment to the market in the last three elections, the emphasis remains modest (around 10 per cent of programme content) in comparison to the market economy offensives of the Scandinavian centre-right. The SPD occupies a similarly centrist position, averaging −9.2 on the market economy–welfare scale, marginally less welfare-oriented than its Swedish and Danish and Dutch counterparts (−10.5, −12.3 and −11.4 respectively). The absence of a market-oriented party is even more marked in the Netherlands. The CDA inclines slightly towards welfare, standing at −6.1 on the market economy scale, whilst the VVD registers −0.2. As in Germany the leading market liberal party (D 66) is relatively insignificant in electoral terms.

In sharp contrast to the centrism of the German party system, the Scandinavian systems are highly polarised, with the distance between the dominant centre-right party and the social democrats averaging 33 percentage points. Polarisation peaks occur in both Denmark and Sweden, precipitated generally (though in the Swedish case not exclusively) by a centre-right party. Denmark is notable in that polarisation can be triggered by either of the centre-right parties. In the German party system, the average distance between the CDU/CSU and the SPD (11 percentage points) is barely one-third of the distance between dominant centre-right party and social democrats in Sweden and Denmark. In the Netherlands, polarisation is even weaker, with a gap of just 6 percentage points between centre-right leader and Labour on the market economy.

TABLE 5
PARTY POSITIONS (MARKET ECONOMY AND WELFARE AS % PROGRAMME CONTENT)

Germany																
	1976				1980				1983				1987			
	Mkt	Wel	E	O	Mkt	Wel	E	O	Mkt	Wel	E	O	Mkt	Wel	E	O
SPD	3.1	19.3	22.4	−16.2	2.8	17.9	20.7	−15.1	4.6	11.0	15.6	−6.4	6.1	17.6	23.7	−11.5
CDU	9.0	11.7	20.7	−2.7	11.8	11.7	23.5	0.1	20.2	10.2	32.4	10.0	5.1	12.6	17.7	−7.5
Emphasis (party average)			21.6				21.1				24.0				20.7	
Polarisation				13.5				15.2				16.4				4.0
	1990				1994				1998				2002			
	Mkt	Wel	E	O	Mkt	Wel	E	O	Mkt	Wel	E	O	Mkt	Wel	E	O
SPD	2.7	10.6	13.3	−7.9	3.3	17.8	21.1	−14.5	9.1	9.8	18.9	−0.7	6.4	7.9	14.3	−1.5
CDU	2.0	11.9	13.9	−9.9	9.8	2.9	12.7	6.9	12.1	3.7	15.8	8.4	9.7	4.2	13.9	5.5
Emphasis (party average)			13.6				16.9				17.4				14.1	
Polarisation				2.0				21.4				9.1				7.0

(continued)

TABLE 5
(cont'd)

Denmark

	1973				**1979**				**1981**				**1984**			
	Mkt	**Wel**	**E**	**O**	**Mkt**	**Wel**	**E**	**O**	**Mkt**	**Wel**	**E**	**O**	**Mkt**	**Wel**	**E**	**O**
Soc	3.0	19.7	22.7	−16.7	0	12.1	12.1	−12.1	4.7	10.4	15.1	−5.7	1.2	23.7	24.9	−22.5
Lib	34.9	1.5	36.4	33.4	12.8	8.5	21.3	4.1	27.2	7.4	34.6	19.8	10.1	1.7	11.8	8.4
Con	38.7	9.7	48.4	29.0	22.6	0	22.6	22.6	40.7	1.1	51.8	39.6	14.3	4.1	18.4	10.2
Emphasis (party average)			35.8				18.7				33.8				18.4	
Polarisation				50.1				34.7				45.3				32.7

	1987				**1988**				**1990**				**1994**			
	Mkt	**Wel**	**E**	**O**	**Mkt**	**Wel**	**E**	**O**	**Mkt**	**Wel**	**E**	**O**	**Mkt**	**Wel**	**E**	**O**
Soc	4.0	13.8	17.8	−9.8	5.0	7.2	12.2	−2.2	1.6	22.6	24.2	−21.0	0.5	9.2	9.7	−8.7
Lib	27.5	9.2	36.7	18.3	17.5	2.5	23.0	15.0	0.6	0.0	0.6	0.6	35.9	0.5	36.4	35.4
Con	11.2	6.7	17.9	4.5	12.0	0.0	12.0	12.0	13.8	6.4	20.2	7.4	8.0	4.4	12.4	3.6
Emphasis (party average)			24.1				15.7				14.7				19.5	
Polarisation				14.3				14.2				28.4				44.1

(continued)

TABLE 5
(cont'd)

Sweden

	1976				1979				1982				1985			
	Mkt	**Wel**	**E**	**O**	**Mkt**	**Wel**	**E**	**O**	**Mkt**	**Wel**	**E**	**O**	**Mkt**	**Wel**	**E**	**O**
Soc	15.7	15.7	31.4	0	10.6	22.5	33.1	−11.9	4.0	17.3	21.3	−13.3	9.8	16.0	25.8	−6.2
Con	17.7	15.5	33.2	2.2	23.8	11.9	35.7	11.0	29.2	7.8	37.0	21.4	46.2	2.9	49.1	43.3
Lib	17.7	3.5	21.2	20.1	4.5	20.1	24.6	−15.6	16.2	21.9	38.1	−5.7	31.3	16.9	48.2	14.4
Emphasis (party average)			28.6				31.1				32.1				41.3	
Polarisation				2.2				22.9				34.7				49.5
	1988				**1991**				**1994**				**1998**			
	Mkt	**Wel**	**E**	**O**	**Mkt**	**Wel**	**E**	**O**	**Mkt**	**Wel**	**E**	**O**	**Mkt**	**Wel**	**E**	**O**
Soc	6.3	39.7	46.0	−33.4	6.8	20.0	26.8	−13.2	20.9	17.7	38.6	3.2	14.5	23.4	37.9	−8.9
Con	22.4	1.6	24.0	20.8	32.3	4.7	37.0	27.6	22.8	1.5	24.3	21.3	36.0	4.8	40.8	31.2
Lib	18.1	13.0	31.1	5.1	9.0	10.4	19.4	−1.4	23.9	26.6	50.5	−2.7	19.0	4.7	23.7	15.3
Emphasis (party average)			33.7				27.7				37.8				34.1	
Polarisation				54.2				40.8				24.5				40.1

(continued)

TABLE 5
(cont'd)

Netherlands

	1972				**1977**				**1981**				**1982**			
	Mkt	**Wel**	**E**	**O**	**Mkt**	**Wel**	**E**	**O**	**Mkt**	**Wel**	**E**	**O**	**Mkt**	**Wel**	**E**	**O**
PvdA	1.8	22.6	24.4	−20.8	5.0	17.5	22.5	−12.5	2.7	19.7	22.4	−17.0	12.8	17.9	30.7	−5.1
VVD	24.6	9.8	34.4	14.8	15.1	8.5	23.6	3.6	5.8	9.5	15.3	−3.7	6.9	10.7	17.3	−3.8
CDA	7.4	20.6	28.0	−13.2	4.8	14.0	18.8	−9.2	4.3	11.7	16.0	−7.4	7.2	12.7	19.9	−5.5
Emphasis (party average)			28.8				21.6				17.9				22.6	
Polarisation				7.6				3.3				9.6				0.4
	1986				**1989**				**1994**				**1998**			
	Mkt	**Wel**	**E**	**O**	**Mkt**	**Wel**	**E**	**O**	**Mkt**	**Wel**	**E**	**O**	**Mkt**	**Wel**	**E**	**O**
PvdA	4.3	13.0	17.3	−8.7	1.5	10.7	12.2	−9.2	2.8	5.2	8.0	−2.4	1.4	17.0	18.4	−15.6
VVD	7.5	8.3	15.8	−0.8	1.8	7.7	9.5	−5.9	4.8	4.4	9.2	0.4	2.4	8.8	11.2	−6.2
CDA	7.3	7.6	14.9	−0.3	3.7	7.9	13.6	−4.2	4.9	2.8	7.7	2.1	1.8	13.1	−14.9	−11.3
Emphasis (party average)			16.0				11.8				8.3				14.8	
Polarisation				8.4				5.0				4.5				9.4

FIGURE 4
EMPHASIS MARKET ECONOMY + WELFARE

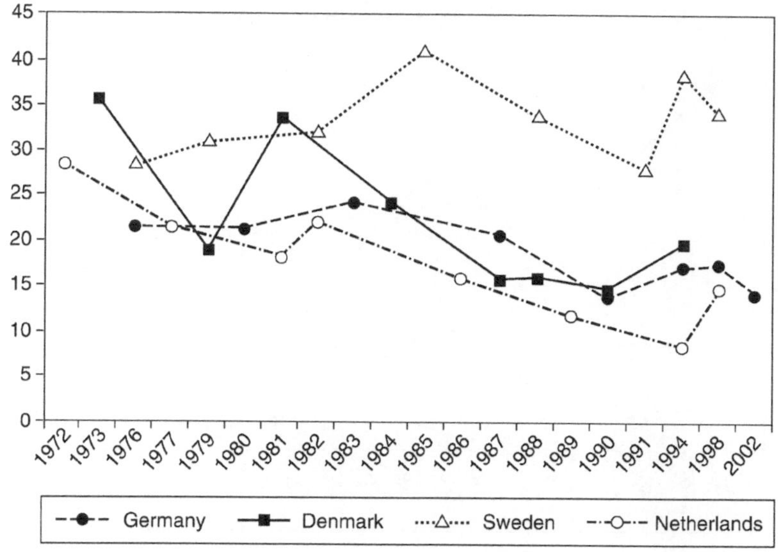

The contrast between Germany and the Scandinavian countries is particularly significant since the experience of Sweden and Denmark suggest that welfare state reform periods tend to be prefaced by market economy offensives by at least one of the centre-right parties, accompanied by sharp party system polarisation. The

FIGURE 5
CENTRE-RIGHT PARTY: MARKET ECONOMY – WELFARE

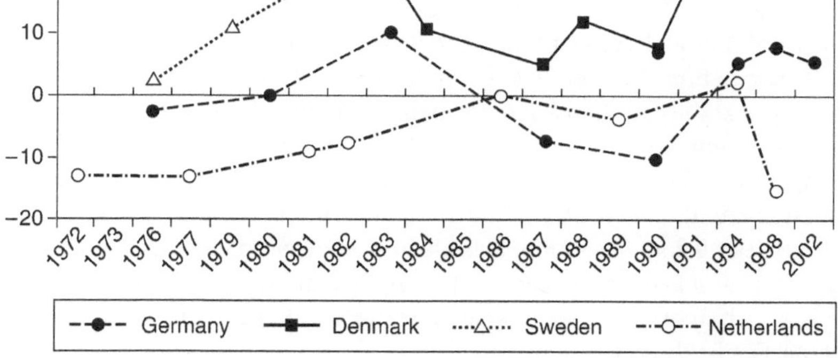

FIGURE 6
POLARISATION CENTRE-RIGHT – CENTRE-LEFT PARTY

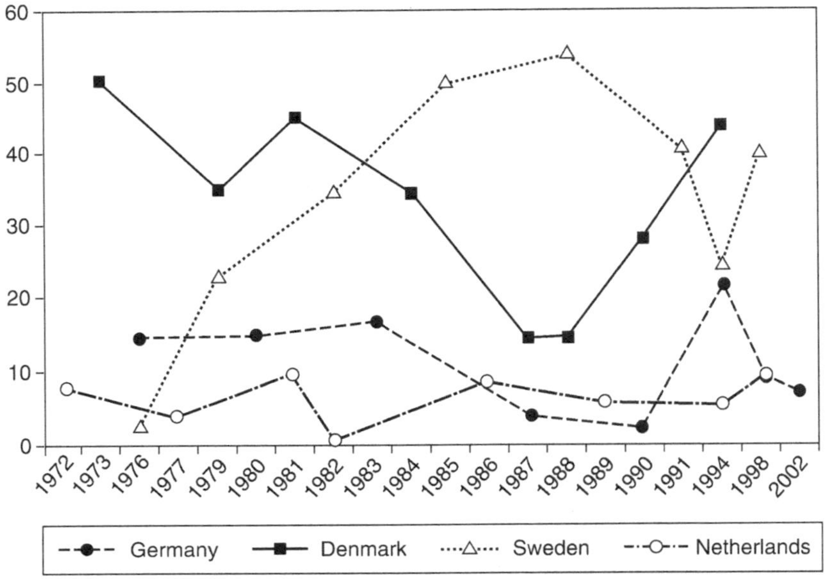

Swedish reforms of the Carl Bildt era (1991–94) were heralded by a conservative party programme in which market economy themes accounted for one-third of the content. Similarly the reforming Schlüter administration in Denmark (1982–83) entered office on the back of a programme in which market economy issues constituted 40 per cent of content. If shifts in voter preferences are catalysed by the politicisation of issues consequent on party polarisation, then the absence of polarisation in the German party system on market economy welfare issues may explain the resistance of German voters to welfare retrenchment. Before we can draw this conclusion, however, we need to explore further the relationship between party positions and public opinion.

PUBLIC OPINION AND PARTY POSITION

Can cross-national differences in support for the welfare state be explained in terms of the intensity of political competition? The data we have just reviewed suggests there may be an association. Sweden has the highest level of support for welfare retrenchment and also exhibits the most intense political competition. Conversely, Germany combines a very low level of support for welfare retrenchment with low-intensity political competition. Denmark falls between Sweden and Germany both in terms of public opinion and the intensity of political competition. The case of the Netherlands, however, suggests a note of caution. Despite low emphasis on market economy/welfare issues and the absence of an electorally significant market-oriented party, public opinion is much more inclined towards welfare retrenchment than in Germany, approaching Danish levels of support.

FIGURE 7
PUBLIC OPINION: REDUCE BENEFITS/CENTRE-RIGHT PARTY (MARKET – WELFARE)

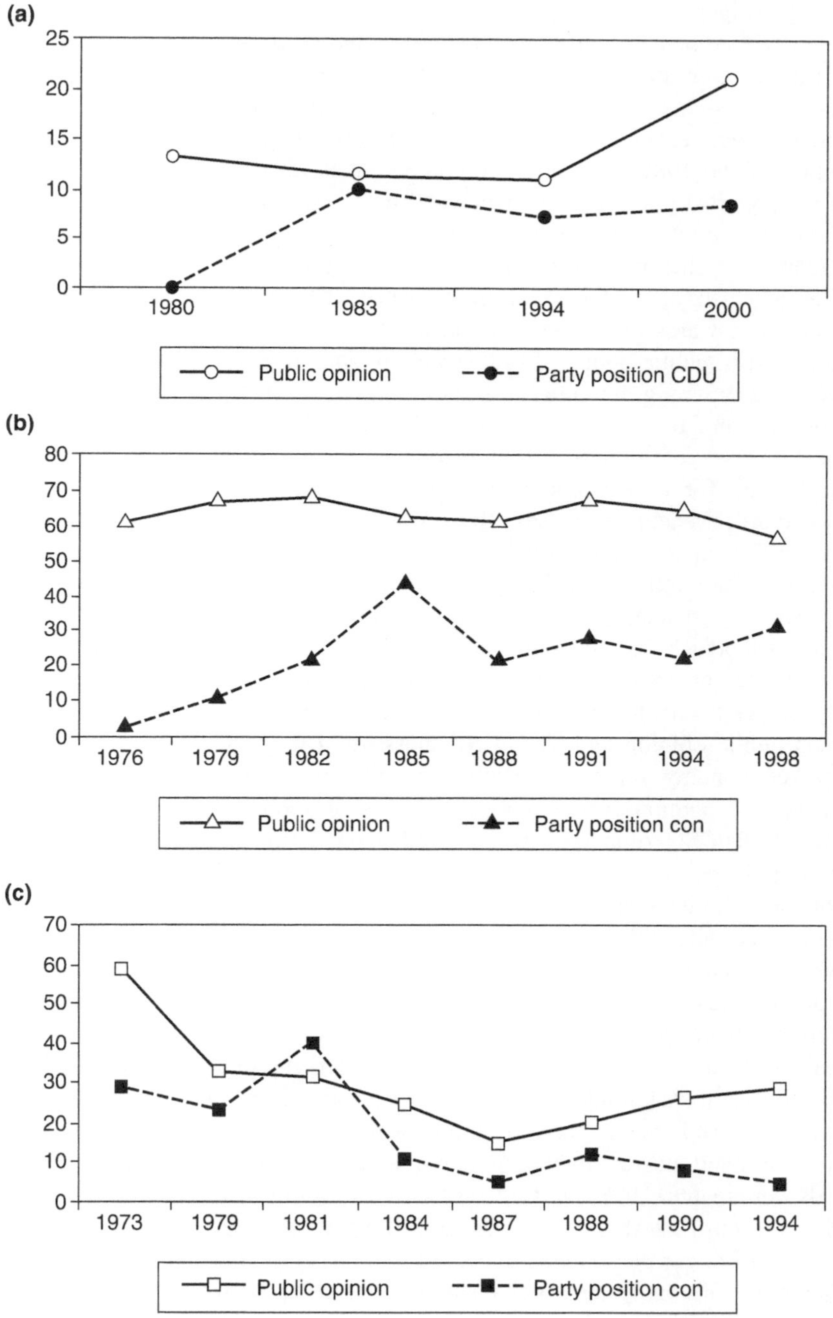

Another way of evaluating the association between public opinion and political competition is by examining longitudinal trends. Denmark provides some evidence of linkage (Figure 3). The high point of support for welfare retrenchment (58 per cent in 1973) coincided with an emphatic orientation to the market economy on the part of the Conservative Peoples' Party. (It also coincided with the emergence of the anti-tax Progress Party.) Thereafter, a decline in support for welfare retrenchment is mirrored in the weakening market bias of conservative party programmes (with the exception of the 1981 election). The conservatives failed to respond to an upward trend in support for welfare retrenchment from 1987. This gave the liberal Venstre party the opportunity to establish dominance of the centre-right, offering an emphatically market-oriented programme in 1994 and going on to form a government in 2001.

The Swedish case shows mixed evidence. The conservatives' programmatic reorientation towards the market economy between 1976 and 1982 coincided with a marked shift in public opinion towards welfare state retrenchment. In 1985 they got it spectacularly wrong, lurching further towards the market just as opinion shifted in the opposite direction. After moderating their neo-liberal instincts in the following election, a renewed emphasis on the market economy coincided with an upswing in public support for welfare cuts in the early 1990s. 1994 saw a parallel shift away from welfare retrenchment in both the conservative programme and public opinion, but the party then *strengthened* its commitment to the market in 1998 against a continuing pro-welfare trend in public opinion. The Swedish experience suggests that periodic increases in support for welfare retrenchment may be linked to the strong positions adopted by centre-right parties on the market economy, although market offensives are not invariably echoed in public opinion.

By contrast with the Scandinavian cases, Germany shows virtually no linkage between public opinion and CDU/CSU message. The party's reorientation towards the market economy in the early 1980s caused hardly a ripple in the flat trajectory of German public opinion. A very marginal increase in support for welfare retrenchment amongst CDU/CSU supporters was cancelled out by an opposite and larger trend amongst SPD partisans, resulting in a decline of two percentage points in overall support for welfare restraint between 1982 and 1984. The only positive linkage between party message and public opinion in this period was a sharp reduction in opinion favouring welfare expansion (44.5 per cent to 24.8 per cent) as expansionists shifted to advocacy of the status quo. The upturn in support for welfare retrenchment in 2000 cannot credibly be attributed to the effects of the CDU 'message'. Whilst their programmes in the three elections from 1994 to 2002 reaffirm a market economy orientation, it is relatively modest in magnitude. Moreover, as we have seen, the *emphasis* on market economy/welfare issues in party programmes receded in the 1990s. SPD positioning, on the other hand, mirrors public opinion quite closely, both in its programmatic bias towards welfare until 1998 and its modest shift towards the market economy thereafter,

A more rigorous test of co-variation between party message and public opinion can be derived from correlation coefficients (Table 6). In the Danish case, a correlation coefficient of .601 indicates a fairly strong relationship between public opinion and conservative positions on market economy/welfare issues. Co-variance between public opinion and the position of the *electorally dominant* centre-right party is even stronger at .634. Sweden offers less persuasive evidence. The tendency of the

TABLE 6
CORRELATIONS: PUBLIC OPINION AND PARTY POSITION (PEARSON'S R)

Public opinion welfare state retrenchment/programme emphasis market – welfare

	Germany 4 elections 1984–2002		Denmark 8 elections 1973–94			Sweden 8 elections 1976–98		
	CDU	**SPD**	**Con**	**Lib**	**Soc**	**Con**	**Lib**	**Soc**
Pearsons r	.182	.771	.601	.462	−.253	−.189	−.797	−.030
Significance	.818	.229	.115	.249	.545	.654	.018	.944

conservatives to campaign vigorously on the market economy *in defiance* of countervailing trends in public opinion is reflected in a weak and negative correlation of −.189 between party position and public opinion. The omission of 'aberrant' elections in 1985 and 1998 from the analysis, however, gives a much stronger, positive correlation of .449. For Germany, a correlation coefficient of .182 suggests little or no relationship between public opinion and CDU/CSU position. Co-variation with SPD positions, on the other hand, is stronger, with a correlation coefficient of .771. Scandinavian social democratic parties, on the other hand have a weak or negative orientation to trends in public opinion (−.253 in Denmark; −.030 in Sweden).

There is, then, some evidence that *cross-national* variations in support for welfare retrenchment are related to *differences* in the intensity of political competition. There is also evidence that *longitudinal changes* in public opinion may be related to *shifts* in party position and *fluctuations* in the intensity of political competition over time. Periodic increases in support for welfare retrenchment in the Scandinavian countries coincided with sustained and emphatic shifts towards the market economy on the part of centre-right parties, suggesting that party position and public opinion react reciprocally, with mutually reinforcing trends in favour of welfare reform. German resistance to welfare retrenchment, and the 'flat' trajectory of public opinion, may thus be attributed, in part at least, to the attenuation of political competition and the muted market economy message of the CDUCSU.

VOTER PREFERENCE AND PARTISANSHIP

What determines the positions that parties adopt on socio-economic issues and the intensity with which they articulate them? It was argued in the introduction that party positions reflect the structure of their electoral constituencies. Parties will take a stand on issues where there is a close relationship between partisanship and issue preference, resulting in sharply defined partisan cleavages. This section tests this hypothesis, using bi-variate correlation analysis to evaluate the strength of the relationship between partisanship and voter preference on market economy/welfare issues. Cross-national comparison is then employed to see whether the intensity of political competition on socio-economic issues reflects the strength of partisan cleavages in attitudes to welfare issues.

Table 7 shows the strength of the relationship between partisanship and voter preferences in terms of correlation coefficients (Pearson's r). In general, the relationship is not a strong one, with r values rarely exceeding .5. The strongest relationship is found amongst Volkspartij voor vrijheit en Democratie (VVD) (Liberal) and Partij van der Arbeid (PvdA) (Labour Party) supporters in the Netherlands. In three out of four elections between 1986 and 1998, correlation coefficients lie in a range from .453 to .644 on income equality and from .385 to .550 on welfare benefits, averaging .472 and .490 respectively. It should be noted, however, that the VVD is not the leading party on the centre-right. The dominant CDA (Christian Democratic Alliance) displays a much less clearly defined preference profile. The cleavage between Christian Democrats and Labour partisans is significantly weaker on both issues, with r values averaging .278 (income equality) and .287 (welfare benefits). Moreover, there is a steep drop in the correlation between partisanship and voter preference in elections from 1986 to 1998 (from .467 to .230 on income equality and from .383 to .201 on welfare benefits). The secular decline of partisan cleavages is particularly sharp in the Dutch case.

Of the electorally dominant centre-right parties, the Swedish Moderate Coalition Party (Conservative) exhibits the strongest preference profile. Amongst conservatives and social democrats, correlations between partisanship and attitude towards *welfare retrenchment* range between .293 and .389, indicating a moderate cleavage. In contrast to the other three countries, partisan cleavages on benefit retrenchment are (marginally) stronger than those over income equality. Sweden is also exceptional in that partisan cleavages on welfare state issues are not subject to the general decline that has occurred elsewhere. An average r value of .161 shows that the cleavage between *liberals* and social democrats is notably weaker.

In Denmark, partisan cleavages on *income equality* are moderate. As in Sweden, *conservative* partisans are more consistent in rejecting equality than *liberals.* Amongst conservatives and social democrats, correlation coefficients vary between .329 and .477. Liberals are slightly less cohesive, with r values averaging .341. On welfare retrenchment, partisan cleavages are significantly less pronounced.

Of the four countries, Germany exhibits by far the weakest pattern of partisan cleavage. Even in the west, the relationship between CDU/CSU and SPD partisanship and preferences on income equality and welfare benefits is tenuous. R values in the range from .144 to .320 (income equality) and .169 to .210 (welfare benefits) indicate only the weakest connection between partisanship and issue preference. Moreover, there is a particularly pronounced decline in the cleavage between CDU/CSU and SPD voters on income equality in 2000, perhaps reflecting shifts in partisanship accompanying the SPD's repositioning towards the centre on socio-economic issues. The West German data confirm the expectations that the cross-class composition of the Christian democratic constituency would be reflected in an ill-defined preference profile on socio-economic issues. It is worth noting, however, that partisan cleavages in Western Germany are significantly weaker than those amongst Christian democrats and Labour Party supporters in the Netherlands. In Eastern Germany, correlation coefficients averaging .113 (income equality) and .154 (welfare benefits) suggest that there is virtually no relationship at all between partisanship and preference on socio-economic issues. CDU and SPD partisans are barely distinguishable

TABLE 7
CORRELATIONS; PARTISANSHIP AND VOTER PREFERENCE (PEARSON'S R)

Germany: Social Democratic Party (SPD) and Christian Democratic Party/Christian Social Union (CDU/CSU) voters.

	1984	1991	1994	1998	2000
West					
Partisanship/inc diffs	.248**	.320**	.251**	.260**	.144**
Partisanship/benefits	.210**	.162**	.201**		.169**
East					
Partisanship/inc diffs	.121**	.148**	.107*	.076	
Partisanship/benefits	.087*	.247**		.128*	
All Germany					
Partisanship/inc diffs	.248**	.212**	.236**	.199**	.139**
Partisanship/benefits	.210**	.118**	.229**		.174**

Sweden: Social Democratic Party (SD), Moderates (Con) and Liberal Peoples' Party (Lib) voters

	1982	1985	1988	1991	1994	1998
SD/LIB						
Partisanship/income diffs			.112**	.137**	.216**	.127**
Partisanship/social benefits	.130**	.174**	.201**	.209**	.137**	.118**
SD/CON						
Partisanship/income diffs			.262**	.276**	.357**	.343**
Partisanship/social benefits	.344**	.366**	.300**	.293**	.348**	.389**

Denmark: Social Democratic Party (SD) Venstre (Lib), and Conservative Peoples' Party (Con) voters.

	1990	1994	1998	2001
SD/LIB				
Partisanship/income diffs	.385**	.310**	.378**	.317**
Partisanship/social benefits	.345**	.241**	.220**	.264*
SD/CON				
Partisanship/income diffs	.411**	.364**	.477**	.329**
Partisanship/social benefits	.238*	.210**	.217**	.254

Netherlands: Labour Party (PvdA), Peoples Party for Freedom and Democracy - Liberals (VVD and Christian Democratic Appeal (CDA) voters.

	1986	1989	1994	1998
PvdA/VVD				
Partisanship/income diffs	.644**	.233**	.561**	.453**
Partisanship/social benefits	.550**		.534**	.385**
PvdA/CDA				
Partisanship/income diffs	.467**	.048	.369**	.230**
Partisanship/social benefits	.383**		.279**	.201**

**Correlation is significant at the 0.01 level.
*Correlation is significant at the 0.05 level.

from each other in their enthusiasm for income equality and resistance to welfare retrenchment.

Variations in the strength of partisan cleavages in attitudes towards the welfare state help to explain the variations in the intensity of political competition that we observed above in the second section. Table 8 summarises the data from previous tables. In Sweden, the contrasting preferences of conservative and social democratic voters are reflected in the high visibility of market economy/welfare issues in party programmes, the strong market orientation of conservative programmes, and a polarised party system. In Denmark, moderate partisan cleavages are reflected in a similarly moderate pattern of political competition. The market bias of centre-right party programmes is almost as strong as in Sweden, and party system polarisation is similar, but market economy and welfare issues receive significantly less emphasis than in Sweden.

It is more difficult to relate the positioning of the Dutch parties to partisan cleavages. The strength of the cleavage between VVD and PvdA supporters on welfare state issues is difficult to reconcile with the low intensity of political competition. In contrast to the marked (if weakening) inclination of VVD partisans to the market economy, party programmes in the 1980s and 1990s show a slight bias towards welfare. This apparent anomaly may be explained by the character of the party system. The cleavage between liberals and social democrats on socio-economic issues may reflect the legacy of 'pillarisation' in Dutch society. The weakness of programmatic messages, on the other hand, may stem from a process of coalition government formation that puts a premium on policy adaptability.[33] Coalition considerations may inhibit parties from staking-out firm pre-election commitments, and election programmes may thus be less reliable indices of party position than elsewhere.

Germany presents no such difficulties of interpretation. The weak linkage between partisanship and voter preferences, and the corresponding weakness in partisan cleavages, goes some way to explaining the low intensity of political competition. Instead of dividing the parties, the fault lines between welfare supporters and advocates of the market economy cut across party electorates. For the CDU/CSU, an emphatic orientation towards the market economy risks activating latent divisions within its own electoral constituency.

TABLE 8
SUMMARY OF DATA

	Political competition: emphasis/ orientation/ polarisation			Public opinion: % support welfare cuts (ave)	Correlation: public opinion/ centre/right party orientation	Correlation: partisanship*/voter preference Pearson's r	
	E	O	P			Inc diffs	Benefit cuts
Germany	18.7	1.4	11.1	14.0	.182	.207	.182
Sweden	33.3	22.4	33.6	39.9	−.189	.309	.307
Denmark	22.6	20.6	33.0	28.7	.601	.395	.230
Netherlands	17.7	−6.1	6.2	27.7	N/A	.279	.288

*Centre-left party/dominant centre-right party voters.

CONCLUSIONS

Welfare retrenchment is unpopular, and cuts in welfare benefits will rarely if ever command plurality support. There are, however, cross-national variations in support for welfare retrenchment, and these can be related to differences in the way that welfare issues are 'processed' in party systems. In particular, the evidence presented above points to the effect of party 'messages', and the intensity with which those messages are conveyed, in shaping voter preferences. It would be unwise to draw definite conclusions about whether parties lead of follow public opinion. There is some evidence, however, that party position and public opinion appear to react reciprocally, with mutually reinforcing trends in favour of welfare reform. Relatively high levels of support for welfare reform in Sweden may thus reflect the intensity of centre-right party messages on market economy issues.

There is also evidence that *fluctuations* in support for welfare retrenchment are related to *shifts* in party position. Thus, in the Scandinavian countries, the peaks in support for welfare roll-back that provided governments with windows of opportunity for economic reform coincided with market economy 'offensives' on the part of centre-right parties. In both Scandinavian countries, but particularly in Denmark, there is some measure of co-variation between public opinion and centre-right party message. Co-variation does not, of course, imply causality. It may be that *both* public opinion and party position are driven by economic 'danger signals' like escalating state debt or rising unemployment. Nevertheless, the above analysis suggests that parties play a role in catalysing shifts in public opinion. In the absence of strong 'cues' from the parties, German public opinion failed to respond to the danger signals until 2004. The extent of German resistance to welfare cuts, and the scale of the electoral backlash against Agenda 2010 and the Hartz reforms may therefore be explained in part by the historic failure of the main German parties to cultivate public opinion to accept reform in the interests of economic competitiveness and employment. Recent *shifts* in public opinion coincide with the urgency imparted to the debate by Chancellor Schröder and those around him, underlining the linkage between public opinion and party message.

This article has identified a number of factors inhibiting the CDU/CSU from embracing welfare state reform in the manner of centre-right parties in Scandinavia and the Netherlands. First, resistance to welfare state reform runs significantly deeper than in the comparator countries. A second factor, compounding the adverse bias of public opinion, is the 'winner-takes-all' character of German elections. In a two-bloc party system in which the two coalition 'makeweights' are more or less even in electoral support, the larger of the two main parties normally forms the government. *Office seeking* parties must therefore adopt *vote maximising* strategies geared to the pursuit of the median voter. In multi-party systems, by contrast, government participation is less contingent on electoral success. The relaxation of the median voter syndrome allows centre-right parties to campaign more vigorously on welfare retrenchment.

The key factor, however, in the CDU/CSU's reluctance to embrace economic reform has been the weakness of partisan cleavages on socio-economic issues. Even in Scandinavia, the relationship between partisanship and voter preferences on market economy issues is little more than moderate. Nevertheless, partisan divisions of opinion are significantly stronger than in Germany, and the relative cohesion of centre-right electorates has encouraged the parties to campaign emphatically for welfare retrenchment. Given the divisions in the electoral constituency of the CDU/CSU, adopting a strong position on welfare state reform would risk a potentially damaging electoral realignment.

It should not be concluded, however, that the absence of political competition and party message precludes economic reform. Cross-national differences in partisan rhetoric, it has been observed, have been much larger than differences in policy outcomes. In the Netherlands, for example, parties have refrained from politicising the issues whilst engaging in cooperative strategies of welfare state reform. Since the 1970s, German governments of both major parties have undertaken incremental measures of welfare retrenchment despite the absence of rhetoric. Incremental reform by stealth, however, has some negative consequences. First, the flat trajectory of German public opinion on welfare issues in the1980s and 1990s suggests that it makes no impact on voter preferences. Second, when welfare state issues are subject to competition, the electorate retains a measure of control by withdrawing support from a reform party once it is perceived as having gone far enough. In the absence of political competition, citizens lack voice. Lacking consent and without offering alternatives, reform by stealth may thus inflict long-term damage on the legitimacy of the democratic process.

NOTES

1. ZDF, 14/05/2004, Sparen statt Schulden, http://www.zdf.de/ZDFde/inhalt/18/0.1872.2126226.00.html reported SPD support at 21 per cent in the March 2004 Politbarometer, the lowest level for either of the major parties since the poll began in 1977.
2. See Gordon Smith, 'Does West German Democracy Have an Efficient Secret?', in W.E. Paterson and G. Smith (eds.), *The West German Model: Perspectives on a Stable State* (London: Frank Cass, 1981), p.74: see also Kenneth Dyson, 'The German Model from Schmidt to Schröder', in S.A. Padgett and T. Poguntke (eds.), *Continuity and Change in German Politics: Beyond the Politics of Centrality* (London: Frank Cass, 2002), p.135.
3. Anthony Downs, *An Economic Theory of Democracy* (New York: Harper and Row, 1957). The neo-Downsian literature is too voluminous to cite comprehensively, but see the following; Ian Budge and Dennis J. Farlie, *Voting and Party Competition*, (London/New York: Wiley, 1973); Ian Budge and Dennis Farlie, *Explaining and Predicting Elections; Issue Effects and Party Strategies in 23 Democracies*, (London: George Allen and Unwin, 1983); Ian Budge, David Robertson and Derek Hearl (eds.), *Ideology, Strategy and Party Change, Spatial Analysis of Post-War Election Programmes in 19 Democracies* (Cambridge: Cambridge University Press, 1987); Ian Budge, 'A New Spatial Theory of Party Competition: Uncertainty, Ideology and Policy Equilibria Viewed Comparatively and Spatially', *British Journal of Political Science*, 24 (1994), pp.443–67.
4. Paul Pearson, 'Coping with Permanent Austerity; Welfare State Restructuring in Affluent Democracies', in Paul Pierson (ed.), *The New Politics of the Welfare State* (Oxford: Oxford University Press, 2001), p.413.
5. For an account of the median voter syndrome in relation to welfare state reform see Herbert Kitschelt, 'Partisan Competition and Welfare State Retrenchment: When do Politicians Choose Unpopular Policies?', in Paul Pierson (ed.), *The New Politics of the Welfare State* (Oxford: Oxford University Press, 2001), p.273. See also Kitschelt, 'Political-Economic Context and Partisan Strategies in the German Federal Elections 1990–2002', *West European Politics*, 26/4 (2003), pp.125–52.
6. Ole Listhaug, Stuart E. Macdonald and George Rabinowitz, 'Ideology and Party Support in Comparative Perspective', *European Journal of Political Research*, 25 (1994), pp.111–49. Stuart E. Macdonald, George Rabinowitz and Ole Listhaug, 'On Attempting to Rehabilitate the Proximity Model: Sometimes the Patient just can't be Helped' *Journal of Politics*, 60 (1998), pp.653–90.
7. Donald Granberg and Mikael Gilljam, 'Implausible Hypotheses in the Directional Model of Issue Voting', *European Journal of Political Research*, 32/1 (1997), pp.31–50.
8. Kees Aarts, Stuart E. Macdonald and George Rabinowitz, 'Issues and Party Competition in the Netherlands', *Comparative Political Studies*, 32/1 (1999), pp.66–8.

9. Bernard Grofman, 'Political Economy: Downsian Perspectives', in Robert Goodin and Hans-Dieter Klingemann (eds.), *A New Handbook of Political Science* (Oxford: Oxford University Press, 1996), p.698.
10. See Patrick Dunleavy, *Democracy, Bureaucracy and Public Choice* (New York/London: Harvester Wheatsheaf, 1991), pp.117–19.
11. See for instance Jurgen Kramer and Hans Rattinger, 'The Proximity and the Directional Theories of Issue Voting Compared; Results for the USA and Germany', *European Journal of Political Research*, 32 (1997), pp.1–21: Russell Dalton, 'Political Parties and Political Representation: Party Supporters and Party Elites in Nine Nations', *Comparative Political Studies*, 18 (1985), pp.267–99: James Adams and Samuel Merrill, 'Modeling Party Strategies and Policy Representation in Multiparty Elections. Why are Strategies so Extreme?', *American Journal of Political Science*, 43 (1999), pp.765–91.
12. Torben Iversen, 'Political Leadership and Representation in West European Democracies: A Test of Three Models of Voting', *American Journal of Political Science*, 38/1 (1994), p.70.
13. Herbert Kitschelt, 'Partisan Competition and Welfare State Retrenchment: When do Politicians Choose Unpopular Policies?', in Paul Pierson (ed.), *The New Politics of the Welfare State* (Oxford: Oxford University Press, 2001), pp.278–9.
14. See Roy Pierce, 'Mass–Elite Linkages and the Responsible Party Model of Representation', in W.E. Miller, R. Pierce, J. Thomassen, R. Herrera, S. Homberg, P. Essaiasson and B. Wessels (eds.), *Policy Representation in Western Democracies* (Oxford: Oxford University Press, 1999), pp.23–4; Edeltraud Roller, 'The Welfare State: The Equality Dimension', in Ole Borre and Eleanor Scarbrough (eds.), *The Scope of Government: Beliefs in Government, Volume 3* (Oxford: Oxford University Press, 1995), pp.165–90.
15. Iversen, 'Political Leadership and Representation', p.65.
16. James Adams, 'A Theory of Spatial Competition with Biased Voters: Party Policies Viewed Temporally', *British Journal of Political Science*, 31 (2001), pp.121–58.
17. Ian Budge and David Robertson, 'Do Parties Differ and How?' in I. Budge, D. Robertson and D. Hearl (eds.), *Ideology, Strategy and Party Change: Spatial Analysis of Post-War Election Programmes in 19 Democracies* (Cambridge: Cambridge University Press, 1987), pp.398–9.
18. For an overview of the debate and empirical test of the respective positions see Jeffrey A. Karp and Susan A. Banducci, 'Issues and Party Competition under Alternative Electoral Systems', *Party Politics*, 8/2 (2002), pp.123–41. See also Jocelyn A.J. Evans, 'In Defence of Sartori: Party System Change, Voter Preference Distributions and Other Competitive Incentives', *Party Politics*, 8/2 (2002), pp.155–74.
19. Arend Lijphart, 'Patterns of Democracy: Government Forms and Performance in Thirty Six Countries (New Haven: Yale University Press, 1999), cited in Karp and Banducci, 'Issues and Party Competition', p.125.
20. Gary Cox, 'Centripetal and Centrifugal Tendencies Incentives in Electoral Systems', *American Journal of Political Science*, 34 (1990), pp.903–35; Karp and Banducci, 'Issues and Party Competition', pp.125–6.
21. Swedish Election Study 1979, SED 0089; 1982, SED 0157; 1985, SED 0217; 1991, SED 0227; 1994, SED 0391; 1998, SED 0470.
22. Danish National Election Study 1990, DDA 1564; 1994, DDA 2210: 1998, DDA 4189: 2001, DDA 812516.
23. Dutch election studies were accessed via the Inter-University Consortium for Political and Social Research (ICPSR). Dutch Parliamentary Election Study 1986, ICPSR 8876; 1989, ICPSR 9950; 1994, ICPSR 6740; 1998, ICPSR 2836.
24. ALLBUS 1982, ZA-S1160; ALLBUS 1984, ZA-S1340, ALLBUS 1990, ZA-S1800, ALLBUS 1991, ZA-S1900, ALLBUS 1994, ZA-S2400: ALLBUS 1998, ZA-S3000; ALLBUS 2000, ZA-S3450. (ALLBUS was used in the absence of items on social equality and welfare benefits in German election studies).
25. See Edeltraud Roller, 'The Welfare State: The Equality Dimension', and Per Arnt Pettersen, 'The Welfare State: The Security Dimension', both in Borre and Scarbrough (eds.), *The Scope of Government*, pp.165–97 and pp.198–230 respectively.
26. Cross-national analysis faces the comparability problem since national surveys formulate questions in different ways (see Pettersen, 'The Welfare State', p.225). By posing the same question across national samples, the ESS provides a comparability check on national data sources.
27. Data cover party programmes from elections between 1945 and 1998 across 23 countries, and is contained in the CD-Rom accompanying Ian Budge, Hans-Dieter Klingemann, Andrea Volkens, Judith Bara and Eric Tanenbaum (eds.), *Mapping Policy Preferences: Estimates for Parties, Electors and Governments, 1945–98* (Oxford; Oxford University Press, 2001).
28. For an outline of MRG methodology see Ian Budge, 'Theory and Measurement of Party Policy Positions', in Budge *et al., Mapping Policy Preferences*, pp.80–81.
29. Where there are two electorally significant centre-right parties, analysis is conducted separately, e.g. conservative/social democratic partisanship.

30. National surveys use differently constructed response scales. In the data presented in Tables 1 and 2, these differences are dealt with by merging response categories to give the percentage of respondents favouring income equality. As a test of the reliability of national election study data, European Social Survey data are given in the right-hand column. In all cases, ESS data corroborate national data.
31. The availability of data in Pettersen, 'The Welfare State', p.210, provides a longer-term perspective on fluctuations in opinion.
32. Politbarometer Nov. 2003, see http://www.heute.t-online.de/ZDFheute/artikel/7/0,1367,HOME-0-2085351,00.html; Politbarometer, May 2004, see http://www.zdf.de/ZDFde/inhalt/18/0.1872.2126226,00.html; Politbarometer, Aug. 2004, see http://www.heute.t-online.de/ZDFheute/artikel/18/0,1367,POL-0-2185682,00.html.
33. Aarts *et al.*, 'Issues and Party Competition in the Netherlands', pp.64–5.

Index